Growth through Structural Reforms

Growth through Structural Reforms

With Leadership and Competence Great Opportunities Exist

Michael Lindemann

Copyright © 2015 michael lindemann
All rights reserved.

ISBN: 150531724X
ISBN 13: 9781505317244

To Cristina, Roy and Nina

Table of Contents

	Introduction	ix
Chapter 1	Under Employment data analysis and measures needs to take a major part in all unemployment improvements in major countries.	1
Chapter 2	Social-economic structural reforms need implementation in practically all major countries.	27
Chapter 3	Monetary policy cannot act alone since it failed doing so.	124
	Conclusions	209
	Addendum	229

Introduction

I WROTE THIS BOOK BECAUSE I have a very strong feeling that a more pragmatic view of some crucial and specific macro situations is necessary, since they are, in general, ignored.

This book is not about "systematic pessimism", it recognizes that many economic factors need to be drastically reviewed first and revised after due in-depth analysis. It is not theoretical, it offers solutions, which are not "ASAP" but gradual and I believe realistic.

Proposed alternative solutions are based on an "active life in international working "in situ" in 3 continents and 7 different countries.

The three subject matters in my book are crucial and curiously enough have not been the object, generally speaking, of the concern they merit because all three have been and are hindering social-economic development and growth and therefore need far more in-depth analysis, review and revision.

- **Under Employment data needs to take a major part in all unemployment data in major countries.**
- **Social-economic structural reforms need implementation in practically all major countries.**

Reforms need to be targeted: general, supply side, demand economics, or a well thought out "mix".

- **Monetary policy cannot act alone since it failed doing so.**

It must follow Economic Strategy and Action Plan and complement it.

Central Banking role to be first totally reviewed and then revised worldwide.

There must be a Focus on Tax Evasion, Tax Breaks, Mobilizing Cash Savings / Hoarding, Predominance of corporate Dividends' Payout versus corporate creation of Investment, all necessary matters to obtain Growth Resources

I have published in 2014 a book entitled "**Why Macro Governance is Obsolete and is Killing the World Economy**" which includes these three major issues, but focuses mainly on a drastic change in approach to Governance, meaning that governments cannot continuously "throw the can forward" and need to take on responsibilities to not only adapt to these huge changes but try to lead, this is and will be increasingly difficult, but if they do not change their political approach they will be losers and accountable to the people they think they are governing.

In this second book I intend to focus on the three above mentioned subjects.

This book is about questioning if structural changes of the economy in the last 30 years have been assimilated and / or are in the process of being better understood by non specialized audiences, and also on whether private business procedures could be *increasingly applied to macro vision*, planning and analysis, and therefore include pragmatic analysis and decision making in major macro points.

I greatly believe that knowledge or "knowing" is a basic factor, that questioning is necessary in a world of affirmations, and that decision making is the result of both, this even more so in a huge crisis situation, which is still continuing, and which has no historical points of reference because of the huge changes in geo economy structure and politics, and in its sectoral / activities categories' structure.

Monetary policies, and Central Banking, overwhelmingly "dictated" the behavior of nations, which is contrary to logic, since financial measures should "complement" financing required by a nations' realistic and also ambitious social-economic view, plan and it's budgeting, and not precede them. By doing it in the contrary sense, there cannot exist financial targeting, because no economic priorities to be financed have been explicitly determined by the governments, which are led financially, mainly by Central Banking, which is senseless!

This is why job creation in general has not been significant, after the 2008 – 2010 maximum Great Crisis periods. Enormous amounts of liquidity were injected into the major economies not sufficiently contemplating the need for crucial structural reforms in many areas, starting with Labor.

Monthly reports on Job Creation and Unemployment have systematically ignored including "Under Employment" in the published data, which has greatly hindered taking adequate measures on Job Creation since the major unemployment problems reside in "Under Employment", which in the US has the same size than the "officially" published data on unemployment, this "omission" being made due to "political" reasons mainly, to make social-economic situations look better than they really are.

In the last 20 / 30 years the structure of GDP and Stock Exchanges changed dramatically: enormous changes in geo-economic structures, great sectoral changes mainly brought about by innovation: i.e. emergence of IT – internet and communications and in the last decade/s social networks, science, and various activity categories.

The three subject matters which are being dealt with in this book are directly related to this meteorically changing environment and if not actualized the economic situations in weak countries, whatever the size, will not only not improve, but will regress.

CHAPTER 1

Under Employment data analysis and measures needs to take a major part in all unemployment improvements in major countries.

MOST MAJOR WESTERN "DEVELOPED" COUNTRIES have used monetary measures of great importance to develop their economies after the Great Crisis initiated in 2007/08 started.

These measures were, in general, not accompanied with the necessary social-economic structural reforms which were required to obtain durable growth and international competivity.

Austerity measures were imposed in the Eurozone some 3 years ago, these being the so called "golden rules", with poor results, the main reason being that most of these "austerity" measures were higher taxation imposed on already high taxes in some major countries and decreases in wages and pensions.

These austerity measures were imposed indirectly by Germany,"de facto" leader in the Eurozone, to the European Commission, the techno bureaucratic inefficient mammoth organization.

All Eurozone countries were given the same mostly unreachable macro goals - deficit and indebtedness ratios on GDP - with the same unreachable timing and to be implemented at the same time for all member countries, a total non sense, which had as a result the contrary effect, or no growth and higher indebtedness.

What was not stressed was that the starting point needed to be the implementation of social-economic structural reforms, starting with Labor.

Germany had gone through the application of these social-economic structural reforms starting in 2000 by then Chancellor Schroeder, and had also benefitted from the longstanding "co –management" system with Labor Unions for decades, which allowed for smoother negotiations on working flexibility, called the "Hartz – VW – rules".

Germany, accordingly, felt that that all other Eurozone member countries and partners should go through the same social "sacrificial" pattern, refusing to "help" them, and being quite indifferent to the diversity in tradition, idiosyncrasies, social-economic situation and realistic possible evolution / trend, with the result that finally only some countries reacted favorably, mainly Spain and to some extent Portugal and Ireland, France being "immobile" after taxing the middle class and the very rich "to death" throughout the last years, and Italy's new Prime Minister started by dispersing himself and is now trying to start implementing structural reforms but having against him the opposition of the classic Italian political class.

This somber picture was further increased by the BCE trying continuously to bring the Eurozone to recovery through solely monetarist expansionist measures, therefore allowing "good excuses" for the "weak" Eurozone governments to defer the necessary structural reforms, this subject matter will be extensively covered in **Chapters 2 and 3.**

US – "Official" Unemployment and "Under Employment" situations
BLS and Wikipedia – data sources

Under Employment refers to an employment situation that is insufficient in some important way for the worker, relative to a standard. Examples include holding a part-time job despite desiring full-time work, and over qualification, where the employee has education, experience, or skills beyond the requirements of the job.

Underemployment has been studied in recent decades from a variety of perspectives, including economics, management, psychology, and sociology.

In economics, for example, the term underemployment has three different distinct meanings and applications. All meanings involve a situation in which a person is working, unlike unemployment, where a person who is searching for work and cannot find a job.

All meanings involve under-utilization of labor which is missed by most official (governmental agencies) definitions and measurements of unemployment.

Underemployment can refer to:

1. "Over qualification" or "over education", or the employment of workers with high education, skill levels, or experience in jobs that do not require such abilities. For example, a trained medical doctor who works as a taxi driver would experience this type of underemployment.
2. "Involuntary part-time" work, where workers who could (and would like to) be working for a full work-week can only find part-time work. By extension, the term is also used in regional planning to describe regions where economic activity rates are unusually low, due to a lack of job opportunities, training opportunities, or due to a lack of services such as childcare and public transportation.
3. "Overstaffing" or "hidden unemployment" (also called "labor hoarding"[1]), the practice in which businesses or entire economies employ workers who are not fully occupied—for example, workers currently not being used to produce goods or services due to legal or social restrictions or because the work is highly seasonal.

Underemployment is a significant cause of poverty: although the worker may be able to find part-time work, the part-time pay is not sufficient for basic needs. This "GDP gap" and the degree of underemployment of labor would be larger if they incorporated the roles of underemployed labor, involuntary part-time labor, and discouraged workers.

Under Employment, is therefore a great factor impacting Unemployment, which is not published "officially" in the BLS highlights every month, nor by the Ministry of Labor, nor by the non existing (in the US) Ministry of Economy (sic).

Analysis by State in the US is very useful, since all the States have varying ratios of unemployment and it is valid analysis to understand the reason for large variances, to improve the whole. This information is available on a monthly basis.

Only once did **FED's** new President, Mrs. Yellen, early on in assuming her job, refer to it by declaring that to look at only "officially" published unemployment only was meaningless, but after this, the FED never again referred to under employment, declaring that job creation was improving and US unemployment was declining, but that a number of issues still remained to be worked on.

The monthly US BLS (Bureau of Labor Statistics) report, which contains very varied and detailed information on all categories of the working population showing different annual periods, is a totally underutilized source of information, which I have been consulting since three years at least.

BLS monthly reports include a wide series of segmented information - please refer to next table - which can cover a certain time period and accordingly allow for evolution analysis and detection of where the "weak" spots are, and provide gradual, adequate and focused improvement.

This type of analysis is not really accomplished by any Government Ministry / Agency, which should be the Ministries of Economy (to be created…) and Labor, working together, and not the FED, who self-appointed itself as "guardian" of employment…

The list of BLS reports is as follows, including information by race, sex and age, education attainment, class of worker and part-time status, selected employment and unemployment indicators, reasons for unemployment, duration of unemployment, occupation, measures of labor under utilization, persons not in the labor force and multiple job holders, average weekly hours and overtime, other criteria (refer to list).

> Employment Situation Summary Table A. Household data, seasonally adjusted
>
> Employment Situation Summary Table B. Establishment data, seasonally adjusted

Employment Situation Frequently Asked Questions

Employment Situation Technical Note

Table A-1. Employment status of the civilian population by sex and age

Table A-2. Employment status of the civilian population by race, sex, and age

Table A-3. Employment status of the Hispanic or Latino population by sex and age

Table A-4. Employment status of the civilian population 25 years and over by educational attainment

Table A-5. Employment status of the civilian population 18 years and over by veteran status, period of service, and sex, not seasonally adjusted

Table A-6. Employment status of the civilian population by sex, age, and disability status, not seasonally adjusted

Table A-7. Employment status of the civilian population by nativity and sex, not seasonally adjusted

Table A-8. Employed persons by class of worker and part-time status

Table A-9. Selected employment indicators

Table A-10. Selected unemployment indicators, seasonally adjusted

Table A-11. Unemployed persons by reason for unemployment

Table A-12. Unemployed persons by duration of unemployment

Table A-13. Employed and unemployed persons by occupation, not seasonally adjusted

Table A-14. Unemployed persons by industry and class of worker, not seasonally adjusted

Table A-15. Alternative measures of labor underutilization

Table A-16. Persons not in the labor force and multiple jobholders by sex, not seasonally adjusted

Table B-1. Employees on nonfarm payrolls by industry sector and selected industry detail

Table B-2. Average weekly hours and overtime of all employees on private nonfarm payrolls by industry sector, seasonally adjusted

Table B-3. Average hourly and weekly earnings of all employees on private nonfarm payrolls by industry sector, seasonally adjusted

Table B-4. Indexes of aggregate weekly hours and payrolls for all employees on private nonfarm payrolls by industry sector, seasonally adjusted

Table B-5. Employment of women on nonfarm payrolls by industry sector, seasonally adjusted

Table B-6. Employment of production and nonsupervisory employees on private nonfarm payrolls by industry sector, seasonally adjusted(1)

Table B-7. Average weekly hours and overtime of production and nonsupervisory employees on private nonfarm payrolls by industry sector, seasonally adjusted(1)

Table B-8. Average hourly and weekly earnings of production and nonsupervisory employees on private nonfarm payrolls by industry sector, seasonally adjusted(1)

Table B-9. Indexes of aggregate weekly hours and payrolls for production and nonsupervisory employees on private nonfarm payrolls by industry sector, seasonally adjusted(1)

Access to historical data for the "A" tables of the Employment Situation Release

Access to historical data for the "B" tables of the Employment Situation Release

HTML version of the entire news release

I will take the September 2014 jobs' and unemployment situation in the US as a representative example of the need to include Under Employment in employment reports.

In September 2014 the steady, but not great, jobs recovery just got a little stronger. But there are still a disturbingly large number of people who aren't feeling the benefits of the recovery.

The US economy recorded 248 000 additional jobs in September 2014 (when average creation in 2014 was 200 000 additional jobs), according to data released by BLS on 10/03//2014. The "officially" published unemployment rate fell below 6 percent for the first time since July 2008, dropping to 5.9 percent from 6.1 percent in August 2014.

BLS Report (colored lettering is mine).

Year	Jan	Feb	Mar	Apr	May	Jun	Jul	Aug	Sep	Oct	Nov	Dec	Annual
	5.7	5.6	5.8	5.6	5.6	5.6	5.5	5.4	5.4	5.5	5.4	5.4	
2005	5.3	5.4	5.2	5.2	5.1	5.0	5.0	4.9	5.0	5.0	5.0	4.9	
	4.7	4.8	4.7	4.7	4.6	4.6	4.7	4.7	4.5	4.4	4.5	4.4	
2007	4.6	4.5	4.4	4.5	4.4	4.6	4.7	4.6	4.7	4.7	4.7	5.0	
	5.0	4.9	5.1	5.0	5.4	5.6	5.8	6.1	6.1	6.5	6.8	7.3	
2009	7.8	8.3	8.7	9.0	9.4	9.5	9.5	9.6	9.8	10.0	9.9	9.9	
	9.7	9.8	9.9	9.9	9.6	9.4	9.5	9.5	9.5	9.5	9.8	9.4	
2011	9.1	9.0	9.0	9.1	9.0	9.1	9.0	9.0	9.0	8.8	8.6	8.5	
	8.2	8.3	8.2	8.2	8.2	8.2	8.2	8.1	7.8	7.8	7.8	7.9	
2013	7.9	7.7	7.5	7.5	7.5	7.5	7.3	7.2	7.2	7.2	7.0	6.7	
	6.6	6.7	6.7	6.3	6.3	6.1	6.2	6.1	5.9				

The 5.9% "official" unemployment rate peaked to 10% of US non-farm civilian working population in October 2009 (in the midst of the "Great Crisis"), having been between 4.4% and 5.6% in the 2004 mid 2008 pre –crisis period, or close to the September 2014 ratio of 5.9% at its peak ratio.

If you only have this "official" data it is obvious that comments will be very favorable in terms of unemployment decreases since 2009.

But, as before mentioned this ratio is far from telling the "whole story".

According to the US BLS (Bureau of Labor Statistics) unemployment is classified into 6 increasing categories:

BLS, U1-U6

U-1 Persons unemployed 15 weeks or longer, as a percent of the civilian labor force

U-2 Job losers and persons who completed temporary jobs, as a percent of the civilian labor force

U-3 Total unemployed, as a percent of the civilian labor force ("official" unemployment rate)

U-4 Total unemployed plus discouraged workers, as a percent of the civilian labor force plus discouraged workers

U-5 Total unemployed, plus discouraged workers, plus all other persons marginally attached to the labor force, as a percent of the civilian labor force plus all persons marginally attached to the labor force

U-6 Total unemployed, also includes all persons marginally attached to the labor force, plus total employed part time for economic reasons, as a percent of the civilian labor force plus all persons marginally attached to the labor force

Those definitions are straight from the BLS site.

Become familiar with these definitions, and it will become clear to you that they measure very different levels of unemployment, which explain why to correctly measure Under Employment is so important, because the major problems of unemployment reside in Under Employment: workers leaving the jobs' market because they cannot find a job because the sectoral activities which progress most require know –how they have not acquired, part-time employment increasing at a rapid pace, longstanding unemployment, youth unemployment, senior unemployment, etc...

What is more meaningful is the size of the gap between the two numbers – and that has swollen over the last five years:

Here's the U-3 rate, the U-6 rate, and the difference between them, which corresponds to Under Employment, for three different points in time:

- **Sept. 2002** (when the recovery from the 2001 recession was well underway): U-3: 5.7%; U-6: 9.6% - **underemployment: 3.9 percentage points.**
- **Sept. 2007** (right before the latest recession started): U-3: 4.7%; U-6: 8.4% -**underemployment: 3.7 percentage points.**
- **Sept. 2014** (the most recent numbers): U-3: 5.9%; U-6: 11.8% - **underemployment: 5.9 percentage points.**

Underemployment **on September 2014 is 2.2 points higher** than it was seven years ago (2007), **the "official" unemployment (U-3) rate is only 1.2 points higher** – or underemployment's evolution is nearly double.

That corroborates several trends for which there's already a lot of evidence:

A lot of part-time workers would prefer a full-time job, but can't find one.

Companies are relying more on part-timers, freelancers and consultants than on permanent staffers with full benefits.

And many people are working at lesser jobs for lower pay than they were before the recession.

Other crucial employment data that needs recurrent - monthly "public" reporting, and mainly in-depth analysis of following points:

- **GDP Growth level required to stabilize unemployment.** Most economists expect it will remain at, or maybe be at least 2% for 2014, but this rate seems insufficient to diminish unemployment significantly.
- **Sectoral / Per Activity evolution** in-depth analysis is crucial, to detect and orientate education and training priorities.
- **Participation rate,** which is the ratio of the civilian labor force to the total non institutionalized civilian population 16 years of age and over.
- **Employment in total nonfarm activities'** evolution.
- **Employment in private sector and government sector** evolution.
- **Age, Education, Income, "Race" categorizations** of unemployment situation, these being great priorities for in-depth analysis.

The major unemployment / underemployment ratios are in the **Young, Black /Afro, Hispano / Latin, poorly educated, and senior categories**

- **Out-of-work length** - More than 5 million people have been out of work for six months or more, or higher than 2.7 million 4 years ago. Before 2009, in records dating to 1948, the number of long-term unemployed had never reached close to 3 million people.
- **Pay for private-sector employees**, when adjusted for inflation, has dropped 1.6% since 2009. In a weak job market, employers have little reason to offer significant raises.

Percentage of Americans either working or looking for work fell to a 31-year low of **62.8%** in August 2014; in **December 2012 it was still 63.6%**.

That is partly because the vast generation of baby boomers has begun to retire.

Another key factor is that hundreds of thousands of Americans have given up looking for work.

More than 23 million Americans are either unemployed, stuck in part-time jobs because they can't find full-time work or want a job but have stopped looking.

If the **percentage of the American population who were in the workforce were the same today as in 2008, the "official" unemployment rate would be above 11%, is a fact (?) that is being evoked several times.**

This appears to relate to the **workforce – participation rate, which is 63.6% in December 2012 and in April 2013 (and 63.5% in June 2013), compared with 65.7% in January 2009.**

This very important ratio is not incorporated into the monthly unemployment number released by the government, and wasn't before President Obama took office.

It is being contended that the reason for the decline in the unemployment rate is primarily that people unable to find work have abandoned their search and left the workforce — not that jobs are being created.

It is obvious that much more analysis (sectoral / by activity for instance, data which exists) is needed on the whole Unemployment and Underemployment mainly and related Job Creation "matter", which is crucial to the social-economic development in any country, which have been dealt with far too less in-depth and lacking profound analysis and reaching corrective measures.

This is where" politics" get in the way for electoral purposes mainly.

What needs to be done is to – in depth –analyze the reasons for this huge difference between "official" unemployment and underemployment, which the BLS report includes, showing categories very understandably, please see BLS reporting further on.

The following chart – **2008 – 2012**, clearly shows that **"Total" Unemployment** (column U-6), which started at 11% in September 2008, peaked in September 2009 (in full Crisis) to +17%, and slowly fell to 15 -16% by April 2010, to fall to 11.8% (not in chart – see further on) in September 2014, a ratio which is close to that in September 2008, when the Great Crisis starting "developing" job wise.

The same happened with **"Official" Unemployment** (column U-3) which started at 6% in September 2008, peaked at 10% at the end of 2009, and is at 5.9% (not in chart – see further on), in September 2014.

The difference between columns U-6 and U-3 is **"Under Employment"**, which started at 5% in September 2008(or 45% of total Unemployment) peaked at 7% in September 2008 (or close to 41% of Total unemployment), and was at 5.9% in 2014 (not in chart –see further on), or exactly 50% of total unemployment, which clearly shows the big and increasing importance of Under Employment.

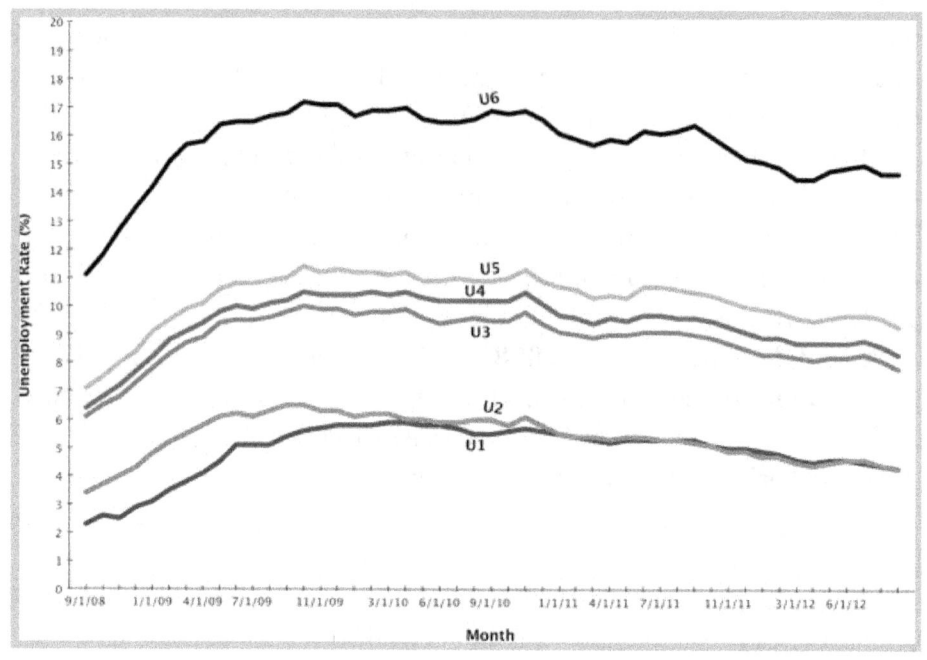

Another BLS report – 2004 – 2012, also on Total Unemployment (column U-6), which includes Under Employment, shows its evolution from 01/01/2000 to 01/ 31/ December 2013 – a 13 years long period.

Same comments as for first chart, noting that at 11.8 in September 2008 , the Total Unemployment ratio, at 11.8% is still 4.8 points higher (nearly 70%) than the 2000 September 7% rate.

It is true that the situation improved when compared to the height of the Great Crisis in 2009 / 2010, but it is still far way from retrieving the year 2000 situation.

Unemployment Rate - U6

2000 - 2014

Year	Jan	Feb	Mar	Apr	May	Jun	Jul	Aug	Sep	Oct	Nov	Dec	Year
2000	7.1	7.2	7.1	6.9	7.1	7.0	7.0	7.1	7.0	6.8	7.1	6.9	2000
2001	7.3	7.4	7.3	7.4	7.5	7.9	7.8	8.1	8.7	9.3	9.4	9.6	2001
2002	9.5	9.5	9.4	9.7	9.5	9.5	9.6	9.6	9.6	9.6	9.7	9.8	2002
2003	10.0	10.2	10.0	10.2	10.1	10.3	10.3	10.1	10.4	10.2	10.0	9.8	2003
2004	9.9	9.7	10.0	9.6	9.6	9.5	9.5	9.4	9.4	9.7	9.4	9.2	2004
2005	9.3	9.3	9.1	8.9	8.9	9.0	8.8	8.9	9.0	8.7	8.7	8.6	2005
2006	8.4	8.4	8.2	8.1	8.2	8.4	8.5	8.4	8.0	8.2	8.1	7.9	2006
2007	8.4	8.2	8.0	8.2	8.2	8.3	8.4	8.4	8.4	8.4	8.4	8.8	2007
2008	9.2	9.0	9.1	9.2	9.7	10.1	10.5	10.8	11.0	11.8	12.6	13.6	2008
2009	14.2	15.1	15.7	15.9	16.4	16.5	16.5	16.7	16.7	17.1	17.1	17.1	2009
2010	16.7	17.0	17.0	17.1	16.6	16.5	16.5	16.5	16.8	16.7	16.9	16.6	2010
2011	16.2	16.0	15.8	16.0	15.8	16.1	16.0	16.1	16.3	16.0	15.5	15.2	2011
2012	15.1	15.0	14.5	14.5	14.8	14.8	14.9	14.7	14.7	14.5	14.4	14.4	2012
2013	14.4	14.3	13.8	13.9	13.8	14.3	14.0	13.6	13.6	13.7	13.1	13.1	2013

Coming back to the September 2014 Unemployment situation in the US, as before mentioned, "Official" unemployment at 5.9% was exactly the same size as "Under employment", equally at 5.9% of nonfarm civilian working population, adding to Total unemployment at 11.8% (please refer to above comments), this showing an improvement as compared to the Great Crisis, but still being much higher than in pre Crisis years.

Labor Force Participation Rate – BLS report – is the share of the working-age population either employed or seeking a job

It has been at 62.8% on average throughout 2014 (62.7% in September 2014). At 62.8%, the participation rate matches the lowest since March 1978 (three and a half decades ago), having reached its peak of 67.3% in January 2000, accordingly showing that unemployment is still far away from getting out of the woods".

Due to the jobs' market deterioration, **Wages** are "going nowhere".

Average hourly earnings increased by 2% in 2014 compared to 2013. But if you take inflation into account – it's running at 1.7%– wages actually stayed essentially flat.

This leaves you with an isolated view of how many workers are not looking for a job because they don't think they will find one, have looked for a job in the past year but not recently, and part-time workers who can't find full-time work.

These are workers on the fringes. Until more of these people find jobs, or full-time jobs, it's possible that wages will be stuck for a while.

What we've seen since the recession is a huge rise in the number of American workers who are on the sidelines of the job market.

During the recession, the number of workers on the fringes of the job market increased. This happened in the last recession, too. But this time around, the jump was massive. It's declined from its peak, but has been flat at a still elevated level for the past few months.

As significantly, the number of American workers who are on the job-market sidelines is a full 2 percentage points above its pre-recession levels.

That's a worrying state of affairs and may help explain why job growth continues to chug along, unemployment falls, and yet Americans are barely making any more money.

All this should greatly worry FED's President, Mrs. Yellen, because the US Central Bank, the "savior", the FED, bases its future monetary moves on the state of employment and growth!

This is why I believe that one of the major "roles" of Central Banks is to boost markets, and that they, knowingly, keep "silent" on the magnitude of underemployment?

Here are questions about the job market future evolution:

How many people who have stopped looking for work — or never started — will start looking if the economy improves further?

This, perhaps more than any other question, has confounded economists. Since the Great Crisis began in late 2007, the proportion of adults either working or seeking work has sunk from 66 percent to 62.8 percent — a 35-year low. That's equal to about 7.5 million fewer people.

But a debate has raged over how many of them are waiting for the economy to strengthen further before they look.

At least half the exodus is due to retirements by the vast baby boom generation.

Younger adults are now also likely to stay in school.

And some jobless people who aren't seeking work are now receiving disability aid.

To some economists, this means that most of the dropouts aren't coming back. If so, employers will soon have to pay more because the pool of potential workers has shrunk.

Others think employers still regard many of the dropouts as potential hires and partly for that reason, feel scant pressure to raise pay.

Andrew Levin, an economist at the International Monetary Fund, points to surveys showing that many of those not looking for work would return for the right job.

At a news conference last month, Fed President, Mrs. Yellen said she thought a "meaningful" number of the dropouts would take jobs if more were available.

What's happened to 3.8 million people who had been unemployed for over six months but no longer are?

European Union and Eurozone – "Official" Unemployment and "Under Employment" situations

Wikipedia and Eurostat – data sources

Recent - August 2014 - Developments in Unemployment (Which Excludes Under Employment) at a European Union / Eurozone and Member State Level

Eurostat estimates that 24.6 million men and women in the European Union - 28 countries, where 18.3 million were in the Eurozone - 18 countries, were unemployed in August 2014.

The Eurozone's seasonally-adjusted unemployment rate was 11.5 % in August 2014.

The European Union's (EU) unemployment rate was 10.1 % in August 2014, the lowest value since February 2012.

Among the Member States, the lowest unemployment rates were recorded in Austria (4.7 %) and Germany (4.9 %), and the highest in Greece (27.0 % in June 2014) and Spain (24.4 %).

In August 2014, the unemployment rate in the **United States** was 6.1 %, down from 7.2 % in August 2013, falling to 5.9% in September 2014.

Unemployment trends

At the beginning of 2000, above 20 million persons were unemployed in the EU, corresponding to 9.1 % of the total labor force, compared to 24.6 Million, or an increase of 23%.

A long period of increasing unemployment followed. At the end of 2004 the number of jobseekers available for work reached 21.4 million, while the unemployment rate was 9.2 %.

At the beginning of 2005 a period of steadily declining unemployment started, lasting until the first quarter 2008.

In 2008, EU unemployment hit a low of 16.2 million persons (equivalent to a rate of 6.8 %) before rising sharply in the wake of the economic crisis.

Between the second quarter 2008 and mid-2010 the unemployment level went up by more than 7 million, taking the rate up to 9.6 %, at that time the highest value recorded since the start of the series in 2000.

The decline of unemployment in the following three quarters was a deceptive sign of an end of the crisis and of a stable improvement in labor market conditions in the EU.

In fact, since the second quarter of 2011 and until the first quarter of 2013 UE unemployment steadily and markedly increased taking it to the record level of 26.6 million, corresponding to a record rate of 10.9 %. Since then the rate has started to decrease, reaching 10.7 % at the end of 2013.

The unemployment rate in the Eurozone followed roughly the same trend as in the EU.

Please refer to coming Table 1 showing "Official" Unemployment plus Underemployment.

However, between 2000 and the beginning of 2004 the unemployment rate in the Eurozone was below that recorded in the EU.

This pattern was subsequently reversed as, between 2005 and the beginning of 2008, unemployment declined more rapidly in the Countries which did not yet have the euro.

As in the EU, during the economic crisis unemployment increased at a considerable pace, with the exception of the period between mid-2010 and mid-2011 where it temporarily declined.

The unemployment level peaked at 19.2 million in the second quarter of 2013, before going down in the second part of the year.

YOUTH UNEMPLOYMENT SITUATION AND TRENDS

In August 2014, 5 million young persons (under 25) were unemployed in the EU, of whom 3.3 million were in the Eurozone.

In August 2014, the lowest rates were observed in Germany (7.6 %), Austria (8.2 %) and the Netherlands (10.1 %), and the highest in Spain (53.7 %), Greece (51.5 % in June 2014), Italy 42.2 %) and Croatia 43.9 % in the second quarter 2014).

Youth unemployment rates are generally much higher, even double or more than double, than unemployment rates for all ages.

As for the rate for the total population, the youth unemployment rate in the EU sharply declined between 2005 and 2007, reaching its minimum value (15.1 %) in the first quarter of 2008.

The economic crisis, however, severely hit the young.

From the second quarter of 2008, the youth unemployment rate has taken an upward trend peaking to 23.6 % in the first quarter of 2013, before receding to 23.1 % at the end of the year.

The EU youth unemployment rate was systematically higher than in the Eurozone between 2000 and mid-2007.

Since then and until the third quarter 2010 these two rates were very close.

Afterwards the indicator moved more sharply in the Eurozone than in the EU, first downwards until mid-2011, then upwards until the end of 2012.

In the middle of 2012 the Eurozone youth unemployment rate overtook the EU rate, and the gap increased until the end of the year.

The gap became even larger in the second part of 2013, when the rate for the Eurozone went down less than the rate for the EU.

High youth unemployment rates do reflect the difficulties faced by young people in finding jobs.

However, this does not necessarily mean that the group of unemployed persons aged between 15 and 24 is that large, as many young people are studying full-time and are therefore neither working nor looking for a job (so they are not part of the labor force which is used as the denominator for calculating the unemployment rate).

This is a debatable situation, whereas youth unemployment is a very serious problem, it gets over valuated by including in all under age 25, those who are students, which distorts both comparable ratios with other age groups and magnifies the problem, which anyhow is real.

The leaders of France, Germany and Italy have pledged in October 2014 to commit some 6.4 billion euros towards tackling youth unemployment.

The trio made their promises at an EU jobs summit in Milan in October 2014 which had threatened to be overshadowed by their differences over fiscal discipline and austerity politics.

French President Mr. Hollande said the stakes have never been higher: "We must consider the program for youth employment as one of the programs for supporting growth in Europe. It's what's at stake for Europe. If Europe is not capable of offering hope to the next generation, people will turn their backs on Europe. We see the risks, we see the danger. Europe must once again become an opportunity for young people."

France and Italy had reportedly called for the EU to allocate more funds to boost job creation but Germany's Chancellor Angela Merkel said there was enough cash in the coffers.

"There's no question that there is sufficient money. But we will have to get the money flowing. This is our main target…" German Chancellor Mrs. Merkel said. "Of course we have to invest, yes. But as important is (the question of) which directions we invest in. For this, we need to know, which are the jobs of the future and not those of the past."

Officials said the meeting was a "stock-taking exercise" to maintain momentum on measures such as the Youth Guarantee Scheme, an EU-wide initiative aimed at helping people under the age of 25 into work.

One of the biggest problems in dealing on an area basis with Youth Unemployment is the great disparities between the 28 European Union countries – please refer to next **Table 2** – (2011 – 2013).

	Youth unemployment rate				Youth unemployment ratio		
	2011	2012	2013	2013Q4*	2011	2012	2013
EU-28	21.4	23.0	23.4	23.1	9.1	9.7	9.8
Euro area	20.8	23.1	24.0	23.8	8.7	9.5	9.8
Belgium	18.7	19.8	23.7	23.9	6.0	6.2	7.3
Bulgaria	25.0	28.1	28.4	28.1	7.4	8.5	8.4
Czech Republic	18.1	19.5	18.9	18.9	5.4	6.1	6.0
Denmark	14.3	14.0	13.0	12.8	9.6	9.1	8.1
Germany	8.6	8.1	7.9	7.9	4.5	4.1	4.0
Estonia	22.4	20.9	18.7	19.1	9.1	8.7	7.4
Ireland	29.1	30.4	26.8	25.5	12.1	12.3	10.6
Greece	44.4	55.3	58.3	57.3	13.0	16.1	16.6
Spain	46.2	52.9	55.5	54.9	19.0	20.6	20.8
France	22.6	24.4	24.8	23.7	8.4	8.9	9.0
Croatia	36.1	43.0	49.7	48.6	11.3	12.7	14.4
Italy	29.1	35.3	40.0	41.8	8.0	10.1	10.9
Cyprus	22.4	27.8	38.9	40.8	8.7	10.8	15.0
Latvia	31.0	28.5	23.2	23.9	11.6	11.5	9.1
Lithuania	32.6	26.7	21.9	20.6	9.2	7.8	6.9
Luxembourg	16.4	18.0	17.4	17.2	4.2	5.0	4.0
Hungary	26.1	28.1	27.2	24.8	6.4	7.3	7.4
Malta	13.8	14.2	13.5	13.5	7.1	7.2	7.0
Netherlands	7.6	9.5	11.0	11.4	5.3	6.5	7.7
Austria	8.3	8.7	9.2	9.0	5.0	5.2	5.4
Poland	25.8	26.5	27.3	27.2	8.6	8.9	9.1
Portugal	30.1	37.7	37.7	34.8	11.7	14.3	13.5
Romania	23.7	22.7	23.6		7.4	7.0	7.3
Slovenia	15.7	20.6	21.6	19.9	5.9	7.1	7.3
Slovakia	33.7	34.0	33.7	33.5	10.1	10.4	10.4
Finland	20.1	19.0	19.9	20.0	10.1	9.8	10.3
Sweden	22.8	23.7	23.4	22.6	12.1	12.4	12.8
United Kingdom	21.1	21.0	20.5	19.7	12.4	12.4	12.0

: data not available
* The quarterly youth unemployment rate is seasonally adjusted.

MALE AND FEMALE UNEMPLOYMENT TRENDS

Historically, women have been more affected by unemployment than men.

In 2000, the unemployment rate for women in the EU was around 10 %, while the rate for men was below 8 %. By the end of 2002, this gender gap had narrowed to around 1.5 percentage points and between 2002 and mid-2007 this gap remained more or less constant.

Since the first quarter of 2008, when they were at their lowest levels of 6.3 % and 7.4 % respectively, the male and female unemployment rates in the EU converged, and by the second quarter of 2009 the male unemployment rate was higher.

The decline of the men's rate during 2010 and the first half of 2011 and the corresponding stability in the women's rate over the same period brought the male rate below the female one once again.

Since then the two rates have risen at the same pace until mid-2013, when they reached their highest value, both at 10.9 %. In the second half of 2013 both the male and the female rates declined, reaching respectively 10.6 % and 10.8 % at the end of the year.

Unemployment Plus Under Employment in the EU and the Eurozone

There are basically three forms of unemployment in the European Union (EU) which are not covered by the ILO (International Labor Office) definition of unemployment.

They are: underemployed part-time workers, jobless persons seeking a job but not immediately available for work and jobless persons available for work but not seeking it.

These three groups do not meet all criteria of the ILO unemployment definition i.e. being without work, actively seeking work, and being available for work.

However, while not being captured through the unemployment rate, these groups still represent a form of unmet demand for employment. For this reason they are part of unemployment.

While underemployed part-time workers form already part of the labor force, persons seeking work but not immediately available and persons available to work but not seeking are outside the labor force, but could be seen and termed as a 'potential additional labor force'.

Underemployment and potential additional labor force are indicators designed to supplement the unemployment rate to provide a more complete picture of the labor market.

- **Ratios excluding Under Employment – "Official" Ratios**

The Eurozone's seasonally-adjusted unemployment rate was **12.2 %** in the first quarter of 2013

The European Union's (EU) unemployment rate was **10.9 %** in the first quarter of 2013

- **Ratios including Under Employment – "Realistic" Ratios**

The Eurozone's seasonally-adjusted unemployment rate was **21.9 %** in the first quarter of 2013

The European Union's (EU) unemployment rate was **19.9 %** in the first quarter of 2013

- **Under Employment Ratios**

Eurozone under Employment was **9.7% or 44%** of "Realistic" Total Unemployment in 2013 1rst Qtr.

EU under Employment was **9.0% or 45%** of "Realistic" Total Unemployment in 2013 1rst Qtr.

As can be noticed Under Employment is close to "Official" Unemployment rates as percentages of nonfarm civilian working populations, which represents a very high percentage, which has not and is not brought to the attention of the Eurozone countries populations in general, for political and electoral reasons, accordingly falsifying all economic planning and budgeting.

Table 1 – Unemployment and Under Employment – First Quarter of 2013

2014Q1	Unemployed		Underemployed part-time workers		Persons seeking work but not immediately available		Persons available to work but not seeking	
	Rate (% over labour force)	Change compared with previous year (percentage points)	Rate (% over labour force)	Change compared with previous year (percentage points)	Rate (% over labour force)	Change compared with previous year (percentage points)	Rate (% over labour force)	Change compared with previous year (percentage points)
EU-28	10.9	-0.4	4.1	0.0	0.9	0.0	4.0	0.2
EA-18	12.2	-0.2	4.4	0.1	0.9	0.0	4.4	0.6
BE	8.7	0.2	3.1	-0.6	1.0	-0.1	2.1	0.1
BG	13.0	-0.8	1.1	0.2	0.9	-0.3	7.7	-1.1
CZ	6.8	-0.7	0.7	0.0	0.3	0.0	1.2	-0.2
DK	7.4	-0.3	2.7	-0.1	0.9	0.1	2.4	-0.2
DE	5.5	-0.3	4.0	-0.2	1.2	-0.1	1.3	0.0
EE	8.5	-1.4	(1.4)	(0.1)			5.6	0.8
IE	12.1	-1.6	6.6	-0.7	0.8	0.0	1.3	-0.6
EL	27.9	0.5	4.7	0.2	0.9	-0.1	2.0	-0.2
ES	25.9	-1.0	6.9	0.3	0.9	0.0	4.9	0.0
FR	10.2	-0.2	5.5	0.2	1.0	0.0		
HR	18.9	0.7	(1.4)	(-0.5)	(0.9)	(0.4)	10.2	-2.9
IT	13.6	0.8	2.9	0.3	0.4	-0.2	12.8	1.1
CY	16.9	1.0	8.1	2.3	1.2	-0.1	4.8	0.8
LV	11.9	-1.1	3.1	0.1	(0.6)		5.3	-1.1
LT	12.4	-0.7	2.3	-0.3	0.6	-0.3	0.7	-0.3
LU	6.6	1.1	1.8	-0.5	0.6	0.1	5.2	-1.3
HU	8.3	-3.4	1.8	-0.3	0.2	0.0	4.2	-2.0
MT	6.0	0.0	2.4	-0.1			1.7	-0.6
NL	7.5	1.0	2.0	0.1	1.1	0.1	4.2	0.4
AT	5.4	0.0	4.1	0.4	0.9	0.0	3.9	0.2
PL	10.6	-0.7	2.3	0.1	0.5	-0.1	3.9	-0.2
PT	15.3	-2.6	4.8	-0.1	0.5	-0.1	5.4	0.5
RO	7.2	-0.3	2.5	0.2			4.6	-0.8
SI	10.8	-0.3	2.4	0.2	(0.2)	(-0.1)	3.5	1.8
SK	14.1	-0.4	1.4	-0.3	0.5	0.1	1.6	-0.2
FI	9.0	0.3	3.5	0.6	4.5	0.3	5.1	0.8
SE	8.5	0.0	4.8	-0.4	2.4	0.0	2.7	-0.4
UK	6.7	-1.1	6.8	-0.2	1.1	0.2	2.1	-0.3
IS	5.8	-0.1			1.6	0.2	4.5	0.5
NO	3.5	0.0	2.3	-0.1	0.6	-0.1	2.1	-0.7
CH	4.9	0.2	5.8	0.0	1.0	-0.2	3.7	0.2
MK	28.4	-1.5	2.1	0.7	(0.4)	(-0.2)		
TR	10.2	0.8	1.7	0.3	0.3	-0.1	7.1	0.2

Note: Unemployment figures in this table differ from those published in online data codes: (une_nb_a) and (une_rt_a) because they do not cover French overseas departments and they are not adjusted to ensure break-free time-series.

It will be important to follow up closely on the number of **FTE** *(Full Time Employment)* jobs during in the future, because Obamacare provides a huge incentive for businesses to replace full-time employees with part-time help.

"Replacing full-time people with part-timers will reduce the reported employment rate, but it will not do anything for incomes or economic growth."

Next chart will show reflects following evolution:

Year	Population	Labor Force	Not in LF	Employed	FT Employed	PT Employed	Unemployed	SNAP
2008	232,809	152,503	80,306	144,550	119,452	25,098	7,953	26,316
2009	234,913	153,804	81,109	140,105	112,947	27,158	13,699	28,223
2010	236,998	153,194	83,804	137,203	109,100	28,103	15,991	33,490
2011	238,851	152,635	86,216	138,093	110,731	27,361	14,542	40,302
2012	242,435	154,114	88,322	140,684	112,587	28,096	13,430	44,709
2013	244,828	154,727	90,100	142,228	114,191	28,037	12,500	46,609
Change	12,019	2,224	9,794	-2,322	- 5261	2,939	4,547	20,293
OC	9,915	923	8,991	2,123	1,244	879	-1,199	18,386

With a total labor force population (*) in 2013 of 154.7 million, Part-time employed at 28.0 million represent 18% of total Labor Force.

(*) Not total population of 244.8 million.

FTE (fulltime employed) decreased a little over 5 Million between 2013 and 2008, whereas **PTE** (Part-time employed) decreased by "only» 3 Million, demonstrating that the larger decrease is in **FTE**.

"**There is no way that the number of FTE jobs can increase much unless the economy starts growing considerably faster than this.** In fact, if the stagnation in RGDP that the BEA reported for 4Q 2012 (a 0.1% annualized growth rate) continues, the number of FTE jobs will continue to fall."

Total "Realistic" Unemployment including Under Employment had reached nearly 22% at the beginning of 2013 in the Eurozone, whereas the same ratio was 12.5% in the US mid- 2013.

The Eurozone ratio of Total Unemployment was accordingly 76% (!) higher in the Eurozone than in the US.

This is mainly explained by the fact that the Eurozone was "wrongly put to life" in 2000 (Maastricht Treaty), reuniting in 2002 countries with extremely different social-economic structural situations and lacking an efficient Central Government, the now - 2014 -18 Eurozone member states not wanting to relinquish an inch of their sovereignty, whereas the US, even being a Federal Government has a President for "all", with a Congress and Senate reflecting different partisan policies, but still the US being one country and not 18...., which facilitates decision making.

Recent developments at European and Member State level

In 2014 Q1 in the EU, the rate of underemployed part-time workers was 4.1 %. This rate is calculated over the population in the labor force. The rate of persons seeking a job but not immediately available for work in 2014Q1 was 0.9 %. The rate of persons available for work but not seeking it was 4.0 % in 2014Q1.

Under Employment accordingly reaches 9.0%, in comparison, the unemployment rate was 10.9 % in 2014Q1.

While EU unemployment increased sharply since 2008 and the beginning of the economic and financial crisis, the three underemployment categories have experienced far more stable trends during this turbulent period.

The proportion of underemployed part-time workers in the labor force has grown slightly from 3.1 % in 2008Q1 to 4.1 % in 2014Q1.

The percentage of the population available but not seeking work followed the same trend, reaching 4.0 % in 2014Q1.

People seeking work but not immediately available has remained close to 1 % over the whole time span, showing no noticeable change since the start of the economic crisis.

Two factors explain this more stable trend compared to the unemployment rate.

Firstly, the three indicators supplementing unemployment have by construction looser requirements than "Official" unemployment itself, because they look at groups of persons who do not simultaneously fulfill all the criteria of the ILO (International Labor Organization) unemployment definition.

This "softer" definition makes the indicators more stable, as people in those three categories are less likely to leave the group.

Secondly, persons in underemployment and persons available for work but not seeking tend to have structural reasons for their situation, e.g. because they believe no work is available, they are fulfilling domestic tasks etc.

In the case of persons seeking work but not available the explanation is different, because they are a very dynamic group with high rotation. What happens is that the flow of individuals entering the category is very much balanced out by the flow of individuals leaving the category. This is because many of them are students starting to look for a job before the end of their studies. There is a fairly steady outflow of students finishing their studies and joining the labor market (hence leaving the indicator possibly to become employed or unemployed), balanced out by another steady inflow of students approaching the end of their studies and wanting to work but not being available to work yet.

Conclusion

All this explains that while in 2013 and 2014 the "Official" unemployment rate diminished and governments applauded, the "Under Employment population" remained rather stable, and showed an increase as a percentage of the labor force, this making total" realistic " unemployment remain at a high level.

Accordingly, it stands to reason that if governments do not take measures to diminish Under Employment (measures which will be analyzed extensively in Chapter 2), Total Unemployment will remain very high, and the social-economic situations in countries with very high "realistic" total unemployment will have a real hard, if not impossible, time in growing on a durable basis

CHAPTER 2

Social-economic structural reforms need implementation in practically all major countries.

WHY ARE THESE STRUCTURAL REFORMS NECESSARY?

GOVERNMENTS IN MAJOR COUNTRIES, so called "Governance" in an area like the Eurozone, supranational "organizations" like IMF, OECD, and also G20 meetings, all referred and refer to the need for structural reforms, but the main Recovery tools since the Big Crisis began 2007 – 2008 were huge increases in **solely** monetary expansion, call it QE, LTRO, TLTRO, purchase of covered bonds, ABS (not yet the case…) (all at close to zero refinancing interest rates), accompanied by "austerity" measures, which consisted mainly in major tax increases of all kinds, decreases in wages and pensions, but no social-economic structural reforms like the ones made in Germany in the 2000 decade.

On mid - October 2014, all these governmental instances are "surprised and disappointed" that all these above described measures have had no favorable repercussions in getting a recovery in the Eurozone, which is at best stagnant, and stronger results in other major countries like China, Japan, Brazil, etc…, the US showing the best" picture", but still retaining high "total realistic" unemployment (please refer to **Chapter 1**).

What they do not comment upon, because from a political / electoral basis it would be extremely negative for them, is that, at least, 5 years have been wasted by not implementing these social-economic structural reforms, starting with those related to Labor, and allowing Central Banking to "do" what they wanted with their "independent" status (please refer **to Chapter 3** on this matter).

One argument always used is that these structural reforms did not provide short-term results and needed large financing, whereas monetary expansion would allow major banks particularly, and banks in general, to make more credit available to corporations in need of financing for investing or working capital purposes.

The sector needing most credit which is the biggest employer in any country, the SMEs, received a small share of all this liquidity, because the remuneration that major banks obtained with domestic financing credit was far less than in continuing lending to weak nations allowing them to renew or create sovereign bonds, financing them with below open markets and making nice spreads with the cheap BCE "money" offer, plus continuing with speculation.

Refer to all the of major banks' speculation which appeared in 2013 /2014, with huge Trillion fines, quite easily absorbed by these giant banks, demonstrating huge profits, same as hedge funds, without any control from Central Banking as to "usage", since Central Banking mainly "works " for these major banks and to boost markets - far more extensive analysis in **Chapter 3.**

The week of 10/ 06 -11/2014 showed the greatest fall in markets since the beginning of 2014, recognizing – for the time being (sic) - that the recovery, especially in the Eurozone, was not "present" and not "coming".

For the time being, since opinions change rapidly, reactivity being king, what is definitely needed is to urgently implement social-economic structural reforms, and as IMF's VP, Mr. Blanchart, says, identify "which" are feasible or not, because it has always been said they are very costly and do not produce immediate (sic) results.

The urgent and pragmatic structural reforms ones are gradual, they basically consist in negotiations with Unions, which could be much shorter if top politicians did not back track all the time when Unions disagree or organize manifestations and strikes, they are "time costly" but not "money costly" (except for losing days of work in case of strikes).

These "not costly - in money reforms" are to making work more easy, which means work flexibility and mobility, decreasing unemployment benefits and their duration which creates longstanding unemployment, eliminating some (many) past and present subsidies to create jobs which failed (which means - savings), diminishing far more determinedly huge government apparels (including the mammoth and very costly European Commission and Union), etc...

It also includes diminishing social charges and taxes which bog down both corporations and mainly the middle class populations. These are very costly and require financing, but not through "new" tax hikes, like VAT increases, as is being proposed (!), these measures having also been hurting corporations and middle class populations.

I will analyze far more extensively in this Chapter the measures that can be taken, dividing them into those who are not only "low cost" but will bring in savings and will accelerate recovery, and those which are costly, need financing, and should to be regionally tested before application.

Part of these reforms can be partially financed by Germany (*), who will be ready to commit if countries like France, Italy and other smaller countries will firmly commit to implementing social-economic structural reforms (see above). France has not done any (other than inefficient "reformettes") in many decades, and Italy's Prime Minister has referred to them, but has not initiated any, so far.

Germany cannot do it all and even more so with a deteriorating economic situation in 2014, it is increasingly suffering from lack of exports to its weak Eurozone partners plus the effect of negative societal reforms after the Grand Coalition since 2013, but since the Eurozone area still must represent close to 20% of world trade, if the Eurozone can "justify" that these structural reforms will be implemented, it will again attract private investment from ex – Eurozone major countries, instead of solely issuing massive Central Banking liquidity inflows.

I basically am in agreement with Germany's policy, even if it requires some changes (please refer to a more extensive comments further on in this Chapter), but only for Germany itself in terms of how they are applied.

Germany has been and still is the "de facto" leader of the Eurozone and has indirectly pushed, through the totally inefficient and techno bureaucratic European Commission, the "golden rules" some 2 to 3 years ago, which turned out to be a "fiasco, because the actual application was mainly higher taxation without comprehensive planning and only reactive and piece meal (France having the record on this) and decreases in wages and pensions, or a totally "sacrificial" call it "policy"- with no stressing of the urgent need for social-economic structural reforms (which Germany itself had applied since 2000).

On top of it, these "rules" were applied equally to all Eurozone countries, same macro goals in deficit and indebtedness, same timing (!), not taking into consideration the economic situation in every separate Eurozone member country, nor the differences in history, traditions, idiosyncrasies, mentality, etc...

The result was very bad and did not further growth obviously, the contrary in effect.

This is when the BCE, under Mr. Dragui's leadership, started with the massive liquidity inflows, late 2011 and in March 2012 with two LTROs for 1 Trillion euros at refinancing rate close to zero, and over 3 years, liquidity offers that were badly used, since most of it went to financing sovereign bonds and increase indebtedness, with Mr. Dragui continued pushing now for another 1 Trillion euros liquidity inflows in covered asset and ABS, and insisting of issuing printed money as the QEs in the US.

These solely monetarist actions will, once more (!), be the excuse for the weak Eurozone countries to not implement the social-economic structural reforms on a gradual basis, which are the most realistic and productive approach to obtain durable and internationally competitive growth.

Social-economic structural reforms – *the leitmotiv in this book*

Opportunities for Increasing Job Creation

The phrase **"job creation"** has been so overstated by politicians that this "misnomer" needs to be dispelled and uncluttered.

When in the US the pre-dawn of the recession began to show a loss of jobs following the passage of NAFTA, this became a highlight for nearly every person running for office. Of course, this meant much more to a smaller community whose income and economy was reliant upon one major manufacturing or industrial plant in their locale.

Governments recognize that the loss of jobs is relevant and at the origin of the depressed economy (sic). But governments cannot create jobs when employers are unable to expand their business. Job creation is only as good as the business owner not being regulated into the demise of his business plan.

Most middle-class population, are "job holders," not job creators, investors are job creators.

Statistics vary but the average percent of employers to employees is around 1 to 3 percent of the total in the US.

Unless the increasing regulations are not overhauled to stop paying tribute to special interest groups, it is likely that there will be low expansion or growth and even stagnancy – Eurozone -of jobs. The governments should not be the largest employers, but they still are (in 2012 and 2013 the tendency reversed a little in the US), and that is the primary reason why they will never "create" jobs.

They are too busy regulating and passing new laws that stifle production, expansion, and destroy the capability to create more jobs or even keep prevailing jobs for Americans, even more so in most Eurozone countries.

Creating jobs should be the business strategy of the employer. Continuing to write and pass new laws, regulations, and taxes are counterproductive to private sector job creation.

It is high time that politicians should be endorsing and sponsoring "business de-regulation and de-taxation" which would promote a decrease in joblessness and increase job creation.

What solutions – what to "do" – on a realistic and pragmatic basis, without spending Billions beforehand?

Governments in major "Western" countries need to define what they will "do" on a short, medium and long-term basis, and "let their people" know.

This will, at least, provide a necessary "guide" and help to regain confidence.

Without confidence, to reform is much harder, because the people will not understand and will consider they are being "victimized".

Confidence in the government and its defined planning for constructive development will set a different picture in any country, for employers and make them more amenable to both hiring and help provide "transition" formation and training.

Priorities are the following:

Start with remedying what I consider as a fundamental one, which, I believe, consists in the **Re Orientation of Education / Schooling at all levels**, its coordination with "productive" and targeted Formation and Training, with Sectoral / Activity needs, labor unions, employers' associations and per activity branch, to adapt to the needs of the historically meteoric changes in geo-economic structures and in countries' sectoral / per activity evolution.

This is a long-term evolution, but needs to be started far more seriously now, because if this does not happen the gap between the "scholars – at different levels of education - entering the market and their acceptance by activity sectors which are the most dynamic, will widen.

Not enough, by far, is made by Government to "make working easier", social-economic structural reforms should be agreed upon and implemented. The "politicking" should cease and "normal" politics should "come back", formal budgets for 1 year, 5 years, and maybe 10 years (?), should be finally agreed upon, to lift the ceaseless anxiety of the population.

Too Big Government and Regulations

Entrepreneurs can be far more capable than Government to create "real" jobs. But for this to happen, Government needs "to get out of the way out" and let private business be the employers.

Public policy should be geared more toward encouraging entrepreneurship and small-business creation rather than to supporting the small business sector per se.

This is based on the observation that most small firms don't grow, once they reach capacity, and that during any given period of time, net new job creation comes more from the growth of new firms, and not so much in existing firms.

Most large firm, in say "IT", but it should not be limited to this sector of activity, started off small. As business picks up, and unless the enterprise has a total innovative product, there is a need for working capital financing which will enable both local and export expansion. In the US, this is more reachable than in most of Europe and in the Eurozone.

The US adds 3 million new people to the population every year, so more "business" is required. That's why in the US "small firms" have continued to account for over 60% of job creation." The increased population also drives more cars, but unlike the small firm, those cars are produced with little new job creation. Without population growth, there would be no job growth. Jobs would change over time, but there would be no job growth with a static population.

During the "Big Crisis" which started in 2007-08, 8 million workers lost their jobs in the US. Large firms were not responsible for most of this - small firms mostly were, the trend continues…

This is, to me, mainly caused by the fact that selective markets (Dow Jones, Nasdaq, Footsie Dax, CAC 40, etc…) which list only large international corporations do increasingly more than half of their total business outside of their "home" country.

It also shows that FED's huge monetary efforts / "stimulus" were not discriminated and properly targeted and favored large banks who "served/

allowed credit" far more to the "safer" big corporations, and not to the biggest employer in any country: the SMEs, and to growing innovative corporations

The 50 largest employers in the **Fortune 500** employ only about 12 million people **(8%** out of 156 million civilian workers employed), and about half of those are overseas. If the new firms had to resolve this problem and put those unemployed back to work, it would take net 1.6 million new firms to be added to the 6 million now in existence; that would re-employ the 8 million workers who lost their jobs in the "Big Crisis", provided those firms started with an average of 5 workers which most do not. The jobs problem we face today is that employment is below capacity in existing firms and public policy should focus on what might be done to get existing firms to re-employ those that had jobs at their firms at the peak of the expansion.

The "start up" rate for new firms has declined in the US from about 12% in 1980 to only 8% in 2001 / 2012. The growth of government may well be a cause. Over the same period, government's share of our GDP has grown steadily as has the volume of regulations. Regulatory compliance per worker is much higher for small firms than for large ones, according to the SBA, and affirmed by the millions of small firms all over the nation.

Dealing with government is a "regressive tax," favoring "largeness" and discouraging the entrepreneurship that the authors feel is critical to our future economic success.

With 90% of US employer firms having fewer than 20 employees, government, through taxes, tax complexity and regulations, handicaps existing employers and discourages new ones from starting.

The same problem, and worse in terms of "red tape" and no social-economic structural reforms, exists in a majority of Eurozone weak countries.

Tax rates and regulatory costs and paperwork burdens impact all small firms, **new or old,** every year and "tax" the important entrepreneurial resources of the small business sector. The Administrations "talk a lot" about reducing this burden, but actions speak louder than words and the evidence is clear that neither tax nor regulatory burdens have been and it is questionable that they are going to be significantly, if at all (?) reduced.

This is something that needs to change to enable the US, and far more the Eurozone, to restore the vitality of their economies.

Hundreds of thousands applications allow users of companies like APPLE to know where is … the next free garage space or…toilet, with information which in many cases is not very useful, but which creates stress, because people discuss them and feel that they should "benefit" from them, when many of them are costly and sometimes quite erroneous.

Information is so extended that for the average person it becomes difficult to digest and handle or manage, this creating real stress.

Politicians, in debates, which in general are insufficiently monitored, throw all kind of statistical numbers at each other, where few moderators are able, or "permitted" (sic), to question them.

The end result is that most of the audience cannot understand, and even less retain, most of the macro "numbers", and do not know which are correct or not, because most politicians tend to use the numbers which favor them, these being in a great number of cases also wrong.

All this creates increasing confusion, and there is an increasing feeling of doubt on what politicians say to their "people", this justifying the great loss of confidence that people have in politicians, which polls show in 2014.

Since over a quarter of a Century, a long period of time, there has not been a per country or area "vision" of what type of evolution a country / area should have in terms of various factors like its history, mentality, idiosyncrasy, particular know-how, etc…, to develop in the medium and long-term future.

INNOVATION

Innovation companies are job makers – IT / Software as the example

To develop the subject of a "product segment" which is representative of the above meteoric evolutions, I will refer to IT development.

IT has and will continue so having a great impact on the evolution of the US economy and to a lower extent with Eurozone, a gap thus area needs to fill with entrepreneurship and lower regulations, in spite of rumors that very high market caps from Apple and Google, plus social media leaders like Facebook, Twitter with their enormous audiences and estimated huge market value valuations, are remainders (or reminders) of the "bubble" of the end of the 1990's.

Market caps are extremely high for the 1rst 3 "IT": Apple, Google, Microsoft companies, representing together 3 times their Revenues. These very high market caps of these companies bring their PE ratios down to 8-9% for Apple and Google, even if their net profitability is way above average.

This makes some analysts believe that they are too high, and might create a "bubble", this remaining to be seen.

Analysts think that these large IT corporations might be "low employers", and that their meteoric progression might be damaging to job creation progression, this being partially the case from a very short-term appreciation standpoint, but we should try and estimate how many jobs have been and are also indirectly created by large IT corporations, and I would think that it would be considerable.

Too much of the debate is still around financial valuation, as opposed to the underlying intrinsic value of the best of Silicon Valley's new companies. My own theory is that we are in the middle of a dramatic and broad technological and economic shift in which IT / Software companies are poised to take over large swathes of the economy.

More and more major businesses and industries are being run on software and delivered as online services—from movies to agriculture to national defense. Many of the winners are Silicon Valley-style entrepreneurial technology companies that are invading and overturning established industry structures. Over the next 10 years, it is expected that many more industries will be disrupted by software, with new world-beating Silicon Valley companies doing the disruption in more cases than not, add the large Asiatic countries like China, India, South Korea.

A great differentiating factor is that start up costs for new "tech" ventures are minimal when compared with those applying 10 years ago (costs are shown as being 10 times lower than a decade ago in 1 example…), main reasons being that infrastructures exist now that had not existed a decade ago, and vastly expanded market for online services exists.

Taking Amazon as an example of what software can accomplish, this online sales corporation being top seller of, say, books when everybody thought that online books' sales would be unimportant. Amazon having proven that through software they could sell about everything, without a single retail shop, whether this is so good for "humanity" is another story....

Going away from "entertainment and communication oriented services", we can cite Walmart, FedEx, oil and gas companies, financial services, as using software as their basic services "tool".

Health care and education are "lagging behind", they are next up for fundamental software-based transformation.

This is a profoundly positive story for the American economy, in particular. It's not an accident that many of the biggest recent technology companies—including Apple, Google, Microsoft, Amazon, eBay and more—are US companies. The combination of great research universities, a pro-risk business culture, deep pools of innovation-seeking equity capital and reliable business and contract law is unprecedented and unparalleled in the world".

Again, Asiatic countries with differences in how they operate are increasingly creating the same type of giant IT corporations, Europe lagging behind.

India, China, South Korea have been "pushing" very strongly to form their (younger) people to acquire this education and these skills, this not only by making it possible for them to get US education and training, but also locally, and are becoming major competitors with regard to the US, and creating giant corporations.

Europe is lagging behind

The Great Crisis very negative consequences have been milder on this business sector

Still, in the US and around the world there is a crying lack of educated and skilled personnel, which are required to participate in the **great new companies coming out of the IT/ software revolution, this** being a long-term process.

Lack of education and skills, is a "killer" short and medium-term, and will continue increasing-short and medium term-unemployment, for obvious reasons: there will be an enormous quantity of people who will not be able to fill the new jobs created by new "IT / Software", they already now cannot do it.

It is not all that sure that the expansion of social media will continue to increase exponentially as until now, there are signs of "fatigue" already, maybe people in general, even including part of the younger people (who are writing "text?" which is getting harder to "understand", teenagers use practically only abbreviations…), might want to try to come back to more "direct and human" contacts, and be more concerned about their privacy.

The "Occidental" world : i.e. US and Europe, need to put their house in order, meaning: living within their means, and that requires a different "way of living", where consumption of some goods should not be so immoderately promoted by all the "modern communication" means, like "pushing" for all the next "IT"/ Software "novelties", because some of these new developments, which have and will come out increasingly, with more and more "IT applications", always faster and always more, are not all that much of a great improvement, but more of a "gimmick", and also sometimes do not correspond to claims made by this modern communication. It will also increase the stress of "keeping up with it", make people spend more, and this is already, and if continued (which it will until saturation arrives) might become a vicious circle.

So, what to do concretely?

A top priority is putting considerable funding, government and private, into Education and Schooling at various levels, which if focused on competitive skills' formation and also training, would really be "stimulus"!

It remains unclear how rigidly Eurozone governments will stick with austerity measures, especially facing street protests and voter wrath at the polls. What is clear, where data is available, is that the youth in the Eurozone have been disproportionately impacted by unemployment. Even in countries like Austria and Germany, which have low unemployment rates, youth unemployment is significantly higher, although nowhere near as high as the staggering 50 percent youth unemployment rate in Spain.

High youth unemployment not only makes violent protests against austerity measures more likely, it will have a negative impact on the long-term competitiveness of the affected economies. Young workers that are not acquiring the work experience and skills needed to compete in a global marketplace may find themselves falling further and further behind and into greater and greater debt. The policies of an ever closer union in the Eurozone have not helped in bringing down unemployment, which is another key reason why Euro skeptics will continue to gain ground across Europe.

Unemployment in the Eurozone

Figures are for January 2013, seasonally adjusted.

Country	Unemployment Rate	Youth Unemployment Rate (age 25 or less)
Greece	27.0%	–
Spain	26.2%	55.5%
Portugal	17.6%	38.6%
Slovakia	14.9%	35.9%
Cyprus	14.7%	–
Ireland	14.7%	30.9%
Eurozone total	11.9%	24.2%
Italy	11.7%	38.7%
France	10.6%	26.9%
Slovenia	10.2%	–
Estonia*	9.9%	–
Finland	7.9%	19.5%
Belgium	7.4%	19.6%
Malta	7.0%	16.0%
Netherlands	6.0%	10.3%
Germany	5.3%	7.9%
Luxembourg	5.3%	18.5%
Austria	4.9%	9.9%

* Figure is for December 2012.

Source: Eurostat news release, "Euro area unemployment rate at 11.9%," March 1, 2013, http://epp.eurostat.ec.europa.eu/cache/ITY_PUBLIC/3-01032013-BP/EN/3-01032013-BP-EN.PDF (accessed March 7, 2013).

heritage.org

This table is self-explanatory and shows the "terrible "youth unemployment" ratios which are constantly increasing, and will worsen throughout 2013 and has extended into 2014 because European / Eurozone «non Governance" continued doing practically nothing significant, except throwing around unfeasible projects.

The biggest problem is the absence in most Eurozone countries of government orientation programs involving schooling at all levels, labor unions, employers' associations, and last but not least corporations on a per activity branch basis, meaning that targeted programs practically do not exist...

In France, for example, every government for the last 30 years has announced ambitious plans to create jobs for young people. In 2009, for example, President Sarkozy said the government would provide 1.3 billion euros in tax breaks and cash incentives for employers who hired young people. President Hollande, is backing the new EU youth employment initiative, having made a program in France to create 150 000 jobs for disadvantaged youths, plus an over 5 years program for creating 500 000 jobs over 5 years, for corporations who hire a young person and keep a senior one.

All of these very costly and badly (not) organized projects which are government supported programs have failed, and unemployment, and even more so youth unemployment (please see further on) has continued to rise.

Even with tax breaks and loan guarantees, companies will not hire with no growth prospects, which is the case across most of Europe, which is in recession. Nor will targeted incentives offset the serious competitiveness problem faced by businesses in such countries as France, where government-mandated social charges and rigid work rules keep labor costs 20% higher than those in Germany.

Youth unemployment is a very serious issue in the European Union, with nearly 6 million young Europeans out of work and trying to find jobs.

Germany and France had announced a plan to create jobs for young people in the European Union, where 23% of those aged 15 to 24 in the labor force are now listed as unemployed (add the underemployed!). "These young people need an answer now," German Labor Minister Ursula von der Leyden said in a television interview before the effort was unveiled at a 05/28/2013 meeting in Paris.

The youth "official" unemployment data is a real catastrophe. In Spain "official youth unemployment is 50 % of this age group working population, in Greece it is 5%, and in the Eurozone it averages around 20-23% (!), thanks mainly to Germany, and also Austria, Finland, Estonia, Latvia, and Lithuania where youth unemployment seemingly diminished or stagnated at far lower levels.

Accordingly to above shown "official" numbers nearly one in four young people (!) in the European Union is looking for work and can't find it, but this ratio may be overstated, since according to the OECD "only" 13% of EU residents aged 15-24 are neither working nor studying, and not all of those are looking for jobs?

As in the US, the unemployment rate counts the unemployed as EU residents aged 15-24 who are neither working nor studying, and not all of those are looking for jobs, a share of only those who are in the labor force. It thereby excludes 15- to 24-year-olds who are enrolled in school or in training programs and therefore not looking for a job.

A more realistic measure might be the "youth unemployment ratio" developed by Eurostat which takes into account the entire population of 15- to 24-year-olds, and determines how many of them are looking for work but can't find it. In the European Union, in 2012, the ratio was close to an unemployment rate of 10%, and in 2013 it will be higher.

The jobs most readily available to young people are temporary and /or part-time, and because young workers have less seniority they're more likely to be laid off, which means that young workers have a significant problem of underemployment, which is not reflected in the "official" data seemingly.

All this uncertainty about the "real" importance of young people unemployment / under employment clearly shows that this situation has not yet, after six years of persistent crisis, been in depth analyzed by European / Eurozone (non) Governance.

University educated people in countries where their participation is high, like in Spain, France, are not getting more jobs than in Germany, where university educated people have a lower participation, but where there is practically no young unemployment thanks mainly to apprenticeship which has been successfully developed for around 2 decades.

"Ideas", like "guarantees" that all young Europeans get some kind of aid which in practice are totally impossible, are the reason that nothing gets ever decided because they are totally unrealistic and impossible to implement, even with theoretical funding.

It will not require anymore a full-fledged education to be successful in "manual arts", also in "plastic arts", and intermediate diplomas should be made available systematically to show that "credible" education for particular / specific skills can be obtained, with corporations' interventions in the learning process, this preparing far more young people to be immediately accessible for specific jobs.

This will not create jobs - now, so it will be necessary to act short-medium-long term, but start with changes in education orientation.

Short-medium term - Looking at economic factors which affect job creation and which need far more in-depth analysis:

Changing the Banking Sector Use of Funds

This requires really fighting against speculation and "betting against" nations 'efforts, this will enable / force banks to be far more positive and active in addressing their funds to lending to medium / small corporations (SMEs) who are the biggest employers in any "developed" country in the world, and to growing innovation corporations.

Reversing Jobs' Delocalization

Worldwide economic trends are presenting an opportunity for revamping a large range of US manufacturing. **BCG** and **Accenture** reported in 2010 that Chinese net unit manufacturing costs are rapidly converging on US costs (see below **Foxconn** example please).

You can compare Bill Gates and Steve Jobs with Edison and Henry Ford, in terms of creating "ways of living" changes, pure creativity and innovation, purveyors of employment, etc... Job's dedicated, in the mid-80s, to create a heavily automated factory in Fremont, California, that, at the time, employed hundreds of workers to produce PC – MACs, which did not sell fast enough, Jobs was fired, and in 1962 the factory was closed…

Steve Jobs returned to Apple in 1996 and the great story everybody knows started with all his multi product creations whose names are worldwide known. But his i-pods, pads and phones were and are assembled in China by a Taiwanese-owned contractor, Foxconn, that employs 1 Million people, 250 000 of which worked to produce only APPLE products. These people worked 60 hours per week at about 50 cents an hour, until in 2010 when "a wave of suicides" and labor unrest forced Foxconn to both raise wages and cut hours per worker.

Companies should re calculate their cost of off shoring, this requiring that calculations integrate the entire costs of off shoring and not only "end prices/costs". Companies may have off shored more than what was is in their own self interest, and to help them improve decision making I read of a non-profit Re shoring Initiative, www.reshorenow.org, which provides for free Total Cost of Ownership (TCO) software that helps them calculate the real off shoring impact on their P &L. It also shows the fragility of global supply chains, Chinese and other LLCC (Low Labor Cost Country) wages rising rapidly, with volatile exchange rates parities. All this corresponds to very good timing for US – and European / Eurozone companies to reevaluate their off shoring strategies and bring some of the sourcing home."

RE EQUILIBRATION OF "WHO" BENEFITS FROM UNEMPLOYMENT REDUCTION

I have dedicated **Chapter 1** to try to explain the importance of "tacking" Under Employment and the great need of incorporating an in-depth analysis in social-economic planning and decision making.

Now I want to show who benefits - in the US - from the so far low decreases in "total" unemployment.

This coming table shows "who benefited" from the huge FED stimulus monetary programs since the crisis began.

The big problem is that even small GDP and even smaller Jobs recovery after the lowest point in the crisis, did not have the same effect on employment, which is one of the crucial problem the US is facing.

Next table and related comments should provide more understanding for underlying reasons.

RÉSUMÉ TABLE

Trends in the Index of Real Corporate Profits, Stock Price Averages, and Real Hourly and Weekly Wages of U.S. Workers from the End of the Great Recession of 2007-2009 to the Most Recent Quarter (2009 II = 100)

Time Period	(A) Real Corporate Profits	(B) Dow Jones Industrial Average at Close End of Quarter	(C) S&P 500 Index At Close of Quarter	(D) Average Real Hourly Earnings of All Private Sector Workers	(E) Average Real Weekly Earnings of All Private Sector Workers	(F) Median Real Weekly Earnings of Full-Time Wage and Salary Workers
2009 II	100.0	100.0	100.0	100.0	100.0	100.0
2009 IV	118.5	123.5	121.3	99.8	98.7	100.3
2010 II	134.6	115.7	112.2	100.6	101.3	99.0
2010 IV	138.6	137.0	136.9	100.4	101.3	99.6
2011 I	139.6	145.8	144.3	99.8	100.6	99.0
Percent Change 2009 II to Present	+39.6%	+45.8%	+44.3%	-.2%	+.6%	-1.0%

The above summary table shows a very bleak picture in terms of social-economic "recovery".

The US recovery from the 2007-2009 great crises which peaked from the 2nd Qtr. 2009 to the 1rst Qtr. 2011 **is both - a jobless and wage less one.**

Aggregate employment still has not increased above the lowest quarter of 2009, and real hourly and weekly wages have been flat and even negative.

The only major beneficiaries, of the recovery have been corporate profits and the stock market and (some?) of its shareholders.

Productivity gains were, in general, not "passed on" to workers and wage earners, but to corporate profit, this also helping small recovery in GDP.

To put it more clearly, workers' share in companies' productivity gains was extremely low and therefore did not increase their purchasing power.

The gap between hourly compensation and productivity is the highest it's been since just after World War II.

This divergence is one of the major drivers of the nation's growing income inequality. "A bigger share of what businesses in the US are producing is going to corporations' owners, to those who lent money to the corporations, and a smaller share is going to workers.

It is obvious that lower pay by job is not desirable, but the pay is in line with demand and if low - pay sectors are more in demand, the pay will be lower.

It behooves governments to target activity sectors with great potential where the pay is above average, and facilitate working in these sectors with minimum work rule, high job flexibility, and far less red tape.

Productivity, which measures the goods and services generated per hour worked, seemingly (???) rose by 80.4% between 1973 and 2011, compared to a 10.7% growth in median hourly compensation, according to the left-leaning Economic Policy Institute, which provided the numbers in 2012. This data must be (very) inflated seeing the origin, and should only be taken as meaning that the gap has been, and probably still is, "quite large".

Where did the productivity go? Mr. Krugman offered no in-depth analysis as to why this was happening, but did state that "Income stagnation does not reflect overall economic stagnation; the incomes of typical workers would be 30 or 40 percent higher than they are if inequality hadn't soared."

I think that most probably one of the disconnections between markets' increases and nations far weaker social-economic situations, is that listed large international corporations took most of the profit coming from increased productivity and increased their wealth and value, but, even if logical, this still is only supposition.

Recovery "value" would have been greater if "value" of wages and salaries had not decreased substantially: 5% between 2009 -2007 – and 2% between end 2010 and 2007.

The world has totally changed starting with sectoral activity huge participation differences with Services and IT / Software having "emerged" very strongly at the detriment (partially) of manufacturing (because services create "manufacturing" jobs too) and surely agriculture, geo-politics have changed with the huge emergence of BRICSS and other South Koreas and Indonesias, etc... , globalization is here!

Worse yet, a steadily higher share of the jobs created in the current "recovery" are low-wage positions in retail and restaurants, while wages for the new generation of auto workers are half that of their predecessors.

The United States leads the industrial world in the percentage of its jobs that are low-wage.

New jobs equal low wages in general. This is another factor that makes the slow US recovery not effective.

Recovery "value" would have been greater if value of wages and salaries had not decreased substantially: 5% between 2009 -2007 – and 2% between end 2010 and 2007.

These decreases are mainly related to anti-inflation FED measures.

Most holders of savings and money market accounts also are net losers due to declining real interest rates which have been negative for many interest bearing and money market accounts.

Fully 25 percent of the workforce makes less than two-thirds of the nation's median wage —ahead of Britain (where just 21 percent hold such low-paying jobs), Germany (20 percent) and Japan (15 percent). This is not what the "We're Number One!" chant presumably refers to, but it could. While Americans with money are boosting both the housing and auto markets, the growing number of Americans without is curtailing their shopping

The good things in the economy aren't flowing through to paychecks anyplace else in the US economy, either.

Corporate profits — which comprise a larger share of the nation's economy than at any time since World War II — are being plowed into share buybacks or dividend payments, but decidedly not into wage increases.

Unemployment and underemployment, at 12% of total nonfarm civilian population is still extremely high and falling only very slightly in 2014 in spite of FED's flooding markets with huge QE's at close to zero interest rates during over 5 years!. *Please refer to* Chapter 1

It is high-time that governments "understand" that change in making politics is badly needed and that social-economic planning needs to precede financial (monetary) planning, and not the reverse

The Eurozone situation is even more revealing as the US one, and the relation between "officially" declared unemployed and those underemployed is quite similar to the US situation, with a higher September 2014 situation: 11.5% in the Eurozone versus 5.9% "officially" unemployed in the US.

"Total" and "Real" unemployment in the US in September 2014 represented 12% versus over 20% in the Eurozone

But Eurozone member country governments, who succeed one another, invariably are "reactive" and "political", thinking about re election right after they have been elected, and, invariably want to – go back 30 years and more! – trying to solve problems with "supported" jobs, and not by unpopular social-economic structural reforms, which are those which after a transition period will allow – internationally competitive - growth.

For social-economic structural reforms to be successful, it is required to make an in-depth a priori analysis, since all countries' economies are not only different but also in different stages of evolution and therefore these structural reforms cannot be "universal"

It is accordingly essential to divide them into:

- **"Low cost" measures to reduce total unemployment**

These measures accordingly will bring Revenue in due course of time

- **Costly measures, which again need to be classified as General reforms, Supply side reforms and Demand side reforms, which all will be amortized over time with Growth.**

1. "Low cost" Measures to Reduce Total Unemployment

To start with I will show a list of priorities that need to be implemented for Social-economic structural reforms to be able to be successful, further on I will develop more extensively some of these basic requirements.

Since these are the main factors for improvement to gain or / and regain higher growth through reaching international competitiveness, I will discuss next the main problem areas and propose "solutions".

1A. "Rules to Work" or "Work Rules"

While "work rules" are necessary as a protection to workers against eventual abuses by employers, these work rules have been mishandled and abused since the end of World War II by labor unions / syndicates (the exception being Germany, because they have had co-management with labor unions since many decades), making it practically impossible for corporations to make changes in their workers' employment conditions without having practically always systematic opposition by these labor unions, and therefore making most European "Latin" countries, including France, countries where increasingly local companies delocalize and foreign corporation avoid to invest because they will not be able to compete internationally.

Employers have not allowed either labor unions to integrate management meetings (except Germany) with what is called "co-management" in order to exchange more transparent information, which did not help to improve contacts between both corporations, employers' unions (who do not do much either because they –also –are "politically" minded) and labor unions The best solution is to allow negotiations between activity branches and labor unions, without Government intervention.

Collective Bargaining is Neither a Privilege nor a Right.

Labor Union organizers, whose adherents are increasingly diminishing in many Eurozone countries, generally tell workers what they can or cannot do with their time. They even can, if they feel it is needed to fulfill their objectives, dictate what "others" can or cannot do with their time, by calling for number of unfounded strikes which immobilize – transports / education as examples – great pans of the society.

You could resume this by naming five ways of collective bargaining which can trample various unalienable rights:

1. Collective bargaining agreements may take away the right of individuals to pursue a career of their choice (whether realistic or not) void of union affiliation.
2. Collective bargaining agreements may force individuals into organizations against the free will of those members.
3. Collective bargaining agreements may force union dues out of members who do not even want to belong.
4. Collective bargaining agreements may dictate what members can and cannot do with their free time.
5. Collective bargaining agreements may even dictate what non-members can and cannot do with their free time.

Unions insist they won the rights to collective bargaining through negotiation, which is partially true, but they have been abusing these "negotiated" rights for many decades.

Rights work both ways. No one should have to work for a company if they don't want to. People can quit, or they can strike.

Likewise, no employee and no labor board has any fundamental right to tell businesses who they can hire, who they can fire.

The alleged collective bargaining "rights" of unions were attained over the years through "negotiation," which also included tactics of coercion, bribery, fear-mongering, and vote-buying. Regardless of how attained, even in good-faith, politicians have no right to take away unalienable rights.

Rights of unions must not and cannot be allowed to interfere on the rights of others to not belong to a union and to not pay union dues if they do not want to, but minorities are powerful because they "act" and menace.

I believe that Margaret Thatcher gave a very important example when she very forcefully opposed labor unions in the UK, which took great human and political courage - sweat, blood and tears – Mr. Churchill – both very criticized, but great states' women and men, but they changed the economic situation in the UK at different times and occasions. Obviously this formidable opposition to labor unions left a great number of "victims, but then again, big social reforms take a great toll and leave " bloody" consequences.

The Western World, and even more the Eurozone needs badly and urgently to implement reforms on "Work Rules".

It will take great political "will"!

Besides Mrs. Merkel and her predecessor Chancellor Schroeder, no major Eurozone government imposed, during 4 decades at least, social-economic structural reforms.

This will also require a drastic change in the composition and attitude of the countries' governments themselves - and a totally revamped European Governance, which took place and starts on November 1, 2014 but holds no great promise for changes in approach, we will see (or not...).

1B. Labor Flexibility

Summary

This major point can be defined as the corporation's ability to make changes to their workforce in terms of the number of employees they hire and the number of hours worked by the employees. Labor market flexibility also includes areas such as wages and unions.

A flexible labor market is one where firms are under fewer regulations regarding the labor force and can therefore set wages (i.e. no minimum wage), fire employees at will and change their work hours. A labor market with low flexibility is bound by rules and regulations such as minimum wage restrictions and requirements from labor unions

Supporters of increased labor market flexibility argue that it leads to lower unemployment rates and higher GDP. However, its opponents claim that flexibility puts all the power in the hands of the employer, resulting in an insecure workforce.

* "External numerical flexibility"

External numerical flexibility refers to the adjustment of the labor intake, or the number of workers from the external market. This can be achieved by employing workers on temporary work or fixed-term contracts or through relaxed hiring and firing regulations or in other words relaxation of Employment Protection Legislation, where employers can hire and fire permanent employees according to the firms' needs.

* Internal numerical flexibility

Internal numerical flexibility - sometimes known as working time flexibility or temporal flexibility, this flexibility being achieved by adjusting working hours or schedules of workers already employed within the firm. This includes part-time, flexi time or flexible working hours / shifts (including night shifts and weekend shifts), working time accounts, leaves such as parental leave, overtime.

* Functional flexibility

Functional flexibility or organizational flexibility is the extent employees can be transferred to different activities and tasks within the firm. It has to do with organization of operation or management and training workers. This can also be achieved by outsourcing activities.
Job rotation is a label referring to many functional flexibility schemes.

* Financial or wage flexibility

Financial or wage flexibility is in which wage levels are not decided collectively and there are more differences between the wages of workers. This is done so that pay and other employment cost reflect the supply and demand of labor. This can be achieved by rate-for-the-job systems, or assessment based pay system, or individual performance wages.

Other than the 4 types of flexibility there are other types of flexibility that can be used to enhance adaptability. One way worth mentioning is flexibility of place. This entails employees working outside of the normal work place such as home based work, outworkers or "television workers ». This can also cover workers who are relocated to other offices within the establishment."

* Flexibility for workers

However, labor market flexibility does not only refer to the strategies used by employers to adapt to their production / business cycles as in the definitions above.

Increasingly the common view is that labor market flexibility can potentially be used for workers and companies / employers and employees. It can also be used as a method to enable workers to adjust working life and working hours to their own preferences and to other activities.

As companies adapt to business cycles and facilitate their needs through the use of labor market flexibility strategies, workers adapt to their life cycles and their needs through it. (Chung, 2006)

The European Commission also addresses this issue in its Joint Employment Report and its Flexicurity approach, calling for an adequate methods to enhance flexibility for both workers and employers that is capable of quickly and effectively mastering new productive needs and skills and about facilitating the combination of work and private responsibilities. (Chung 2008)

ETUC also emphasize the importance of the development of working time flexibility as an alternative to implementing external flexibility as the sole method of increasing flexibility in the labor market (ETUC, 2007). In their report on working time, TUC has also argued that flexible working should be extended to all workers through stronger regulations (Fagen et al. for TUC, 2006). As authors Gerson and Jacobs agree that "flexibility and autonomy are only useful if workers feel able to use them" (Gerson & Jacobs, 2004, pg. 238). Therefore, if the policies and benefits are being offered, our hope, as management, is that our employees take advantage of the opportunities."

I feel that above quoted definitions provide a very clear meaning of what labor flexibility means.

Problem is that mainly all of "Southern" Eurozone countries and France do not apply labor flexibility (France has made a "timid" reform proposal on "Job Securitization" only), which made no differences

Instead they tend to create taxation which has a counterpart a reduction on labor charges, provided the application is well targeted, which is rarely the case.

This, to me, has two great disadvantages:

One, it does not address the origin or reasons for high labor cost and productivity since it is like a subsidy for corporations to utilize as they seem fit ...

Two, it eliminates necessary dialogue between employers and labor unions, it is pure Government intervention.

Therefore, labor flexibility is a powerful "tool" to increase labor savings, higher productivity and also creates a better labor atmosphere within corporations, and should be applied in all Western countries.

1C. Labor Support – Job Creation – All kinds of Subsidies/ Subventions - to be reviewed in-depth

There have been a huge number of all kinds of subsidies created over the last 3 or 4 decades in Western World countries, and also a large part of these subsidies have piled one on the other and to a great extent have been maintained in annual budgets.

These subsidies are of all kinds:

* **Labor support Programs**

These programs are mainly free or partially government assisted jobs, which in most cases did not work out because not targeted to selected activities sectors, because beneficiaries had not received a priori adequate formation and training and were not retained by the corporations or left their jobs to collect unemployment indemnities, and because beneficiaries were not properly informed of these benefits, since administrative "red tape" continues being unbeatable!

If all these labor support programs were reviewed in depth in terms of their adequacy productivity and affordability, a great number of them would be eliminated, which will provide large savings to be partially (*) retained to be utilized as formation and training programs, which need to be in targeted to economies per activity / sectoral needs, and not created indiscriminately.

In order to orient / target these formation and training programs as productively as possible, there needs to be far greater coordination between representative education / schooling institutions, employers 'associations by branches of activity and labor unions.

In some countries there are so many and various subsidies that potential beneficiaries do not know of the existence of a large part of them, therefore communication needs to improve tremendously and be summarized for public "understanding".

(*) These savings should also be partially used in financing innovation programs by large SMES and also, in some cases in selected start-ups, which have the best chances to be internationally competitive.

- **Apprenticeship programs**

Germany is always cited as being the "model" for apprenticeship programs, and it did work for decades thanks to good understanding between corporations' management, labor unions, employers 'associations, etc....

But times change and nowadays Germany finds itself with non filled jobs for apprenticeship.

It is also a matter of behavior, seemingly many apprentices do not follow elementary rules, like bringing cellular's to the job and using them, not following basic rules on service to customers in spite of having received adequate training. To illustrate "modern non behavior" in activity sectors which in the past had numerous hiring examples in apprenticeship, like the leisure market, including hotels, restaurants, and other services, as an example, apprentices prefer to work in non top hotels, because they can wear their own clothes and not uniforms.

The result is that since some years and increasingly so, there is a great number of unfilled vacancies. Corporations are encouraged to use "speed dating" between corporations and eventual candidates organized by the German Chamber of Commerce and Industry (DIHK). Another alternative is "on the job" training with totally non trained youth and allow them 4 years to perform, including immigrant population;

Apprenticeship continues being an employment alternative that is largely better than providing government subsidized and non targeted jobs, but it is needed to adapt this form of employment to societal changes.

- **Health programs and subsidies**

The national and private health systems vary greatly between the US and Europe and in Europe / Eurozone between countries.

In the US the so called "entitlement" programs, Social Security, Medicare and Medicaid, and lately " Obamacare" have been the object of political discussions over decades as to their coverage, costs and effectiveness in general. This very important issue will not be further discussed here, but the US government needs to reach a decision on both the system and its costs, because budget wise it is the most important "entitlement" item in the US budget.

In Europe there are great disparities in health programs, some are far more generous than others (who may be lacking in appropriate coverage). In these very different national health systems backed up by private or "mixed" type of complementary health insurance programs there are a great number of "unproductive" expenses being incurred, also absenteeism which is abusive and great improvements to be made in adapting remunerations to the different medical acts performed.

The cost of health programs has been increasing in many countries which indirectly has an effect on employment because of unfilled needs of preventive health programs which increase "justified by sickness" absenteeism.

A total re examination of heath programs needs to be made in European countries, like in the US, but hoping for more rapid resolution than in the US, so far.

- **Unemployment Benefits – Amounts and length**

There are large variations between European countries of the length and amounts of Unemployment benefits, these two factors need to be revised because they constitute a very heavy expense in some countries.

- **Tax programs and loopholes, which also can be considered as a kind of subsidy**

Again, there has been a huge build-up of these tax loopholes, and as for labor subsidies there needs to be a large and in-depth review of them, being very discriminate in order not to eliminate "employment productive" taxes.

It also has to avoid the "populist" concepts of taxing outrageously the "very rich", because they can be otherwise solicited by requesting they aid SMES in their development in return of continuing to allow for some tax loopholes.

To make this review work, it requires a complete re examination of the whole direct and indirect tax system, and not to do it reactively - piecemeal, as is the custom unfortunately.

⁌ Other subsidies

There are far more subsidies of different nature in most Western countries, which have been originated through states in the US and governments in Europe "lobbying".

These subsidies need to be first "listed" and then reviewed for "productivity" and also for whatever valid "community contribution" they may provide.

"Latin" Governments, including France, in general, prefer to increase taxes than to review expenses, which is totally incoherent, and political.

Populations seemingly "accept" with less difficulty tax increases because government promise that these increases supposedly are justified to provide lower labor costs for corporations and will therefore increase their competitiveness and end up by creating more jobs, but in reality most of these "programs" have been extremely inefficient, because of lack of targeting – please see above comments

Expense reductions by governments originate, in general, labor unions more or less severe reactions, going from all kinds of street manifestations to more or less harsh strikes, immobilizing parts of the population. Expense reductions mean less "acquired" advantages of all kinds – see list of subsidies above please – and is well known that to take something from somebody provokes very negative reactions.

Governments "know" this well, and will, generally sacrifice implementing these expense reductions, to getting good surveys of popularity for election or re election…

This is why, if there is no real political will, nothing much will happen for these categories of unproductive and becoming increasingly unaffordable types of expenses.

1D. Retirement Age

The age of retirement is a very important issue, because of the generally ageing demography curve in Western countries.

There is quite a bit of confusion about the real meaning of retirement ages in the various Western countries.

Some have a legal age; some have a legal age tied in with the number of years worked, some have no legal age, etc…

It is essential to plan ahead and extrapolate historical curves on birthrate, which is the ratio of total live births to total population in a particular area over a specified period of time; expressed as childbirths per 1000 people, mortality /death age evolution, in terms of the demographic curve in each of the Western countries.

This is vital because of an ageing population, the number of "active" population decreases and this will be a factor of insufficient retirement funds to cover the increasing retirees' pensions.

It is therefore not an option, but a necessity to increase both the employment time and the age level for retirement.

This essential factor is not sufficiently recognized by a series of Western countries in both increasing requirements for retirement by the duration of working periods and the age of retirement and actualize a series of early XX Century about job penuries which due to progress do not exist anymore.

Several countries have adopted capitalization systems to finance partially increase retirement costs, some "mixed "ones with traditional redistribution.

In the OECD an average 20% to 30% of retirement costs is financed by capitalization programs.

I will not stress this point at this time, even if it makes contributors responsible for retirement programs, because to invest funds without risk and at a reasonable rate of return has become extremely difficult nowadays because of increasing macro volatility.

All this ties in with points already covered earlier about the young population formation and training needs to be able to incorporate as "active" workers those young people who do not want to complete "high" education and prefer to take a job.

On the senior age stage – say, 55 or more, it is necessary to provide far better adapted re formation and training methods, in order to allow seniors to perform "decently" in jobs they were not accustomed doing. Over a certain age, seniors who receive adequate (?) formation, need to accept lower remuneration in line with remuneration of younger middle age performers.

It is a real necessity for governments to increase "active" population from both age sides: the under 25 and the over 55 age groups, to increase the base of the "active" population which is required to cover retirement funds for the retirees

1E. Sectoral / per activity evolution – Orientation for Schooling / Education, Formation and Training needs

It requires an in-depth analysis, going back 20 - 30 years at least to determine the evolution of jobs per activity sector and determine a valid trend.

The main objective of this analysis is to determine where the "competitive" pluses and minuses per activity sector are.

The next step is to analyze what can be done to optimize the "pluses", and diminish, if realistically possible, the "minuses.

This will serve as an orientation guide for education / schooling reorganization in terms of setting realistic goals for students to be able to be able to "productively" enter different labor markets.

This will require different ways of setting educational programs, in content and length, to effectively prepare students to enter different job markets with different requirements which they will have to satisfy to obtain jobs.

This will serve as an orientation guide for training and providing government supported apprentice ship jobs and other types of support jobs with young people being hired if seniors are also hired to serve as "guides" (as an example, between many of "supported" by government jobs).

So far, there have been a great number of government "supported" jobs, which have not been at all "productive" and did not last long and consumed high budgets, which could have been differently and productively utilized, if job creation measures had been planned in sufficient depth, and not reactively" to show populations that governments "did" help them.

I do not have sufficient data on sectoral analysis for the same period as the one hereafter shown analyzed (2007 - 2010), much less on, say, the last 20 - 30 years, where analysis and conclusions would be far more significant.

Coming from economic modeling specialists (EMSI) I have seen: An interactive graphic showing changes in employment -2011-2001 - in geographic areas within the US (like where services expanded more - see bigger green globes), which can be related (with additional info) to types of activity.

Charts on sectoral changes between 2008 -2011 which show health care expanding by far the most with close to 20% increase, which is logical with an ageing population and also medicine progress, with finance & insuring and educational services running far away second

This is the type of analysis which needs to be expanded by Ministries of Economics and particularly Ministries of Labor - Change in Employment by Industry: '2001-2011'

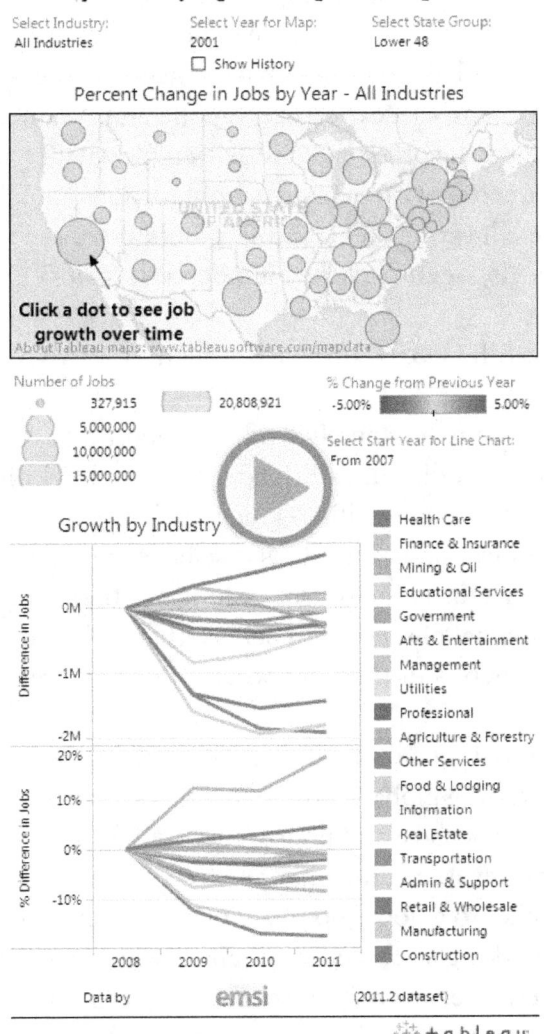

It needs to be focused on because it is vital to know if sectoral change is contributing to high structural unemployment, where no fiscal or monetary stimulus have been able to bring about significant reductions, which demonstrates that focus has not been sufficiently efficient in terms of social-economics and sectoral / by activity analysis.

It is known that non - farm employment has suffered less, that manufacturing's impact on employment has decreased, and that accordingly what is loosely called "Services" has gained considerable impact. But Services in the US enclose: caricature, on one end: Walmart employment ("non tech"), and on the other end: Google employment ("tech"). It should be "easier" for unemployed persons to obtain jobs in Walmart than in Google, because education and training should be easier to implement?

This brings us, again, to the number one priority: **"Education / Schooling"**.

Quotes from Bill Gross – former President of PIMCO Fund:

"If we are to compete globally while maintaining a higher wage base, we must train for "middle" in addition to "high" tech. Philosophy, sociology and liberal arts agendas will no longer suffice.

Skill-based education is a must, as is science and math."

"The private sector is the source of long-term job creation but in the short term, no rational observer can believe that global or even small businesses will invest here - in the US - when the labor over there - Asia - is so much cheaper".

"That is why trillions of dollars of corporate cash rest impotently on balance sheets awaiting global – non - US – investment opportunities. Our labor force is too expensive and poorly educated for today's marketplace."

"Students, however, can no longer assume that a four year degree will be the golden ticket to a good job in a global economy that cares little for their social networking skills and more about what their labor is worth on the global marketplace, an ivory tower for the past half century".

Bill Gross (like Messrs. Krugman, Sachs, Zakaria, Immelt, proposes to set up an "infrastructure bank" for "reconstruction programs", all these being different proposals, but all "rather" Keynesian. The fact that first grade students are brought up with "the computer", has positive sides (it makes using IT "instruments" a natural and will further adaptation to XXI Century requirements), and negative sides (it makes them think less and read less, since a lot of the work is "programmed")

Not being a trained economist, but still having kept somehow up to date on economics, and generally speaking as an experienced international businessman, I definitely am not a Keynesian advocate, because the world has changed tremendously, and relatively obsolete theories do not work anymore.

Also because I believe that free stimulus" programs lately have not been successful, see Employment…

Students across the US are provided access to career services centers, resume workshops, and personality or aptitude assessments throughout high school and college. But far too many young adults leave school without the proper knowledge or ability to successfully apply for jobs, write cover letters, or think strategically in an interview.

According to a Gallup poll, only 18% of Americans believe high school graduates are ready for the working world and only little more than half (54 percent) of Americans believe the same for college graduates.

What their definition of "prepared" is "uncertain", but for sure something's missing from the educational system that prepares students for the "real world". In fact, statistics show that US colleges aren't devoting as much money or employees to these resources as they are in areas such as recruitment. In a 2010 study of for-profit colleges, there were 35 202 recruiters employed, compared to 3 512 career services staff and 12 452 support services staff.

Plus, education costs are at its highest level in the US and require many "mortgage/repaying" years on loans conceded to this young population of students' future after education to repay these fees, creating a serious handicap on spending habits and the increase in demand – please see significant chart on this further on.

What is, generally, falling short in the education of young adults on careers, the job search process, and how to find meaningful work resides in many cases that this young population has the skills to obtain these jobs, but don't have the know-how to be successful in landing them.

This makes following measures (not a limitative "list") necessary to enable this young population to obtain the necessary knowledge to be competitive job seekers out of school:

Integrate required careers courses into every student's curriculum. US high school seniors and college freshmen or seniors could all benefit from taking required courses that prepare them for the job search.

If US high school seniors decide not to pursue college and instead go to a trade school or immediately into the workforce, will they be leaving the educational system with the knowledge to write a cover letter or network? Maybe not, but not all students want to or and can afford a "complete" education, and intermediate degrees can help them to seek jobs if they have had some acquired working know-how in their CVs

Market career counseling at colleges and universities

The disconnection between student and career counselor at colleges and universities is very common. Career counselors stress that students just don't understand or realize the breadth of opportunities and services they provide. Career services centers should focus on not only providing relevant and timely materials, workshops, and strategies to their students. They should be more pro active in reaching out to their students.

Require internships or apprenticeships for graduation.

Employers and educators alike can agree that internships are an integral part of landing a job out of college. While some universities already require students to obtain an internship prior to graduation, others only encourage it. But an internship can make the difference between landing a job and being underemployed. High school students should also be encouraged to do the same. While many of these students may not know what their career path is quite yet, require them to shadow a local business or organization in their field of their interest.

Young population must really realize that they need to learn these skills before graduating and pursuing their first job.

Creating jobs for everyone's interests and skill level is only half the battle. Lets create a more valuable degree for our youth by not only giving them the skills necessary to succeed in their industry, but also to navigate their career competitively and knowledgeable in the future.

In the Eurozone, Youth unemployment is shockingly high in Greece, Spain, and Italy, and other Eurozone countries as shown by Europe's Most Tragic Graph by The Atlantic:

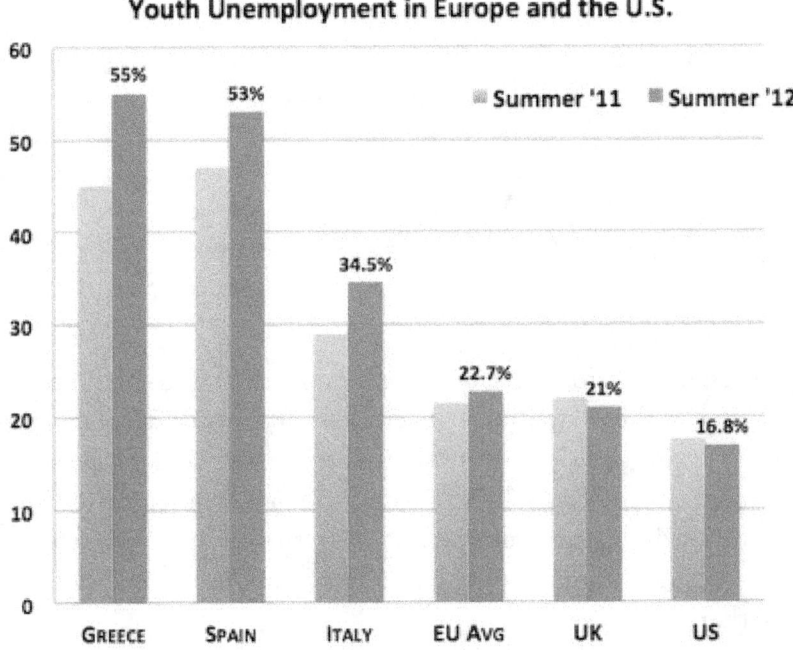

The statistics on Youth Unemployment have already been included in Chapter1

The primary answer is as already several times mentioned before:

Too much work rules, great lack of work flexibility, no motivation to seek jobs because of useless subsidies by governments which are not productive, pension rules, and other rules, that are so harsh that companies simply do not want to hire workers.

A subject which creates "discussion" is the potential (already existing) redistribution of income between the "young" and the "senior / retiree populations" which I will partially summarize, because it shows that the "active" population will increasingly diminish through demographic projections and that if no specific and realistic / productive actions are taken in favor of diminishing radically the problems of insertion of the "young", this will affect the " senior " population as well, and governments will have, for political reasons (seniors" vote counts!...), to provide "subsidies" (which it should not).

These comments do not apply only to the United States - they apply, even much more, to most European countries as well.

1F. Macro Factors Which Will Play in the Evolution of Creating More Jobs

A more slowly growing workforce

The projected labor force growth over the next 10 years will be affected by the aging of the baby-boom generation; as a result, the labor force is projected to grow at a slower rate than in the last several decades.

The recession of 2007–2009, a sluggish labor market, crises in the financial and credit markets, and weakness in the housing sector have combined to create great uncertainty about the future of the US economy and labor market.

Demography

However, despite all these problems, a very important factor in the economy is the size and demographic composition of the population, which together determine the growth and composition of the labor force. As suggested by the saying "Demography is destiny":

Demography is a key driving force in the growth of the US economy, the growth of the workforce and almost all social and economic trends.

Compared with the workforce of the past decades, today's workforce is older, more racially and ethnically diverse, and composed of more women.

These trends are expected to continue to shape the future of the workforce; however, the Work force in the US is expected to grow at a slightly slower rate than in previous decades. The annual growth rate of the US workforce over the period 2010–2020 is projected to be 0.7%, lower than the 0.8% growth rate exhibited in the previous decade.

The labor force is projected to increase by 10.5 million in the next decade, reaching 164.4 million in 2020. This 6.8% increase in the size of the labor force is lower than the 7.9% increase posted over the previous 10-year period, 2000–2010, when the labor force grew by 11.3 million.

The slower growth of the labor force is primarily the result of a slower rate of growth in the US population and a noticeable decrease in the labor force participation rate.

The civilian non institutional population - 16 years and older, had an annual growth rate of 1.1% from 2000 to 2010, but is projected to grow by a lesser 1.0% during 2010–2020.

Labor Force Participation

The labor force participation rate started a downward trend in 2000, and the decrease accelerated during the 2007–2009 crises and its aftermath.

The Bureau of Labor Statistics (BLS) produces its labor force projections by multiplying the civilian non institutional population projections by the labor force participation rate projections. As a result, changes projected in the aggregate labor force are the reflection of changes in both the labor force participation rate and changes in the age, gender, racial, and ethnic composition of the population.

Changes in the labor force participation rate are generally gradual, and population growth is the chief factor in the growth of the labor force. However, during the recent recession, the aggregate labor force participation rate also decreased noticeably and affected the growth of the workforce, as can be seen in above chart and comments.

As a result, the labor force participation rate declined by 2.4 percentage points over the 2000–2010 period and is projected to drop by another 2.2 percentage points between 2010 and 2020. The labor force participation rate is now at the lowest level since 1978 - before women flooded into the workforce, pushing the participation rate to record highs.

AGES AND OPTIONS

So who, exactly, is dropping out of the labor force? It's well-known that male-dominated industries such as manufacturing and construction have endured painful and probably permanent shrinkage, which suggests a lot of middle-aged, blue-collar men are now sitting on the sidelines. Some analysts feel extended unemployment insurance has given a lot of laid-off workers a stronger incentive to collect a government check than look for a job. Then there are critics of the "47 percent" (now the 43 percent) of adult Americans who pay no income tax yet somehow eke out a living.

But the numbers tell a somewhat different story about who the labor force dropouts really are. Here are labor force participation rates for different age groups in 1990, 2000 and 2013:

LABOR FORCE PARTICIPATION RATES (PERCENTAGES)

	January 1990	January 2000	August 2013	Change from 1990 to 2013	Change from 2000 to 2013
All, 16 years and older	66.8	67.3	63.2	-3.6	-4.1
Men 16 and older	76.7	75.0	69.5	-7.2	-5.5
Men between 16 and 24	72.3	69.0	56.2	-16.1	-12.8
Men between 25 and 34	94.9	93.7	89.3	-5.6	-4.4
Men between 35 and 44	94.8	93.4	90.5	-4.3	-2.9
Men between 45 and 54	91.0	88.8	85.5	-5.5	-3.3
Men 55 and older	39.7	40.2	46.5	6.8	6.3
Women 16 and older	57.7	60.1	57.3	-0.4	-2.8
Women between 16 and 24	63.3	63.1	53.3	-10.0	-9.8
Women betweem 25 and 34	73.8	76.5	73.3	-0.5	-3.2
Women between 35 and 44	76.6	77.5	74.6	-2.0	-2.9
Women betweem 45 and 54	71.0	77.0	74.0	3.0	-3.0
Women 55 and older (NO DATA)					

In August 2014 the Total labor participation ("All, 16 years and older") rate is 62.7%, the lowest ever

The biggest drop-off has come among young workers.

The recession and subsequent weak recovery have cut sharply into opportunities for entry-level workers, in virtually all industries. Some simply can't find work. Others have chosen to go to college or graduate school instead of looking for a job.

The job woes of this "Millennial" generation have garnered plenty of attention.

More twenty-something's live with their parents these days, which has torpedoed the rate of new-household formation and left homebuilders and automakers anxiously wondering who will buy their products in five or 10 years

The amount of student debt has mushroomed, as many students pay for college with readily available (and often federally backed) loans. Many grads are starting their careers deep in the hole, since they can't find jobs that pay enough to cover their loan payments while still allowing them to live independently.

Those are legitimate problems, but it's also possible that a better educated workforce will pay dividends in a few years' time. College enrollment rates grew at a moderate pace until 1999, after that it began to increase more sharply. The recession lured even more people into higher education, including a lot of older adults who attended community college to acquire new skills. And sure enough, enrollment rates have begun to drift downward now that more young people sense an improving job market and feel they're more likely to find work.

Potential Benefits

That education bulge could give the economy a boost in the future, much as the G.I. Bill did in the 1950s and '60s. Consulting firm McKinsey, for instance, predicts that by 2020, the US economy will face a shortage of about 1.5 million college-educated workers.

If so, demand (and pay) will rise for those who do have a degree, turning at least some of today's workforce dropouts into tomorrow's productive workers. Also, more students have been choosing math and science majors, which seem more likely to lead to profitable work and perhaps a more innovative economy.

It also stands to reason that some dropouts in other age brackets will return to the workforce when or perhaps if, the job market improves enough to make it worth their while. Some dropouts are still working plenty hard as stay-at-home parents or caregivers to their own elderly parents, having made a pragmatic decision that it's not worth the trouble to work in an iffy economy while paying someone else to help with their family obligations.

Also notable is that the participation rate for men over 55 have gone up considerably. That makes sense, since those close to retirement may have the greatest need to pad their savings. Established workers are also in the best position to simply stay in their jobs instead of retiring, compared with younger workers who haven't even found a job in the first place. If older workers gradually improve their finances and once again begin to retire earlier, that could open the door for younger workers to move into their jobs, which might improve hiring down the entire employment food chain.

The real question about labor force dropouts is whether there would still be an elevated number if the economy were as productive today as it was in the late 1990s or even the late 1980s. It might make sense to drop out when the rewards for your work are fairly low. But if workers leave even when the rewards of work go up, then something fundamental has changed. That could end up being the biggest threat to the nation's future prosperity.

The projected workforce growth over the next 10 years will be affected by the aging of the baby-boom generation (boomers), persons born between 1946 and 1964. The baby boomers will be between 56 and 74 in 2020, placing them in the 55-years-and-older age group in the workforce, with distinctively lower participation rates than those of the prime age group of 25 / 54 year old.

1G. BLS Projects and Profiles US Labor Force Trends in the Next 10 Years.

1. First, on the basis of historical population data and projections from the US Census Bureau, past and future trends in the U.S. population are discussed.
2. Then, current and future estimates of labor force participation rates are presented for detailed age, gender, racial, and ethnic groups.
3. Finally, the median age of the labor force for Civilian labor force, by age, gender, race, and ethnicity, 1990, 2000, 2010, and projected 2020

The major subjects covered in this report are the following

- **US population**

The 2010 census measured the US resident population at 308.7 million, an increase of 27.3 million people over a decade. In addition to counting the population every 10 years, the Census Bureau calculates annual population estimates and periodically produces long-term projections of the US resident population by age, gender, race, and ethnicity.

These projections illustrate the demographic forces that are expected to shape the future of the US resident population. Specifically, the US population is expected to get larger, to continue growing at a slower rate, to grow older, and to become more diverse.

Larger population The Census Bureau projects that the US resident population will grow from 308.7 million in 2010 to 341.4 million in 2020, an increase of 32.7 million people in 10 years.

Slower growth Even though the resident population will grow by large numbers, the annual rate of growth is projected to slow from 0.98% during 2009–2010 to 0.94% over the period 2019–2020. The slower rate of growth is primarily the result of the aging of the US population.

Older population A significant factor shaping the future demographics of the US population is the increase in older population cohorts. In 2020, the 55–years-and older age group will total 97.8 million, composing 28.7% of the 2020 resident population, compared with 24.7% in 2010.

More diverse population Immigration has a major role in the growth and makeup of the racial and ethnic composition of the U.S. resident population. Every race and ethnicity is projected to grow over the 2010–2020 period.

However, the share of White non-Hispanics in the total resident population is expected to decrease.

* **Fertility**

The total fertility rate, which is the average number of children born to a woman over the course of her life, is often the largest component of population change and has the greatest impact on the level and growth of the population. Fertility is derived from the behavioral choices people make in planning their future. Even a minor change in the fertility rate, maintained over a long time, can have a great impact on future population growth. Higher fertility rates result in higher population growth, a lower median age, and a larger share of the population for younger age groups.

Assumptions about the fertility rate affect estimates of the labor force with a lag of roughly 16 years, given that the definition of the labor force encompasses only those members of the civilian non institutional population 16 years and older who are employed or unemployed and are looking for a job.

In the most recent Census Bureau projection of the resident population, used as the basis of the BLS workforce projections, the future fertility rate is assumed to remain close to the present level, roughly the replacement level of 2.1.

Differences in fertility rates among various racial and ethnic groups cause different growth patterns in specific population groups.

Compared with other developed countries, the United States has a rather high fertility rate, primarily a result of higher fertility rates among young immigrants of different racial and ethnic backgrounds. However, this differential in fertility rates ultimately converges to the fertility rate of the native population in the second generation of immigrants.

As a parallel example to extend the analysis of the US:

Eurozone's shrinking populations is one of the big problems that this bloc of 18 countries has been having and will continue having increasingly if no improvements are made in the short-term. These Eurozone difficulties are present in the majority of member countries, this example refers mainly to the "leader", **Germany**, and its population drop which already causes social-economic problems and will cause more severe ones in the future if this situation continues

Follow comments on what Germany has not done and what it has been starting doing, which reflects the ability and commitment to change some deeply ingrained customs, towards non immigration and female working.

Germany has the biggest Turkish community outside of Turkey, and in spite of problems which are natural, it seems to have melted rather well into the communities, which has not been the case with mainly France and a huge immigration, mainly coming from North Africa which has been creating trouble since decades, because the obvious potential immigration and housing problems were badly, if not at all, organized since at least 40 to 50 years, creating worrisome ghettos. Immigration to be "helpful" needs to be thought out in great depth and organized - before - a country appeals to immigrants to come and work in a country that is very different in culture and mentality from their country of origin.

Female working is a benefit to the communities and to women in general, but it is very difficult to organize, especially for married women with child/s, the biggest source of diminishing fertility.

Obviously, countries with economies running "well", have fewer problems, but Germany's case shows that even the Eurozone leader and wealthiest country has big problems which if not remediated will shrink the population heavily in the medium-long term future.

Germany is looking for ways to encourage working mothers. The 24-hour kindergarten, for example, caters to parents who work overnight.

The reality is that the German population is shrinking with increasing low rate of birth and an ageing population.

There is perhaps nowhere better than the German countryside to see the dawning impact of Europe's plunge in fertility rates over the decades, a problem that has frightening implications for the economy and the psyche of the Continent. In some areas, there are now abundant overgrown yards, boarded-up windows and concerns about sewage systems too empty to work properly. The work force is rapidly graying, and assembly lines are being redesigned to minimize bending and lifting.

In its most recent census, Germany discovered it had lost 1.5 million inhabitants. By 2060, experts say, the country could shrink by an additional 19 percent, to about 66 million.

Demographers say a similar future awaits other European countries, and the issue grows more pressing every day as Europe's seemingly endless economic troubles accelerate the decline.

But bogged down with failed banks and dwindling budgets, few are in any position to do anything about it.

Germany, however, an island of prosperity, is spending heavily to find ways out of the doom-and-gloom predictions, and it would seem ideally placed to show the Continent the way.

So far, though, even while spending 265 Billion USD a year on family subsidies, Germany has proved only how hard it can be.

That is in part because the solution lies in remaking values, customs and attitudes in a country that has a troubled history with accepting immigrants and where working women with children are still tagged with the label "raven mothers," implying neglectfulness.

If Germany is to avoid a major labor shortage, experts say, it will have to find ways to keep older workers in their jobs, after decades of pushing them toward early retirement, and it will have to attract immigrants and make them feel welcome enough to make a life here. It will also need to get more women into the work force while at the same time encouraging them to have more children, a difficult change for a country that has long glorified stay-at-home mothers.

There is little doubt about the urgency of the crisis for Europe. Several recent studies show that historically high unemployment rates — in excess of 50 percent among youths — in countries like Greece, Italy and Spain are further discouraging young people from having children.

According to trends' studies it was detected, that many countries in Europe were expected to shrink by 2060; some, like Latvia and Bulgaria, even more than Germany. And the proportion of elderly will become burdensome.

There are about four workers for every pensioner in the European Union. By 2060, the average will drop to two, according to the European Union's 2012 report on aging.

Large families began to go out of fashion in what was then West Germany in the 1970s, when the country prospered and the fertility rate began dropping to about 1.4 children per woman and then pretty much stayed there, far below the rate of 2.1 children that keeps a population stable.

Other countries followed, but not all. There is a band of fertility in Europe, stretching from France to Britain and the Scandinavian countries, helped along by immigrants and social services that support working women.

Raising fertility levels in Germany has not proved easy. Critics say the country has accomplished very little in throwing money at families in a system of benefits and tax breaks that includes allowances for children and stay-at-home mothers, and a tax break for married couples.

Demographers say that a far better investment would be to support women juggling motherhood and careers by expanding day care and after-school programs. They say recent data show that growth in fertility is more likely to come from them.

"If you look closely at the numbers, **what you see is the higher the gender equality, the higher the birthrate**" said Reiner Klingholz of the Berlin Institute for Population and Development.

In the meantime, mothers trying to work here face obstacles that discourage large families. Though Germany recently enacted a law guaranteeing day care for all children over 12 months, compared with 3 years and older before, experts say there is still a shortage of affordable facilities. Further, many schools let out at noon, and there are few after-school programs.

Many working mothers find themselves quickly pushed into poorly paid "mini" jobs — perhaps 17 hours a week for about 600 USD a month. More than four million working women in Germany, about a quarter of the female workforce, hold such jobs.

Another way to adjust to the population decline is to get older workers to postpone retirement.

The German government is increasing the retirement age to 67 from 65, and companies have moved fast to adapt.

The share of people ages 55 to 64 in the work force had risen to 61.5 percent in 2012, from 38.9 percent in 2002, *(way above the Eurozone average!)*

Other companies are offering flexible hours to appeal to older workers. Hans Driescher, a physicist trained in the former East, is 74 and still on the job at the German Aerospace Center almost a decade after he reached the mandatory retirement age. He started out working 55 hours a month, but has now cut down to 24. He spends the summer in his garden and works the rest of the year.

With high unemployment rates across most of Southern and Eastern Europe, Germany is in a good position to increase its labor pool by plucking the best and the brightest from its neighbors, and it has begun to do so.

Yet, with hundreds of thousands of skilled jobs unfilled, some executives believe Germany should change its immigration laws and accept foreign credentials to compete for workers with other aging countries.

Germany's experience with integrating foreign workers in the past, particularly the country's large Turkish minority, has proved difficult, and many government officials and business leaders are examining Germany's culture, eager to do what it takes to be hospitable. But whether they will succeed is unclear. A recent study found that more than half the Greeks and Spaniards who came to Germany left within a year. Many arrivals are young and highly qualified and see a global market for their skills. And many, given the opportunity, will probably go home, experts say. Immigration in general has become more temporary, and moving across borders in Europe is especially easy.

"I think the answer is that we need to look outside Europe," Dr. Klingholz said.

* **Mortality** *(following* **US** *BLS report).*

With changes in the health habits of individuals and continual progress in medicine and technology, the life expectancy of the US population is expected to continue to increase.

In developed countries, mortality happens largely at the very old age cohorts, when people are mostly out of the labor force. As a result, mortality has a lesser effect on the working-age population than fertility has. The Census Bureau projects falling mortality rates and increasing life expectancies for the US population, due primarily to a significant reduction in deaths from infectious diseases, heart conditions, strokes, and cancer.

According to the Census Bureau, mortality rates of second-generation immigrants are projected to converge to that of the general population by 2075.

* **Immigration**

Among the three sources of population growth, immigration is the most volatile, and thus hardest, to project. Immigration can be affected by sweeping changes in immigration policies or by events that happen in other parts of the world, encouraging or discouraging more immigration to the United States. The immigration assumption is a major determinant of population projections and plays a significant role in the growth and composition of the labor force. Immigration is also the main source of diversity in both the population and the labor force. According to the Census Bureau's population projections used in the 2010–2020 projections of the labor force, net immigration to the United States is expected to add 1.4 million people annually to the U.S. resident population.

This figure is a sharp increase over the roughly 800 000 immigrants per year projected in 2004 by the Census Bureau's previous long-term projections of the resident population. As the projected number of immigrants to the United States nearly doubles, a substantial change will occur in both the size and composition of the population. As with previous Census Bureau projections, assumptions about immigration are not constrained by any current policy on international migration patterns.

The assumptions on immigration were developed with the use of a historical time series of data on the age, gender, race, and ethnicity of immigrants.

1H. Key elements in Implementing Structural Reforms on Labor
More important for the Eurozone, who is well behind the US and the UK

Work Flexibility
As mentioned earlier, It seems to me that the key "operating" structural reform point is to make **"working less difficult for... workers"**.

This requires that governments' interventions become far less frequent.

Government interventions have been one great obstacle to allowing for far less work rules and increased work flexibility, both in the US and even more so in Eurozone's 5 "PIIGS "countries and France mainly.

I believe that working through branches by activity sector is by far the best and most practical possibility of advancing more rapidly on this crucial subject, this requires that labor unions become far more integrated with corporations.

This is a major problem in many Southern countries and France, where labor unions, with few exceptions in each country, have very rigid and "protectionist" attitudes, while in most of these countries their memberships decline constantly, as does their real impact percent of worker's representation.

But these minorities are far more aggressive, and achieve to immobilize entire pans of activity, like transports (ground and flying), education, health, etc... through sometimes abusive strikes and manifestations.

Employers' associations have not been very effective either in creating constructive dialogue, and "talk" a lot, are "political", but do not get much done.

In the Eurozone, Germany has been a very good example of this kind on negotiations, as an example in the last decade this being illustrated by successful branch agreements in the automobile industry (see VW and Hartz rules).

But, then, Germany has practiced co-management, allowing for labor union representation in corporations' management for decades, I believe since Chancellor Ludwig Erhardt started with this type of co-management in the late 60's.

It is a difficult change in mentality for Southern countries and France to allow for labor union representation in corporations.

Corporations are generally considered as the "enemy" and "profiteers" (this is a very "general" type of statement), and therefore workers need to be "defended" by labor unions.

But, "something's gotta give"and if workers are to retain their jobs under crisis, they will have to accept to share with employers the burden of their labor and employee benefits.

This can be achieved through **flexibility "deals"** where workers accept temporary remuneration decreases or temporary lower duration of employment, until the corporation comes out of the crisis.

If workers, through representation in management are not aware of the "real" situation of corporations, under crisis or not, they will mostly always tend to consider that they are being exploited by corporations' management, who want to optimize profits for shareholders at the expense of workers.

This kind of situation can also happen to corporations without there being a crisis, but as a result of bad management, and where "new" management needs to apply "corrective" measures to allow for the survival of their corporations.

I am not pretending that corporations are "saints", they have been, are, and will always be cases of management taking advantage of predominant situations and imposing "unfair" corrective measures, this being the reason for the existence of labor unions.

But if constructive dialogue does not exist between employers and workers, these kind of situations will continue, and will finish with "social" (or not) termination plans", and increases in unemployment, which in times of serious crises can be massive, as has been the case since 2009.

It is therefore far more preferable to institute "dialogues" on per branch of activity basis.

Technological Advancement, Globalization and Unemployment

The big question is, if we will ever go back to what is called "full" employment, which necessarily needs to include underemployment.

How should we measure "full« employment (knowing that "official" unemployment plus underemployment, was 12% of the Civilian Working population in August 2014 (6% "official" unemployment plus 6% underemployment – BLS tables).

Should we aim for 6 -7 % total direct and indirect unemployment?

In October 2014, close to 6 years from the "recovery's" (?) start, the number of jobs is still 2 million below the pre-recession peak. Since World War II, this has never happened.

After the harsh 1981-82 recession, employment recouped lost ground in 12 months. Economists are searching for an explanation and feel that high-tech should be one of the main factors to get to "full" employment (they have not set a % of CLV)

Before getting into this very important subject, the internet learning processes should at least be mentioned.

Take the Kahn Academy in the US which is an organization on a mission. They are not-for-profit with the goal of changing education for the better by providing a free world-class education for anyone anywhere.

All of the site's resources are available to anyone. It doesn't matter if you are a student, teacher, home-schooler, principal, adult returning to the classroom after 20 years.

Khan Academy's materials and resources are available completely free of charge. Students can make use of their extensive library of content, including interactive challenges, assessments, and videos from any computer with access to the web. Coaches, parents, and teachers have unprecedented visibility into what their students are learning and doing on Khan Academy.

There are other examples of "flying" classrooms in the US which are accessed through internet.

High-tech is usually seen as an engine of growth, but the spread of automated processes and robots has actually acted as a drag on job creation. Digital technologies are contended by economists to have enabled companies to cut costs, increase productivity (i.e., efficiency), improve profits and slash payrolls. They expect more of the same.

MIT academics foresee dismal prospects for many types of jobs as these powerful new technologies are increasingly adopted not only in manufacturing, clerical and retail work but in professions such as law, financial services, education and medicine," wrote David Rotman in an informative story in the MIT Technology Review.

A gap has opened between productivity increases and employment growth, goes the theory. If it persists, it would confound economic history.

A number of economists and "experts" blame technological advancement and globalization.

On technology, they tend to think (whether they really believe it is rather "unbelievable"?...) that "technological unemployment" is a "new disease" by which job destruction caused by automation exceeds and economy's capacity to create jobs. As rich nations sought to counter cheap Asian labor, "machines and robotics have rather silently replaced humans." They continue saying that accountants, machinists, medical technicians, even software writers that write the software for "machines" are being displaced without up scaled replacement jobs. Retrain, rehire into higher paying and value-added jobs? That may be the political myth of the modern era, there aren't enough of those job, they maintain...

I do not believe in this type of "theories" (which is what they are, to me at least).

Advance technologies obviously replace unskilled labor and an intermediate group which has not yet received pertinent and targeted formation and training to be able to integrate higher skilled jobs, but technological advancement creates a great many jobs – see example on IT / Internet jobs created in France in Chapter 2, and following data and comments.

The "digital "economy presents one of the major opportunities for job creation, the nature of jobs will differ from past work experiences for a majority of the population.

It is generally agreed that the persistent high unemployment rate - the longest such period since the Great Depression - is primarily caused by a fundamental reshaping of the economy. The US and other advanced nations are going through structural changes driven to a large extent, by advances in information technologies (IT).

Companies are able to do their present work with fewer people, as a result of the major improvements in IT- based labor productivity in the past two decades. At the same time, sophisticated IT infrastructures have enabled them to optimize their supply chains and shift work around the world to cut costs.

The US economy now produces more goods and services than it did before the downturn un-officially began in December 2007. But it does so with almost Five Million fewer jobs.

As we know "computers", "internet","IT in general" – and the again alive discussion on "robotics" effects on employment - are now doing many things that used to be the domain of people only. The pace and scale of this "interference" with human skills is relatively recent and has profound economic implications. Perhaps the most important of these is that while digital progress grows the overall economic pie, it can do so while leaving some people, or even a lot of them, worse off.

Computers, Internet, IT in general, will be some sort of replacement for traditional "computers". They are getting and are going to get more powerful and capable in the future, and have an ever-bigger impact on jobs, skills, and the economy. It's about the technologic meteorological race that has started some decades ago and will be ever increasing.

Technologies are racing ahead but many skills and organizations are lagging behind.

Cloud Computing is and will increasingly be a major factor in IT.

Citing wikipedia's definition, it describes a variety of different computing concepts that involve a large number of computers that are connected through a real-time communication network (typically the Internet). Cloud computing is a jargon term without a commonly accepted non-ambiguous scientific or technical definition. In science, cloud computing is a synonym for distributed computing over a network and means the ability to run a program on many connected computers at the same time. The popularity of the term can be attributed to its use in marketing to sell hosted services in the sense of application service provisioning that run client server software on a remote location.

Cloud computing relies on sharing of resources to achieve coherence and economies of scale similar to a utility (like the electricity grid) over a network.[1] At the foundation of cloud computing is the broader concept of converged infrastructure and shared services.

The cloud also focuses on maximizing the effectiveness of the shared resources. Cloud resources are usually not only shared by multiple users but as well as dynamically re-allocated as per demand. This can work for allocating resources to users in different time zones. For example, a cloud computer facility which serves European users during European business hours with a specific application (eg. email) while the same resources are getting reallocated and serve North American users during North

America's business hours with another application (e.g. web server). This approach should maximize the use of computing powers thus reducing environmental damage as well, since less power, air conditioning, racks pace, and so on, is required for the same functions.

The term moving cloud also refers to an organization moving away from a traditional capex model (buy the dedicated hardware and depreciate it over a period of time) to the opex model (use a shared cloud infrastructure and pay as you use it)

Proponents claim that cloud computing allows companies to avoid upfront infrastructure costs, and focus on projects that differentiate their businesses instead of infrastructure. Proponents also claim that cloud computing allows enterprises to get their applications up and running faster, with improved manageability and less maintenance, and enables IT to more rapidly adjust resources to meet fluctuating and unpredictable business demand.

An important change in the software world occurred on the week of 07/22-26/2013.

Microsoft, Oracle, Salesforce and NetSuite introduced partnerships that let imagine a different future for this sector of activity.

When customers choose cloud applications, they expect rapid low-cost implementations; they also expect application integrations to work right out of the box–even when the applications are from different vendors.

This could be big and positive change for independent "cloud vendors", and most of all, for customers. The Software / IT sector has been a ferocious battleground of competing paradigms. Oracle has pushed a service of fully integrated solutions, while comparatively fledgling cloud vendors have offered choice and integrations with other important services. Customers have been forced to choose between these divergent services

To understand this change it is necessary to have a relook at the history of the technology development.

While no period of time is ever fully defined by one "monopoly" (they do not exist anymore) approach), like Microsoft, with PCs, was the one corporation who came closest to a "monopoly" with over 90% of market,

Apple, with mobiles / smart phones, music downloading / streaming and other activities, Google, with research motors and many other developing activities the "Jack of all trades.

Salesmen would offer their vertical combination of software, the company producing them and the customer would decide to buy one and only one proprietary line and not the others.

This was the case because of the level of integration required between components that made up mainframe computing and the lack of industry standards in place, which required vendors to source, build, and define most of the components (software, hardware) themselves to compete efficiently.

But, as technology becomes increasingly cheaper and as efficient, the market moves toward open and modular systems.

Due to this diversity of offers, the rise of heterogeneous software in the client-server era meant that for every new technology implemented, the CIOs and IT teams had to become experts in an all new set of infrastructure, services, and integration. This made supporting and deploying solutions from disparate vendors cost and time-prohibitive.

This was followed by massive integrations / consolidations of companies through financial instruments, which created monoliths.

In some respects, this "development" benefitted customers: the same solutions being offered and less vendors to see, selling the promise of a fully integrated suite of products where everything worked together.

But ultimately, it did not do much for this sector of activity, since with less competition, and probably reduced margins in order to compete with other "giants" (?), it limited innovation.

Cloud computing – please see above comments - over a decade later, is threatening this approach.

Prior to this 07/21-26/2013 week, the customers was faced with difficult choices between the 'fully integrated' suites and the "best of the lot" cloud offers.

With encouraging moves from both "giants" mainly: Oracle and Microsoft, a single offer of open solutions may succeed.

These integrations are very difficult to "build", many corporations failed in a big way when they tried it, and it is even harder with these giant corporations, the future will tell.

There are other precedents, to prove that innovation is a job developer, like:

Airlines and interstate highways decimated railroad passenger service. Between 1945 and 1970, intercity rail travel dropped nearly 90 percent.

Air conditioning drew people and plants from the Northeast and Midwest to the South.

Early in the 20th century, supermarkets — a more efficient form of organizational technology — displaced small grocers. "While selling food cheaply was good for consumers, it was bad for the hundreds of thousands of retailers, wholesalers and manufacturers who needed high food prices in order to make a living," wrote Marc Levinson in his book "The Great A & P and the Struggle for Small Business in America."

But these and other large technological shifts — from steam power to electrification, have not created the permanent rise in unemployment says Harvard economist Lawrence Katz. Some existing workers lost their jobs; it was hard on them. Yet there were always "new sources of labor demand" that prevented a steep rise in unemployment.

11. Subsidies / Subventions of all kinds

As above mentioned, it is urgent to review in - depth and totally – all kinds of subsidies / subventions given in the last 30 years

As mentioned earlier in **this Chapter**, this is a great source for savings to finance effectively selective internationally competitive growth programs:

Determine how many subsidies and their value size – amounts, are still included in current macro budgets, start rationalizing and eliminating all unproductive, all and unknown by those supposed to benefit from them, and determine affordability of all subsidies.

The populations, in general, do not even know all the subsidies that they are good for, since the enormous complexity of mot subsidies is so high that beneficiaries would need technical assistance to determine which benefits are they eligible for, and supposing they know, they will face the huge red tape of being able take advantage of them!

In the meantime, this huge mass of benefits, which over time – decades – pile onto each other, and are, generally, maintained in budgets and weigh heavily on them.

The **real and opportunity cost of subsidies is high.**

A full accounting of subsidies is practically impossible because the incentives are granted by thousands of government agencies and officials, and many do not know the value of all their awards. Nor do they know if the money was worth it because they rarely track how many jobs are created.

"How can you even talk about rationalizing what you're doing when you don't even know what you're doing?" said Timothy J. Bartik, a senior economist at the W.E. Upjohn Institute for Employment Research in Kalamazoo, Mich.

The NYT analyzed more than 150 000 awards and created a database of incentive spending, which is searchable on the newspaper's Web site. The survey was supplemented by interviews with more than 100 officials in government and business organizations as well as corporate executives and consultants.

A portrait arises of mayors and governors who are desperate to create jobs, outmatched by multinational corporations and short on tools to fact-check what companies tell them. Many of the officials said they feared that companies would move jobs overseas if they did not get subsidies in the United States.

Over the years, corporations have increasingly exploited that fear, creating a high-stakes bazaar where they pit local officials against one another to get the most lucrative packages. States compete with other states, cities compete with surrounding suburbs, and even small towns have entered the race with the goal of defeating their neighbors."

While some jobs have certainly migrated overseas, many companies receiving incentives were not considering leaving the country, according to interviews and incentive data.

And this use of incentives is really transferring money from education to businesses.

Despite their scale, state and local incentives have barely been part of the national debate on the economic crisis.

The budget negotiations under way in Washington have not addressed whether the incentives are worth the cost, even though 20 percent of state and local budgets come from federal spending. Lawmakers in Washington are battling over possible increases in personal taxes, while both parties have said that lower federal taxes on corporations are needed for the country to compete globally.

1J. LONGSTANDING UNEMPLOYMENT

This is, together with **youth unemployment**, the worse situation in US and the Eurozone unemployment and under employment.

More than 5 million people have been out of work in the US for six months or more, up from 2.7 million 4 years ago!

Before 2009, in records dating to 1948, the number of long-term unemployed had never reached 3 million.

5 million people represent 3.2 % of Total Civilian employed population of 155 641.

A great number of these people must be included in the "underemployed" population, and are probably the most de motivated of all, they need more than any sector of population different formation and training, whose cost will be partially financed with more rapid employment and less indemnities to be paid.

US'S UNEMPLOYMENT PROBLEM IS BECOMING MORE LIKE THE EUROPEAN PROBLEM.

The rate of short-term unemployment—six months or less—is almost back to normal. In December 2012 it was 4.9% of the labor force. That's only 0.7 percentage point above its 2001-07 average. But the rate of long-term unemployment, 3.2% in December 2012 is precisely triple its 2001-07 average, according to a Bloomberg Businessweek calculation based on BLS data. (Those two rates—4.9 percent and 3 percent—add up to the overall unemployment rate of 7.9 percent in 2012.) A striking statistic: The long-term unemployed made up 38% of all workers without jobs, double the average share and just a few notches down from the 2010-11 peak of 45%.

There are seemingly 2 reasons for this huge increase in long-term unemployment:

The first is about the extension of unemployment benefits from the usual 26 weeks to 99 weeks, which has, again, been reduced in 2013: The rationale for "welfare-to-work" is simple.

If you pay people to be inactive, there will be more inactivity.

So you should pay them instead for being active – for either working or training to improve their employability.

The evidence for the first proposition is everywhere around us.

In 2014 there is, once more, a great "political discussion" on whether to maintain these huge benefits or to cut them down to 27 Months.

For example, Europe has a notorious unemployment problem.

But if you break down unemployment into short-term (under a year) and long-term, you find that short-term unemployment is almost the same in Europe as in the US – around 4% of the workforce.

But in Europe there are another 4% who have been out of work for over a year, compared with almost none in the US.

The most obvious explanation for this is that in the US unemployment benefits run out after 6 months, while in most of Europe they continue for many years – on average 2 years!

This is clearly and obviously true. We know very well that the longer unemployment benefits increase more if we're going to have long term unemployment.

The second reason shows that this is a difficult social problem to solve. Long term unemployment has risen, but does that mean that unemployment pay eligibility shouldn't have been extended?

The human misery saved by the extension is probably larger than that caused by the extension of long term unemployment. But it's entirely possible to disagree on this.

Fact is that once long term unemployment exists it is extremely difficult to get rid of. Skills will decline and rust when not in use. Thus those who have been out of contact with the labor market for a year or more find it extremely difficult to get back into it. Employers tend to look at the long term unemployed as the "no hopers": if they were any good then they would have found a job, some sort of job, surely? And there's some justification for it. And the long term unemployed themselves: the habits of work have to be learned and if not continually reinforced do decline.

There is no easy or simple solution.

Given this disconnection from the labor market it's entirely possible to have the "normal", i.e. short-term, unemployment rate down to just frictional levels (that is, the 2%, perhaps 3%, which is the result not so much of there not being jobs but of the inevitable gaps between one employment and the next, the weeks, month or two that it takes to chase a job, interview for it, get hired and so on) and yet still have a "high" unemployment rate as a result of all people who are long-term unemployed.

The "solutions" consist in, either the hard approach, to cut back on the length of time someone can claim unemployment, or to especially create jobs only and exclusively for those long term unemployed in order to get them back into the labor force, which I believe is rather unrealistic.

The real solution, but for the future, and which needs to start now, is to make integration of workers far more easy, by re orienting Education (at all levels of schooling), Formation and Training which is the top priority, and has been mentioned already several times.

Retirees Benefits

In the US protecting retiree benefits is the left's political equivalent of the right's "no new taxes" pledge. Congressional Republicans are partially abandoning their position, and President Obama and congressional Democrats should do the same in the name of national interest

Supporting retirees is now the federal government's main activity. There's a huge redistribution from young to old - a redistribution that will be made worse if retiree programs are largely excluded from deficit reduction, as many liberal groups urge. Either taxes will rise steeply or other federal programs (defense, food stamps be cut sharply. The young will pay more and get less. Or, given these non productive choices, true deficit reduction won't happen.

In fiscal 2012, non-interest federal spending in the US totaled 3.25 Trillion USD Of that, 762 Billion went for Social Security, 469 Billion for Medicare (insurance for the 65 and over population) and 251 billion for Medicaid (insurance for the poor — two-thirds goes for long-term care for the aged and disabled). Altogether, that's 46% of non-interest spending. Defense, $651 billion and declining, was 20 percent.

As baby boomers retire and health costs rise, this spending will increase.

In 2010, there were 40 million Americans 65 and older. By 2020, that number is projected to be 55 million, by 2030, 72 million.

If benefits' cutting had started years ago, changes could have occurred slowly. People would have received ample notice, now time urges. **Benefit cuts will be unfair to retirees; but avoiding cuts will be unfair to the young.** That the US has arrived at this juncture indicts our democratic system. What could justify it?

One argument is that most elderly are poor; benefit cuts will further impoverish them.

Not so. The Administration on Aging reports that in 2010, 25.9% of households headed by someone 65 or older had incomes exceeding USD 75 000, 19.4% had incomes from USD 50 000 to USD 74 999, and 18.8% had incomes from USD 35 000 to USD 49 999.

From a Citi Group study – the average earnings for full-time workers ages 25-34 with Bachelor's degrees has dropped 14.7% since 2000 (+1.6% annually), while tuition fees increased by 72% (+5.6% annually). The chart below from Citi shows this striking and very worrying situation.

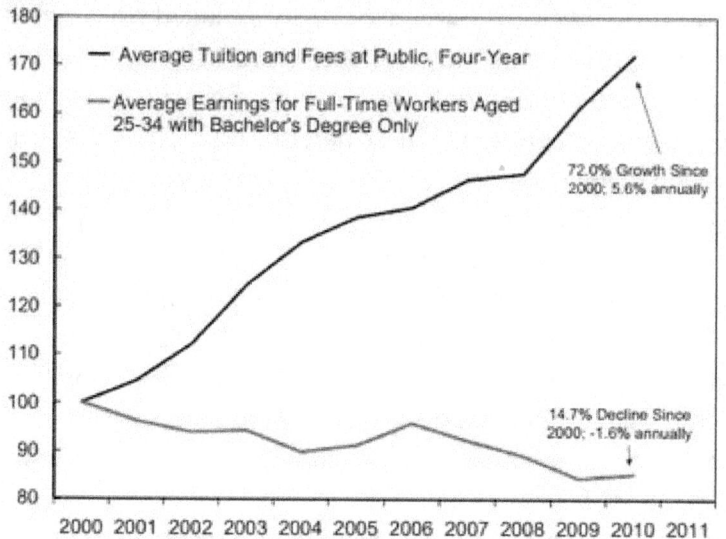

Figure 5. Real Tuition and Fees at a Public, Four-Year College and Average Earnings for Full-Time Workers Aged 25–34 with Bachelor's Degree Only (Indexed, 2000 = 100)

Sources: College Board, U.S. Department of Education, Census Bureau, and Citi Research. Note: Both tuition and earnings were weighted in 2010 dollars, and tuition and fees were enrollment-weighted.

First Conclusions for Decline in Labor Force Factors, which all relate to Underemployment

- Young people have great difficulty in finding jobs
- Discouraged workers stop looking for jobs.
- People retire because they cannot find jobs.
- People go back to school hoping it will improve their chances of getting a job
- People stay in school longer because they cannot find a job.

What the BLS tables - and other types of statistics and analyses - provide, see all the above shown data in **this Chapter** - is a long and rather complete categorization by age, sex, education, income, race, ethnology, which are the main "factors" to be examined to determine the real reasons for such high unemployment and underemployment rates, in order to start providing orientations to follow and solutions to be implemented.

This very large databank does, seemingly, not receive the "proper" attention.

This very worrisome total unemployment situation is to a great extent structural because it is originated by the ageing age curve - the boomer situation - whose effects will last for 2 decades at least, the FED re financing massively without targeting even if it self-appointed itself as " guardian of employment", and failed, this low re financing cost and the high cost of President Obama 's health reform pushed employers non hiring policies, trying to replace it with software and robotics and, finally, the worldwide increasing debt situation makes this crisis a structural and not cyclical one, contrary to FED's beliefs and possible actions.

In the US there is no Ministry of Economics and no effective Ministry of Labor, working jointly, to centralize this data, on which social-economic policies should be adopted, ad hoc study groups are not adequate and lack permanency.

In the Eurozone, the majority of countries do not undertake the necessary structural reforms and on top of it, the European and Eurozone "Governance" is incapable of providing guidelines, and even less appropriate analyses to determine the measures and reforms to be taken

All this different and necessary data needs to be analyzed and controlled in-depth before reaching conclusions, but shows the great need for Government and Congress to examine Unemployment, Underemployment and Job Creation and its reasons and problems far more profoundly, since economic planning and budgeting should be based on realistic current data and trends.

All these types of analyses show the improvements to be made and this helps to far better target the efforts to be made to reduce unemployment. If these numbers would include "underemployment" results would be far worse.

"Universal" Macro Goals – should they continue existing?

I believe that fixing universal macro goals as percent of GDP is outdated and does not make any sense anymore.

I believe that these so called " economic rules" have no foundation anymore, because the world is changing far too fast in many social-economic structural aspects, to "fix" all around "universal" percentage points goals on GDP, like the other "golden rule" of 3% **Deficit** as % of GDP, the 0.5% "primary" (before cost of interest expense) deficit, and the now called "structural" deficit, which is far too vague as a ratio and mainly a "concept" and opens to overspending and less revenues caused by "extraneous" reasons (which are not defined) as % of GDP.

Every country has a different GDP structure (call it accumulation of wealth) and financial situation, these being always the points of reference of all these "macro goals". Some GDP structures are far more vulnerable or potentially susceptible to obtain growth increase than others.

In other words I believe that to use ratios as percentage of GDP "universally" does not make sense anymore, because every country is in a different situation and with different problems and opportunities to seize upon.

Referring to **Debt**, the Eurozone's overall debt stands at 90% plus of GDP, and is increasing (goals have always been set at 60% of GDP), compared to 70% in early 2010.

All 5"PIIGS" countries have debt being way over 90%, some exceeding 130% of GDP, except Spain, who has doubled the amount of its debt in 2 to 3 years and is at 84% of GDP.

The US indebtedness exceeds their GDP.

Economists "blame" far too high indebtedness, which is an evident reality, but has been recognized as such with a decade delay, and continuously set up "rules", one of these "economic rules" being Ken Rogoff's rule, who maintains that debt-to-GDP ratios above 90% (why 90%?) cut real economic growth by nearly two percentage points for about a decade.

If **structural reforms** are not started in earnest in 2014 in most of the Western "advanced" world countries, too much debt and unfavorable demographic trends, counter-intuitively coupled with the effects of globalization and technological advancement (see further on please), are said by many economists to lead to a five to year period (most of them say "a decade"?) of US economic growth averaging at best 2%, Europe is, in total, in recession, and both the US staying with "official" structural unemployment averaging 6% in the US and 11-12 in Europe in general (to which, at least, 80-90% more needs to be added for underemployment – please refer to **Chapter 1**).

2. COSTLY STRUCTURAL REFORMS

These reforms will bear costs at the beginning and for a certain period, which requires due financing, but they will allow for durable and internationally competitive growth.

They should be divided into:

2A. GENERAL REFORMS – like reducing significantly government apparels

2B. DEMAND ECONOMIC REFORMS which relate to the utility for a good or service of an economic agent, relative to his/her income

Demand is a buyer's willingness and ability to pay a price for a specific quantity of a good or service. Demand refers to how much (quantity) of a product or service is desired by buyers at various prices. The quantity demanded is the amount of a product people are willing to buy at a certain price; the relationship between price and quantity demanded is known as the demand. The term demand signifies the ability or the willingness to buy a particular commodity at a given point of time. Source – Wikipedia

2C. SUPPLY-SIDE ECONOMICS REFORMS which relate to a school of macroeconomics that argues that economic growth can be most effectively created by lowering barriers for people to produce (supply) goods and services as well as invest in capital.

According to supply-side economics, consumers will then benefit from a greater supply of goods and services at lower prices; furthermore, the investment and expansion of businesses will increase the demand for employees. Typical policy recommendations of supply-side economists are lower marginal tax rates and less regulation. Source – Wikipedia

2A - GENERAL REFORMS

Introduction
Deflation has been one of the big "excuses" for this bad economic situation in the Eurozone situation, for me at least.

DEFINITION OF DEFLATION
Source: **Investopedia**
Deflation is a general decline in prices, often caused by a reduction in the supply of money or credit. Deflation can be caused also by a decrease in government, personal or investment spending. The opposite of inflation, deflation has the side effect of increased unemployment since there is a lower level of demand in the economy, which can lead to an economic depression. Central banks attempt to stop severe deflation, along with severe inflation, in an attempt to keep the excessive drop in prices to a minimum.

The decline in prices of assets is often known as Asset Deflation.

David Ricardo, a great economist born in 1772 (…) wrote his first economic article ten years after reading Adam Smith and ultimately, the "bullion controversy" gave him fame in the economic community for his theory on inflation in 19th-century England. This theory became known as monetarism, the theory that excess currency leads to inflation. He was also a factor in creating classical economics, which meant he fought for free trade and free competition without government interference by enforcing laws or restrictions.

I believe that the real definition of the macro big problem should be **Diminishing Inflation** and not Deflation.

Money in Trillions have been issued, around 4 Trillion US dollars have been issued by the FED since 2008, the last QE will (?), allegedly, end money inflows in the US on October 2014, but refinancing rates have been practically zero.

The BCE has issued a Trillion euros over 3 years in two LTROs late 2011 and in March 2012 at also close to zero rates (0.5%), and have even been lowered to 0.25% some months ago. As the 1 Trillion euros offer comes to maturity in late 2014 and in March 2015, the BCE is going (?) to issue covered securities' loans and maybe ABS (which can include toxic assets) and is also is trying to launch a QE, to re establish its balance sheet by at least 1 Trillion euros.

In fact, the Central Banks are those who are increasing indebtedness have had very "mixed " (mostly bad) results.

One, they provide refinancing at rates close to zero, and Banks have not accomplished the "intended" usage for these cheap money inflows.

Two, the cheap money has induced speculative placements.

The problem, to me at least (a not trained economist, but very experienced international businessman with good notions in Macro Economy), is with the usage that the beneficiaries – the large private Banks – give to these Central Banks' very large offers.

I believe that main credit usage is still given to large banks which allow little credit to the biggest employers in all countries: SMEs and to small innovation companies.

Large Private Banks do not receive high remuneration with these kinds of, say, "domestic" loans, preferring to lend to the large international companies listed in the selective markets, to "weak "countries to allow them lower financing costs than in open markets to renew or enlarge sovereign bonds, and accordingly increase already very large countries' indebtedness, and to make speculative placements.

It has been proven that in big cases with huge fines to the large US and also Eurozone banks, the fines have been absorbed rather "easily", even continuing paying dividends to their shareholders and continuing with very large remunerations to their executives, proof that very large benefits have been obtained from these big risk speculative operations.

Capitalization of Big Banks needs to be reviewed in-depth.

BCE declared they will issue a full report beginning November 2014, but anticipated that banks having undergone surveys had fortified their capitalizations already. We will see how capitalization requirements were calculated and the results?

The biggest problem is caused by Uncertainty about the future, because "people" in general have no clue where their governments are leading to their countries, because decision making, with honorable exceptions, are reactive and volatile, there not being any "vision", or "guiding" strategy on which modus operandi budgets can rely on.

It is a matter of continued "politicking", which, in an accelerated manner is making citizens not trust any more their political "leaders "(sic) and due to uncertainty there is quite a bit of money hoarding, waiting for matters to clarify...?

People, in general, are not restricting their purchases of essentials, a large part of budgets, and increasingly so the more you descend social classes, because they need all types of products for "daily life"' and are not waiting for prices to fall further as many economist claim.

The so call luxury or hedonistic / entertainment products will not fall all that much either, because when in crisis, people try to buy them and even restrict essentials, the matter nosing itself far less for "high" medium classes, and not at all for the "very rich".

What all these huge money inflows have caused in general is to continue increasing Indebtedness and allowing weak countries to live beyond their means, which causes an increase in deficits, even with rather low financing costs due to low interest rates brought about by Central Banking huge liquidity expansions.

This whole subject will be extensively commented in Chapter 3.

I have mentioned it here because I do not consider that this subject is part of positive" General Reforms"

General reforms, to me, include following type of macro measures:

- **Government Apparels' significant reduction**
- **Reductions in terms of numbers of public employees**

Governments are Too Big in most major countries, also in Areas like the Eurozone, mostly inefficient and with no "vision" and macro guidance.

They create big inefficiency with laws that once approved are not implemented, with "thousands" of rules that citizens cannot absorb and do not understand, with increasingly more red tape which is contrary to what most governments promised in terms of simplification.

Most governments in major countries intervene far too much when trying to direct businesses and resolve conflicts.

Governments should not be employers, but help to create jobs.

Investors are employers.

Most of the attempts to decrease the size of governments have failed, the US having done more than Europe, mainly the Eurozone – both in terms of Brussels and Luxembourg mammoth "organizations" (sic) in this respect, and major countries in general.

There have been countries like Canada, to some extent the UK, some of the European Nordic ones, others, who have managed to diminish very strongly their Governments' sizes, but major countries like France (fifth in the world) do not have the political will to do it, and Italy has lost much time and now, seemingly, wants to start doing it, but will have the political class against them.

Massive unemployment also plays against reducing significantly government personnel, since it will aggravate considerably already high unemployment, and most of those who would be dismissed lack the skills to be hired in stagnant economies.

Still, there are public employees, mainly among the younger ones, which can be trained to take offers in private business, these are productive investments.

To promote decentralization and send them to regional governance does not solve anything, because all you do is transfer the problem of dismissals to the regions.

So the only immediate solution is not to replace a single public worker who retires, awaiting economic improvement to go further with real reductions, decades have been lost!

- **Reductions in terms of <u>costs</u> of public employees**

Here are realistic opportunities to heavily cut down the cost of Governments' apparels.

- Freeze all increases in COL (cost of living) during a certain period.
- Freeze all pensions' increases during certain period.
- If differences exist between remunerations' in general with the private sector, negotiate agreements that public employees will have to accept temporary decreases in remuneration with prior levels not completely recovered at the end of the "frugality" period.
- If benefits, of all kinds, favor public employees compared to private corporations' employees, these should be negotiated to achieve equalization with those received by private business workers.

This refers to pensions' and other social benefits being higher in duration and in amount of how they are calculated.

What is hindering all these above mentioned governments' apparels reforms / reductions?

Lack of government's will, being afraid that such "revolutionary" changes might make them lose the next elections, going from, community / region, to Congress, Senate and President ones.

Power held by Unions of all kinds, extreme left to moderates, all types of sectoral activities.

This power has been declining over the last decades, unions having less and less representative power.

But minorities have always been far more active than "silent majorities" and been able to take to the streets hundreds of thousands people, and have through strikes immobilized total pans of different activity sectors, mainly transportation.

The time has come to do something about this exaggerated power of decreasingly representative organizations, like Mrs. Thatcher managed to do in the UK.

I am definitely not advocating suppression of Unions, but to put them in the place that they should belong to, and obtain their understanding – and mainly acceptance - that the world economy has changed totally in few decades and that they need to be far more aware of private businesses opportunities and problems, and accept to work in some sort of way that could be similar to the German co-management system, which took decades to install itself.

2B. Demand-side economic reforms

These Demand reforms advocate use of government spending and growth in the money supply to stimulate the demand for goods and services and therefore expand economic activity.

Classic definitions summarized – based on Wikipedia

Macroeconomic policy instruments refer to macroeconomic quantities that can be directly controlled by an economic policy maker.

Instruments can be divided into the following two sub titles:

1. Monetary policy instruments
2. Fiscal policy instruments.

Monetary policy is conducted by the Central Bank of a country or supranational region (Eurozone).

Fiscal policy is conducted by the Executive and Legislative Branches of the Government and deals with managing a nation's Budget.

Monetary policy instruments consists in managing short-term rates (i.e. FED Funds and Discount rates in the US), and changing reserve requirements for commercial banks. Monetary policy can be either expansive for the economy (short-term rates low relative to inflation rate) or restrictive for the economy (short-term rates high relative to inflation rate). Historically, the major objective of monetary policy had been to manage or curb domestic inflation.

More recently, Central Bankers have often focused on a second objective: managing economic growth as both inflation and **economic growth** are highly interrelated.

Fiscal policy consists in managing the national **Budget** and its financing so as to influence economic activity. This entails the expansion or contraction of government expenditures related to specific government programs such as building roads or infrastructure, military expenditures and social welfare programs. It also includes the raising of taxes to finance government expenditures and the raising of debt (Treasuries in the U.S.) to bridge the gap (Budget deficit) between revenues (tax receipts) and expenditures related to the implementation of government programs.

Raising taxes and reducing the Budget Deficit is deemed to be a restrictive fiscal policy as it would reduce aggregate demand and slow down **GDP** growth.

Lowering taxes and increasing the Budget Deficit is considered an expansive fiscal policy that would increase aggregate demand and stimulate the **economy**.

These reforms are therefore consumer oriented and their "mission" is to increase their purchasing power, and accordingly would, if well implemented, make more demand and economy growth possible.

Demand policies, as currently seen in some of the major weak countries in the Eurozone, and to some extent also in the US, follow the expansive fiscal policy.

My opinion is that the Eurozone social-economic and financial situations are not sufficiently stable, and relative ignorance of deficit in favor of growth expansion does not make sense because it will continue to increase already huge indebtedness and will continue allowing these weak countries to live above their means.

It puts the cart before the horses, because it will not be based on solid economies and will last a certain time only, like all the huge money inflows made or maybe being made as QEs, buying covered assets, ABS, etc.., which all basically failed and only gave respite being to a great extent artificial, helping big banks to getting even bigger and pushing a bull market for over three years, while "total" Unemployment (including Under employment) continues being far too high (even more so in the Eurozone).

DEMAND-SIDE INNOVATION POLICIES

Since the "new - November 1, 2014 - European Commission (EC) president, Mr. Juncker, has declared that the EC will create a 300 Billion fund for pan –Eurozone investments I have used some elements of an OECD study to as comments on demand policy on Innovation projects.

The following is based on the rationale and scope for public policies to boost demand for innovation.

Historically, Western governments have tended to rely on macroeconomic policies (i.e. monetary and fiscal policy – see above short comments please) and framework conditions (i.e. competition, tax or entrepreneurship policies) to support market demand.

Demand for innovation in this context emerged from the removal of barriers to corporations' entries, allowing potential entrepreneurs to enter the market with new or improved goods and services - based on innovation - and meet unmet or latent demand.

As such, much of the role of government on the demand side of innovation has focused on "getting prices right" in order to foster markets for innovation.

In recent years, however, several Western and "emerging" countries have used more targeted demand-side innovation policies such as public procurement, regulation, standards, consumer policies and user-led innovation initiatives, as well as "lead market" initiatives, to address market and system failures in areas in which social needs are pressing.

This interest in demand-side innovation policy has emerged as part of a greater awareness of the importance of feed-back linkages between supply and demand in the innovation process.

Demand-side innovation policies are part of an evolution from a linear model of innovation, usually focused on R&D, to a more broad-based approach that considers the full scope of Innovation cycles.

This focus on the demand side also reflects a general perception that traditional supply-side policies **have not been able to bring innovation performance and productivity to desired levels.**

Furthermore, current high pressures on fiscal budgets in mainly some of the major Eurozone countries have generated interest in using demand-side innovation policies to boost innovation performance while increasing the productivity of public spending, through innovation, in areas of strong societal demand, such a health, security, population ageing and the environment.

However, with few exceptions, experience in OECD member countries shows that the use of such policies remains limited to areas in which social-economic needs are not met by market mechanisms alone (i.e. health, environment) or in which private and public markets intersect (i.e. energy supply, transport).

The evidence to date suggests that the likely success of demand-side innovation policies depends on a number of strategic factors. First, because government is (should) be only one of several factors that influence demand.

What is important is to consider whether the action undertaken is efficient from a market - budget type point of view and whether it improves social welfare.

Therefore, demand-side innovation policies should be targeted to clearly articulated policy objectives and their impacts should be carefully evaluated.

In addition, complementarities between demand - and supply-side measures are essential.

As innovation dynamics are sector- specific, the sectoral level may be the most promising for policy making.

The scale of demand-side innovation policies should be carefully assessed as it is easier to match demand-side and supply-side policies in a certain sector than across the economy as a whole.

The timing and duration of government intervention also need to be considered: different policy measures supporting the demand and/or the supply side are needed along the different phases of the innovation cycle.

Adopting demand-side innovation policies has several implications for the public sector. The combination of policy measures (sectoral, supply- or demand-oriented) to support demand for innovation makes good governance and policy co-ordination within the public sector essential.

The systemic nature of demand-side innovation policies also implies that alignment needs to be achieved not only across levels of government, but also with industry and other influential stakeholders.

It is therefore necessary to establish shared visions and roadmaps between the public sector and corporations to implement demand-side policy instruments successfully.

A demand-side innovation policy gives a more pivotal role to public administrations (i.e. by procurement, regulation, and setting and certifying standards).

This requires investments in skills and competencies in public administration, as well as a different approach in Governance.

Consumer policy and consumer education play a role in promoting innovation in innovative markets and can help ensure that confident consumers make informed choices. Consumer policy is thus an important policy instrument which can be used to counter inertia and skepticism about new goods and services and help improve the flow of information between users and developers.

Public procurement is at the centre of recent demand-side innovation policy initiatives. Because of their large purchasing power governments can pull demand for innovation and can also create a signaling effect as lead user and influencing the diffusion of innovations more broadly.

However, using public procurement as a policy instrument to promote innovation is challenging.

The traditional focus on value for money as well as the problem of fragmentation of public demand (often between different levels of government) can limit the potential scale effects of innovation projects' procurement.

The general principles and recommendations for demand-side innovation policies are the following:

- Government should assess the rationale and opportunity for policy intervention. Demand-side measures can represent costs for corporations, but can also provide new business opportunities.
- Policies to foster demand for innovation need to consider market and sectoral issues. Some demand-side measures are appropriate to stimulate the uptake of innovations, while others will act on their diffusion.
- Scale, timing and duration of policies to foster demand need to be determined carefully and address the risks of protectionism, large player dominance and technological lock-in.
- Demand-side innovation policies need to be matched with adequate supply-side policies and measures. This will require good organization to enhance government co-ordination and stakeholders' involvement.
- There exists significant potential to boost demand for innovation by increasing the innovation capacity of the public sector to meet social economic mainly and even global challenges.
- Adequate incentives and regulatory frameworks can help foster innovative public procurement in line with good governance, transparency and accountability.

- Mobilizing public administrations in favor of innovation – through supply-side or demand-side measures – requires establishing strong incentives, administrative reform and upgrading competencies of human resources.
- Consumer policy and education ought to be emphasized as a means of enhancing users.

My opinion, once more, is that I consider the European Commission's basically techno bureaucratic approach is unfortunately not sufficiently hands on, pro active, dynamic and managerial to be able to handle such wide purpose and to some degree organizationally difficult to handle large projects, and that they should start with implementing social-economic structural reforms in all Eurozone countries.

Demand management occurs when governments attempt to influence the level and growth **of AD (Aggregate Demand) (*) hence the levels of national income, employment, rate of inflation, growth and the balance of payments position.**

(*) **AD (Aggregate Demand)** – Is the total amount of goods and services demanded in the economy at a given overall price level and in a given time period. It is represented by the aggregate-demand curve, which describes the relationship between price levels and the quantity of output that firms are willing to provide. Normally there is a negative relationship between aggregate demand and the price level.

Reflationary policies seek to increase AD **and raise the level of planned spend at or near the GDP potential level.**

Demand management requires some sort of equilibrium between GDP, Employment, Inflation rate, Growth and the Balance of Payments.

Three out of four major countries in the Eurozone – France, Italy and Spain, except Germany, the Eurozone leading country - have no GDP increase, very high unemployment (including Under employment), have no growth (except Spain's exports) and negative Balance of Payments.

They are accordingly, as already many times before mentioned, weak countries.

To establish a "pure" demand management policy by these country themselves seems rather difficult under these circumstances, since all the support needs to come from the other countries, which countries like France and Italy request, and Germany denies to do without social –economic structural reforms committed by these countries.

The new European "organizations" have not emitted an opinion so far, mid-October 2014.

From where would the financing of funds necessary to increase populations' purchasing power come from?

Increased Taxation?

The results of the famous "Golden Rules", which were not applied in most Eurozone countries, and if applied, mainly set up higher taxation on already high taxation, which results in fine in "taxing a country to death", because at a certain level of taxation, the revenue on taxation decreases and makes growth impossible and pulls countries into recession.

Too much taxation kills taxation revenue because the money recovered from increased taxation, on an already prohibitive one, is generally used in reactive and populist spends which neither bring total unemployment down nor provoke growth.

Taxation should be differentiated into direct taxes and indirect ones, **best example for latter being VAT**, which should take into account the level of VAT in similar type and size countries in order not to be uncompetitive.

Taxation applications should be extremely targeted, they should apply mainly to selective groups / niches which benefit from not paying taxes, with "unproductive" benefits that can be abusive in favor of the beneficiaries, and correspond to tax loopholes which do no benefit the economy in general.

Take the 2nd biggest country in the Eurozone: France, total taxation is 57 / 58% of national wealth, on average, which means that on average a taxpayer works 7 months out of 12 for the Government!

It takes 230 euros gross salary including employer's charges to obtain 100 euros net in purchasing power in France. This compares with 186 for the total European Union (EU), or 24% more, and 57 in the UK as a low percentage.

France with this huge total imposition is second only to Denmark in Europe, who has a different "social model", and most probably will surpass Denmark in 2014!

How can France be competitive, with this situation?

Only by changing radically its social-economic labor "model", including a full review and revision / elimination of proven inefficient and now unaffordable subventions and subsidies, a "system «which has been left practically unchanged through many decades.

No Government in at least 4 decades (!) has been willing - for electoral purposes mainly - to approach this number one priority seriously, there has evidently been a lot of "talk".

France is by no means "alone" in this situation, only that in France it is "now" seriously damaging eventual progress, due to the rapidly increasing taxation on already high taxation, and with no underlying medium - long term plan, just being reactive mainly...

Tax Evasion

To fight more against tax evasion can be a considerable source of revenue.

The increasingly higher taxation induced tax payers to evade tax whenever possible, and to activate "intelligently" more in-depth controls will bring in considerable amounts of money.

Investments

Private Investments are the best source of, call it, liquidity inflow.

But, for corporations to invest in Eurozone "weak" countries, they need far more reassurance than the one now existing, which always brings us back to the need of implementing real and complete social-economic structural reforms, to provide ex – Eurozone investors with the motivation and credibility to put their money on Eurozone private ventures in selective sectoral / per activity areas.

Europe, and the Eurozone, have excellent top corporations, practically all those listed in the various selective Stock Exchanges like the Footsie, Dax, CAC 40, etc.., but, in general, in Latin Eurozone countries there is a great shortage of support for entrepreneurship, not like in Anglo Saxon countries, not even mentioning the US!

Major Private Banks have not done their job with respect to supporting entrepreneurship, with all the huge and "generous" refinancing interest rates offered by the ECB, which has shown no capacity to control usage of funds "offered".

Neither have these major private banks supported SMEs which are the biggest employer in any country, and this being so, the ECB would do better to institute concrete controls for lending, and even establish some type of quotas for SME support lending, until the much talked about "Eurozone Banking Union" is implemented, which is urgent and a "must".

Public Investments are necessary as a medium – long –term **complement**, but will not have any short term results.

This is another of the wishful thinking priorities of the "new" European Commission president, Mr. Juncker, the 300 Billion euros fund, with no financing source defined, which under their "supervision" will most probably never develop with 18 Eurozone countries or 28 European Union countries giving opinions as to what projects should be financed on a pan – Eurozone basis.

On this subject, please refer to all my comments above on **Innovation demand management** and its complexities.

Private Investment is required.
But large possible and durable investors will not be attracted with the great uncertainty that prevails in the Eurozone, and will require assurances in terms of seeing implementation of social-economic structural reforms

which will make the modus operandi of their eventual investments in corporations or new projects more "workable" and fluid.

Private bank backing is also essential, but with large international corporations' investments, this is no problem.

Conclusion

I would think that following a logical order of reasoning, that **Supply -Side Management** should be applied first viewing that, at least in this book, priority is given to Implementing real and complete **Social –Economic Structural Reforms**, and that **Corporations need to be backed up** first in order to be able to fulfill demand and growth from local consumers and export markets.

2C. Supply-side economic reforms

Supply-side Policies

Supply-side economic policies are mainly micro-economic policies designed to improve the supply-side potential of an economy, make markets and industries operate more efficiently and thereby contribute to a faster rate of growth of real national output. Most governments accept that an improved supply-side performance is the key to achieving sustained economic growth without a rise in inflation.

But supply-side reform on its own is not enough to achieve this growth. There must also be a high enough level of aggregate demand so that the productive capacity of an economy is actually brought into play.

Taking into account the Western economies' situation, and in particular that of the Eurozone, which is by far the most preoccupying "advanced" area worldwide, it seems to me that "supply-side" economics is the most appropriate policy to follow to obtain recovery, which will not be ASAP, but a medium –long-term process.

5 to 6 years have been lost since the Great Crisis began to finally undertake decisions on which policies to follow, all was monetary "policy" (sic) and reactivity so far, and the current project of Mr. Juncker, president of the "new" European Commission, of undertaking a 300 Billion euros pan European or Eurozone investment, is putting the cart before the horse, one more time, and besides the Eurozone has to construe leverage ability for this kind of project in terms of financing.

Supply-side economics, in general, are in line with what I have so far been proposing in this book on making social-economic structural reforms the absolute priority to obtain durable recovery and growth and be internationally competitive

Supply side policy includes any policy that improves an economy's productive potential and its ability to produce. There are several individual actions that a government can take to improve supply-side performance.

IMPROVING PRODUCTIVITY OF FACTORS

Measures to improve factor productivity, which is the **marginal** output generated by factors inputs, include the following:

1. Use **the tax system** to provide incentives **to help stimulate factor output, rather than to alter demand**, is often seen as central to supply-side policy.
   - This commonly means reducing direct tax rates, including income and corporation tax. Lower income tax will act as an incentive for unemployed workers to join the labor market, or for existing workers to work harder.

   Lower corporation tax provides an incentive for entrepreneurs to start and so increase national output.

2. **Better education and training to improve skills, flexibility, and mobility** – also called human capital development. Spending on education and training is likely to improve labor productivity and is an essential supply-side policy option. A government may spend money directly, or provide incentives for private suppliers to enter the market. Government may also set and monitor standards

of teaching, and force schools to include a skills component in their curriculum.
3. Other supply-side policies include the promotion of greater competition in labor markets, **through the removal of restrictive practices, and labor market rigidities**, such as the protection of employment.
4. Measures to **improve labor mobility** will also have a positive effect on **labor productivity**, and on supply-side performance. **This improves labor market flexibility.**
   Government can encourage local rather than central pay bargaining. **National pay rates rarely reflect local conditions, and reduce labor mobility.** For example, national pay rates for, say, Postmen do not reflect the fact that in some areas they may be in short supply, while in other areas there may be surpluses. Having different rates would enable labor **to move to where it is needed most.**
5. The adoption of performance-related pay in the **public sector** is also seen as an option for government to help improve overall productivity.
6. To reduce first and end second **pay differences between public and private sectors** as with all kinds of **benefits** is a measure that will allow better funding for education and training – Point **2**.

Measures to improve competition and efficiency in product markets, especially in global markets, are a significant part of supply-side policy. Examples of measures include:

- Government may help to improve supply-side performance **by giving assistance to firms to encourage them to use new technology, and innovate.** This can be done through grants, or through the tax system.
- **Deregulation of product markets** may be implemented to bring down barriers to entry, encourage new and dynamic market entrants, and improve overall supply-side performance. The effect of this would be to make markets more competitive and increase efficiency.

- **Privatization of state industry** was a central part of supply-side policy during the 1980s and 1990s, mainly in the US, and helped contribute to the spread of an enterprise culture. As long as privatization is accompanied by measures to promote competition, there are likely to be efficiency gains for the firm, and productivity gains for the employees. Before privatizing, contracts need to be reviewed in great depth to protect tax payers' interests and avoid abuses.
- Supply side performance can also be improved **if there is a constant entry of new firms**. Small businesses are often innovative and flexible, and can be helped in a number of ways, including start-up loans by capital ventures firms and selective tax breaks.

The effects of supply-side policy - Evaluation

Advantages
- Supply-side policies can help reduce inflationary pressure in the long term because of efficiency and productivity gains in the product and labor markets.
- They can also help create real jobs and sustainable growth through their positive effect on labor productivity and competitiveness. Increases in competitiveness will also help improve the balance of payments.
- Finally, supply-side policy is less likely to create conflicts between the main objectives of stable prices, sustainable growth, full employment and a balance of payments. This partly explains the popularity of supply-side policies over the last 25 years.

Disadvantages
- **However, supply-side policy can take a** long time **to work its way through the economy.**

As with the implementation of social-economic structural reforms, this book's leitmotiv - a similar concept

For example, **improving the quality of human capital, through education and training**, is unlikely to yield quick results. The benefits of deregulation can only be seen after new firms have made their market entry, and this may also take a long time.

- Supply-side **policy is very** costly **to implement**. For example, the provision of education and training is highly labor intensive and extremely costly, certainly in comparison with changes in interest rates.

The costliness of having trained personnel in both education and training to be able to follow up on progress of both these fundamental "instruments" is nearly always understated or better said not "faced".
How many times Presidents of "advanced" countries said that every young person needed to be followed up on an individual basis, this is blatant "populism" and a total impossibility!
It is like trying to give the same personal attention to every visitor of a MEGASTORE versus one to a small and normal store…

- Some specific types of supply-side policy may be strongly resisted as they may reduce the power of various interest groups. For example, in product markets, profits may suffer as a result of competition policy, **and in labor markets the interests of trade unions may be threatened by labor market reforms.**

Conclusion

Supply-side policies correspond better to the situation in which most major countries in the Western "advanced" world are, being aware that the worst problems resides with Eurozone.

- From the previous analyses of Demand-side and Supply-side policies it is clear that there is no perfect option, and that some characteristic of Demand-side policies are also adequate with obtaining a real, durable and internationally competitive recovery, which in any case will be medium – long-term, but a great amount of time has been lost by not taking decisions and being reactive.

Over half a decade of loss in time having as a result the bad social-economic and financial situation in which the Eurozone finds itself today – 2014.

Germany, and not so much the weak French and Italian economies which are the object of endless discussions, is a good case to rapidly review that situations can change rapidly to negative if social-economic developments conflict with policies which have allowed Germany to lead the Eurozone for at least one decade.

The German economy is showing in the second and third quarters of 2014 clear signs of weakening.

GDP declined by 0.2 per cent in the second quarter of 2014 and German business sentiment fell for a fifth straight month in September 2014 to its lowest level in 17 months. Manufacturing orders dropped during August 2014 to the lowest level since May 2013.

Germany's problems will remain and get worse if no "corrective" actions are taken by the German government, who is capable of self-corrective decision making contrary to other major countries.

Much of the success of the German economy during the last years –last decade - can be attributed to harsh social-economic structural reforms in the labor market and in social protection. These were introduced by the Social Democrat Chancellor Gerhard Schroder (mandate in 1998-2005) in 2003 with his 'Agenda 2010' – refer also to the so called "Hartz" VW reforms.

The centre-right / centre-left "grand coalition" which allowed German Chancellor, Mrs. Merkel, to continue heading the government, has modified- going backwards – the "Agenda 2010" by reintroducing early retirement, granting extra pensions for mothers and installing an unprecedented legal minimum wage of 8.50 euros per hour in all sectors and all regions of Germany.

These different direction reforms have had as a result that the minimum wage implementation will increase labor costs by about 10 Billion euros and it is still not clear how many jobs will be lost after its introduction in 2015.

The new pension benefits will cost around 200 billion euros - until 2030.

Early retirement could take up to 250 000 "seniors" off the job market over the coming years when skilled and experienced labor is becoming increasingly scarce and valuable.

Demographic decline will be Germany's greatest challenge in the long run: coming decades could see Germany's workforce shrink by about 200 000 every year. The old age dependency ratio - between those older than 65 ("seniors") and those of working age - could increase from 31 per cent in 2013 to 57 per cent – in 2045.

This means that only 1.75 working persons in 2045 will be available for the senior population instead of 3.2 persons currently – a 54 percent decrease (!), unless social planning is changed, which I believe will be the case, but cannot bring back the current ratio.

Immigration to boost the workforce will be essential. Experts calculate that net-migration of around 400 000 people a year - preferably young and educated - would be needed to avoid this demographic decline.

The picture has changed, Germany is not anymore the "cash cow" - old BCG case study, it will first of all need to take care of itself, which the Eurozone "organization" (sic) does not want to recognize, and neither France and Italy want to either.

They all want Germany's help, but they will have to take care of themselves with far more "aggressive" (in the good sense of the word) social-economic structural reforms, which have not even started, France being a notch worse than Italy in this respect.

Germany will have to invest far more than during the last decade in productivity improvement "instruments" and innovation in the short-term, because labor productivity, labor participation rates and also, and to great extent, entrepreneurship will have to increase dramatically over the short – medium term.

The decrease in investment have made Germany less competitive, this reflects itself in low productivity which leaves Germany low in this type of ranking

Its education system orientation will have to change to adapt to coming sectoral changes which innovation will bring.

All these changes are necessary and urgent to allow Germany to replace a dwindling working population with far more productive workers and staff.

Germany's government will not increase its public debt, like many so called "analysts" have been requesting from Germany, when they ask the German government to abandon its "austerity obsession" and take advantage of the historically low interest rates, artificially financed by the huge BCE money inflows of all kinds, one of the big macro errors since late 2011, made for more debt-financed "stimulus".

Domestic industrial investment is also increasingly discouraged by Germany's policy to reduce systematically both fossil and nuclear energy, and this also will have to change.

It is obvious that this places the German government in a "new" situation, from that of the last decade, since these reforms will be extremely costly to the "economy" – businesses, consumers, taxpayers, but Germany is a disciplined and rigorous country which will make these necessary reforms, they have already done so twice since the fall of the "Wall" in 1989.

What the above illustration of Germany's situation reveals is that Germany cannot continue being the "de facto" leader in the Eurozone, which means that both the "new" European Commission and Union, and mainly the governments of the major Eurozone countries cannot count anymore to have Germany as a possibility of "banking" them.

To continue putting the Eurozone economic and financial situations in perspective, before concluding, I am referring to **Markit's October Eurozone Survey of October 2014.**

Markit's October 2014 "Flash" Survey reflects, even being a "purchasing managers' survey", quite well how very worry some the situation is in the Eurozone.

This is a "Flash" Survey, not backed up by factual October 2014 data, but it seems "in line " with an extension to October 2014 of preceding months in 2014, which show a very negative trend for the Eurozone, which, unfortunately, is not "news", except for the "eternal optimists" who do not want to face economic facts.

This trend shows France "starring" and also Italy, and, at a much higher level also Germany – please refer to my preceding comments on Germany above.

The decrease in Prices is shown as being the steepest since January 2010, while input prices / costs are up, in spite of oil dropping from USD 112 to around USD 85 since June 2014(!), and USD 98 to USD 85 since the end of September 2014(!).

The decrease in prices by a great number of retailers in different sectors of activity is either a result as punctual "promotions" or of real price decreases to reduce heavy stocks. This is a normal reaction of trying to lift falling sales or sales not meeting objectives.

The great problem is that this price lowering is done at a time when input costs are going up, which has a very bad consequence with falling margins and no investments.

Economists, analysts, supranational "organizations" like IMF, European Commission, OECD, ECB, in spite of all these facts, are still requesting prices to go up, because of low inflation!

They argue that if prices fall, consumers will wait until prices reach bottom (sic) to buy, and ignore seemingly that a great majority of products will be bought by necessity - "essentials" - and others (middle class), say, hedonistic ones, will be bought to "cheer up" and "have some pleasure", even if essentials' purchasing has to go down / suffer.

If "in the real world" retailers would increase prices, they would go broke!

ECB continues with its "plans" to continue with huge money inflows, this becomes ridiculous, since it is obvious that the number of credit takers has and is increasingly diminishing at full speed, and that private banks will refuse to take risks on "domestic" loans.

Major Western nations, in general, (the US, the UK, and Germany (with problems) being in a better situation than "average") and each one differently in accordance with its specific needs, will have to bite the bullet and put "their house in order", social-economically and financially (in this order) in order to have a viable future, in other words they will have to implement social-economic structural reforms.

Mr. Juncker, European Commission's new president (November 1, 2014) "great" and so far only "idea", at least the only one that has been published x number of times, to proceed with a 300 Billion euros pan-Eurozone investment program, where all the ingredients are so far unknown, does not seem a viable "solution" in view of the "real" economic and financial situation in the Eurozone, this being my personal consideration at least.

Markit's comments

The Eurozone saw a marginal upturn in growth of business activity in October, according to the flash

The headline Markit PMI™ rose from September's 2014 ten-month low of 52.0 to 52.2, signaling the first upturn in the pace of expansion for three months.

However, the index remained below the average seen in the third quarter of 2014, and was the second-weakest reading seen so far this year.

Manufacturing output expanded at the fastest rate for three months, while growth of service sector activity was unchanged on the six-month low seen in September 2014.

In both cases, rates of growth remained historically weak and below the averages seen in the year to date.

Furthermore, although output rose at a slightly faster rate, new orders barely rose in October, registering the smallest monthly improvement since orders began rising in August of last year.

Manufacturers reported a second consecutive monthly drop in new orders, albeit again only modest, while inflows of new business in the service sector showed the smallest rise since January.

Backlogs of work fell at the fastest rate since June of last year, dropping in both services and, to a lesser extent, manufacturing.

Subdued demand prompted firms to cut staffing levels. Although only marginal, the reduction in headcounts was notable in being the first since November of last year.

Service providers reported the first cut in payroll numbers since March, though manufacturers reported a slight upturn in employment.

Prices were increasingly being cut in order to help boost sales.

Average prices charged for goods and services showed the largest monthly fall since February 2010, having now fallen almost continually for just over two-and-a-half years.

Charges for services fell at the steepest rate since January 2010 while a more modest decline was seen in the manufacturing sector, where prices fell only marginally and to a lesser extent than in September.

Price cuts occurred despite overall input costs rising in October, pointing to a further squeeze on operating margins.

That said, manufacturing input prices fell for the second month running.

Finally, business optimism about the year ahead in the service sector fell to the lowest since June 2013.

The outlook is perhaps a little brighter in manufacturing.

New business and employment suffered the largest fall since June and April of 2013 respectively.

French selling prices dropped at the fastest rate since October 2009.

There was better news out of Germany, where the PMI rose to its highest for three months. While services saw the slowest pace of expansion since June, growth of manufacturing output rebounded to a three-month high.

However, German companies also reported that new business rose at the slowest pace since September of last year, while employment growth slowed and prices charged were cut to the greatest extent since September 2012.

Elsewhere across the region, output growth partially recovered from the slide to a ten-month low in September.

But new business growth was the weakest for 11 months, employment barely rose and prices charged fell at the steepest pace since July of last year.

Commenting on the flash PMI data, Chris Williamson, Chief Economist at Markit said: **"The Eurozone PMI rose in October but anyone just watching the headline number misses the darker picture painted by the survey's other indices, which show the region teetering on the verge of another downturn.**

"Growth of new orders slowed closer to stagnation and backlogs of work fell at a faster rate, causing employment to be cut for the first time in nearly a year.

"Business confidence in the service sector also slid to the lowest for over a year and prices charged fell at the fastest rate since the height of the global financial crisis, adding to an increasingly downbeat assessment of business conditions.

"While the survey suggests the euro area has so far avoided a slide back into recession this year, a renewed downturn cannot be ruled out. Growth is so anemic that increasing numbers of companies are being forced into dismissing staff and slashing prices in an attempt to cut costs and boost sales

The Markit Flash Eurozone PMI shows the steepest fall in output prices through discounting, since global crisis and renewed job losses, in spite of an otherwise stable PMI.

Conclusion

Chapter 2 includes
- General Reforms
- "Low cost" measures to reduce total unemployment
- Costly measures, which again need to be classified into:
- General reforms
- Supply-side reforms
- Demand-side reforms

I believe that the Eurozone, and in particular major countries like France and Italy and to a lower extent Spain, and also at a far lower degree the United States, cannot continue without implementing real and complete Social-Economic Structural Reforms which have been described in this **Chapter 2** and initiated in **Chapter 1** with an extensive analysis why Under Employment analysis and corrective actions needs to be given priority since it is of similar size than "Official" published unemployment, and is where the major problems reside.

Following this reasoning I believe that all called "Low cost measures to reduce total unemployment, with special emphasis on reducing "Under Employment" are priority number one.

So called "General Reforms" need to be undertaken since they will bring very necessary cost reductions.

Reforms shown under "Supply-side" Reforms should be undertaken, because they follow the Social-Economic Structural Reforms "logic".

Some reforms shown under "Demand-side" like those shown as part of Innovation, are complementary.

I tried to segment the different possible and realistic Reforms, but they are not "universal" and need to be taken as a "package" and each government must choose those which are priority for their stage of evolution and will improve most social-economic situations in each country

It is obvious that none of these reforms are with immediate effect, and therefore require Savings and Financing.

Considerable possible realistically speaking **Savings** are shown under review and revision (elimination) of all kinds of **Subsidies** in **this Chapter**, but they require political will to change, which has not existed during the whole Great Crisis and before.

All above mentioned Structural Reform measures, if appropriately implemented and executed will provide Savings over time, but not in the very short-term, except decisions on Subventions / Subsidies.

Financing should come out of a mix of private investments channeled through the IMF mainly, with leverage being brought about by very firm commitment to all above mentioned Structural Reforms and taking into account that the Eurozone represented before the Great Crisis over 20% of world trade, this being the most single important "bloc " worldwide and not to be neglected.

Central Banking should stop their money expansionist measures until Structural Reforms are underway and that private investment starts, then they should be a complementary source of very targeted financing through private banking and controlling firmly the usage given by the major private banks, a role that has not been well accomplished so far, and that will be commented far more extensively in the following and last **Chapter 3**

CHAPTER 3

Monetary policy cannot act alone since it failed doing so.

IT MUST FOLLOW ECONOMIC STRATEGY and Action Plan and complement it.

Central Banking role to be first totally reviewed and then revised worldwide.

Focus on Tax Evasion, Tax Breaks, Mobilization of Cash Savings to get Growth Resources.

Opportunities for increasing Macro Growth - Premises

- Can these vital questions be dissociated from necessary changes in "Politics"/ Governments' "Vision", strategy, analysis, execution, and follow up –necessary corrections on deviations?
- Monetary policy alone cannot continue driving the world through "independent" Central Banks

Financing needs to follow economic policy which practically does not exist since most decision making is stop gap and reactive.

Major Banks in US, together with real estate government agencies and the biggest US insurance corporation were saved by the Treasury and the FED with unprecedented capital injections to avoid major banks runs, and if no financial regulations are imposed worldwide, with the next (?)

Bubble break up there will be a repe at.

The problem is basically that greed is lobbying to avoid this legislation, because risky business is far more profitable, and until the "bubble" broke everybody thought, before the crisis that real estate prices would be going up indefinitely!

- Debt reduction is number one priority, but needs to be done gradually
- Financial Regulations need to be developed and applied – worldwide.
- Central Banking Limitations and inherent risks if their "independence" continues.

Central Banking has proved to be a hindrance because it's flooding market with exaggerated Liquidity is not caring about solvability, provides excuses for areas and major nations to Implement necessary and urgent social-economic structural reforms which will bring durable competitive growth.

- Banking Union Eurozone Project – a necessary and good project, but it needs that a modern Eurozone Government a priori analyzes as to realistic functionality, technicalities, and its implementation.
- Too much taxation kills taxation revenues.

Poor "management" ("governance") of most Western, mainly Eurozone countries during at least 3 to 4 decades have left most of these major countries (Germany being an exception, which is changing in 2014) and "not economically integrated areas" in a very bad social-economic state.

I am using the word "management" for macro purposes because the world has changed globally, international / worldwide competition is ferocious and will be increasingly so, a majority of "Western" major countries' governments policymaking and the composition and even more the attitudes of the supranational organizations will have to change quite radically from "traditional politics" which are failing, to be able to compete with BRICS (Brazil, Russia, India, China and South Africa) and other "emerging" (I would call them "emerged") upcoming giants like South Korea to name the biggest one.

The big "emerging" countries have one big advantage over "traditional" Western countries, especially "old world" European countries, in that they have greatly suffered for various reasons in the past and have emerged because they could reform themselves and accordingly develop rapidly, either (quite) freely (Brazil) or (quite) dictatorially (China).

Western countries, especially Europe, are "tied" down by their traditions, idiosyncrasies, mentalities and change for them is very difficult because they are still very rich countries if you compare GDP (Gross Domestic Product) per capita with that of emerging countries, and therefore are extremely opposed to any kind of change which will affect past and current "benefits" to which they have been accustomed and which are to some extent not anymore affordable, since their huge indebtedness makes them live above their means, and this cannot continue.

The disadvantages of big "emerging" countries are that they are still very poor - comparatively - in per capita GDP, and that through increasingly improved Information technology and the first generation of more affluent workers are now traveling to "developed" countries and are far more aware of "what they are missing" in terms of worldly consumption goods and services", and therefore are already and will increasingly be more demanding higher remuneration and more free time (like the Western world …), not to speak about free expression and democracy …

This will affect their international competitiveness in terms of costs and export pricing, but these countries do not "copy" anymore as the main base for their growth anymore, but are innovating in new products due to a rapid development of schooling at all levels, and mainly in the modern digital sector, but are still very competitive in "designing" existing products.

In résumé, there will most probably be less disparities and imbalances over the medium-long term, but if the Western traditional countries do not change far more rapidly they will lose the international trade war.

Add to this that most Western countries social-economic behavior has been very lax, because Governments have followed to a great extent monetary measures which have a short and temporary effect and have disguised the real problems of non manageable indebtedness, that is why this huge crisis finally arrived, a big exception being Germany who is a very constitutionally minded and disciplined country, which has not been able to "convince" its Eurozone partners to adopt their policies, because they "act alone" and there is no a real and effective European / Eurozone "Governance".

Not being able to convince millions of adults they "do need or want a job" has been Washington's biggest failure, despite at least 3 to 4 Trillion USD in "stimulus" spending, industrial policies, targeted tax cuts, and social programs intended to boost demand, which shows that monetary measures do not solve - alone - unemployment problems, if properly geared and even more, targeted, they can help to partially finance structural measures like re orientation of schooling / education at all levels, far better coordination with labor unions, employers' associations, corporations on a per branch level, but not by trying to be an employer using unproductive and artificial "job creations, financed by government, who have always failed and been extremely costly.

During the early years of the recovery consumer demand did expand as the household deleveraging process ended, but too many of those funds were spent on imports that did not return to buy US exports—the gap between new imports and new exports was lost demand for US goods and services.

At about USD 500 Billion in 2012, the trade deficit is almost entirely attributable to the gaps in trade with China and on oil. Confronting China more forcefully about its undervalued currency and other mercantilist practices is very difficult because unilateral actions will be retaliated in other ways in a globalized world, and it would not work.

Other opportunities exist, like opening up more offshore and Alaskan oil reserves for development, continuing developing shale gas which represents in 2010 20% of total natural gas supply in the US and whose progress looks very promising. All these opportunities could cut the trade deficit in half, jump start robust growth and create 5 million new jobs, and offer the opportunity for more substantial deficit reduction

Still, the logical conclusion being - and developed in **Chapter 2** of this book – is that what is urgently needed to be done first is to implement social-economic structural reforms which in due course of time would render a selective number of economic sectors / activities in each country internationally competitive, and not further increase already very heavy stimulus spending, which, in general, is not "by sector of activity" and not job targeted.

Without strong "political will", these social-economic structural reforms will not be made and the imbalances will continue.

THE BASICS OF MONETARISM – QUOTES FROM INVESTOPEDIA

Monetarism is a macroeconomic theory borne of criticism of Keynesian economics. It was named for its focus on money's role in the economy. This differs significantly from Keynesian economics, which emphasizes the role that the government plays in the economy through expenditures, rather than the role of monetary policy.

To monetarists, the best thing for the economy is to keep an eye on the money supply and let the market take care of itself. In the end, the theory wants to show that markets are more efficient at dealing with inflation and unemployment.

Milton Friedman, a Nobel Prize-winning economist who once backed the Keynesian approach, was one of the first to break away from commonly accepted principles of Keynesian economics. In his work "A Monetary History of the United States, 1867-1960" (1971), a collaborative effort with fellow economist Anna Schwartz, Friedman argued that the poor monetary policy of the Federal Reserve was the primary cause of the Great Depression in the United States, not problems within the savings and banking system.

He argued that markets naturally move toward a stable center, and an incorrectly set money supply caused the market to behave erratically. With the Bretton Woods system's collapse in the early 1970s and the subsequent increase in both unemployment and inflation, governments turned to monetarism to explain their predicaments. It was then that this economic school of thought gained more prominence.

Monetarism has several key tenets:
- Control of the money supply is the key to setting business expectations and fighting inflation's effects.
- Market expectations about inflation influence forward interest rates.
- Inflation always lags behind the effect of changes in production.
- Fiscal policy adjustments do not have an immediate effect on the economy. Market forces are more efficient in making determinations.
- A natural unemployment rate exists; trying to lower the unemployment rate below that rate causes inflation.

Quantity Theory of Money

The approach of classical economists toward money states that the amount of money available in the economy is determined by the equation of exchange:

MV=PT
Where: M = the amount of money currently in circulation over a set time period V = the "velocity" of money (how often money is spent or turned over during the time period) P = the average price level T = the value of expenditures or the number of transactions

Economists tested the formula and found that the velocity of money, V, often stayed relatively constant over time. Because of this, an increase in M resulted in an increase in P. Thus, as the money supply grows, so too will inflation.

Inflation hurts the economy by making goods more expensive, which limits consumer and business spending. According to Friedman, "inflation is always and everywhere a monetary phenomenon." While economists following the Keynesian approach did not completely discount the role that money supply has on gross domestic product (GDP), they did feel that the market would take more time to react to adjustments. Monetarists felt that markets would readily adapt to more capital being available.

Money Supply, Inflation and the K-Percent Rule

To Friedman and other monetarists, the role of a central bank should be to limit or expand the money supply in the economy. "Money supply" refers to the amount of hard cash available in the market, but in Friedman's definition, "money" was expanded to also include savings accounts and other on-demand accounts.

If the money supply expands quickly, then the rate of inflation increases. This makes goods more expensive for businesses and consumers and puts downward pressure on the economy, resulting in a recession or depression.

When the economy reaches these low points, the central bank can exacerbate the situation by not providing enough money.

If businesses – such as banks and other financial institutions – are unwilling to provide credit to others, it can result in a credit crunch.

This means there is simply not enough money to go around for new investment and new jobs.

According to monetarism, by plugging more money into the economy, the central bank could incentivize new investment and boost confidence within the investor community.

Friedman originally proposed that the central bank set targets for the inflation rate. To ensure that the central bank met this goal, the bank would increase the money supply by a certain percentage each year, regardless of the economy's point in the business cycle. This is referred to as the k-percent rule.

This had two primary effects: It removed the central bank's ability to alter the rate at which money was added to the overall supply, and it allowed businesses to anticipate what the central bank would do. This effectively limited changes to the velocity of money. The annual increase in money supply was to correspond to the natural growth rate of GDP.

Expectations

Governments had their own set of expectations. Economists had frequently used the Phillips curve to explain the relationship between unemployment and inflation, and expected that inflation increased (in the form of higher wages) as the unemployment rate fell.

The curve indicated that the government could control the unemployment rate, which resulted in the use of Keynesian economics in increasing the inflation rate to lower unemployment.

During the early 1970s, this concept ran into trouble as both high unemployment and high inflation were present.

Friedman and other monetarists examined the role that expectations played in inflation rates; specifically, that individuals would expect higher wages if inflation increased. If the government tried to lower the unemployment rate by increasing demand (through government expenditures), it would lead to higher inflation and eventually to firms firing workers hired to meet that demand bump. This would occur any time the government tried to reduce unemployment below a certain point, commonly known as the natural unemployment rate.

This realization had an important effect: monetarists knew that in the short run, changes to the money supply could change demand. But in the long run, this change would diminish as people expected inflation to increase. If the market expects future inflation to be higher, it will keep open market interest rates high.

Monetarism in Practice

Monetarism rose to prominence in the 1970s, especially in the United States. During this time, both inflation and unemployment were increasing, and the economy was not growing.

Paul Volcker was appointed as chairman of the Federal Reserve Board in 1979, and he faced the daunting task of curbing the rampant inflation brought on by high oil prices and the Bretton Woods system's collapse.

He limited the money supply's growth (lowering the "M" in the equation of exchange) after abandoning the previous policy of using interest rate targets. While the change did help the inflation rate drop from double digits, it had the added effect of sending the economy into a recession as interest rates increased.

Since monetarism's rise in the late 20th century, one key aspect of the classical approach to monetarism has not evolved: The strict regulation of banking reserve requirements.

Friedman and other monetarists envisioned strict controls on the reserves held by banks, but this has mostly gone by the wayside as deregulation of the financial markets took hold and company balance sheets became ever more complex.

As the relationship between inflation and the money supply became looser, central banks stopped focusing on strict monetary targets and more on inflation targets. This practice was overseen by Alan Greenspan, who was a monetarist in his views during most of his near-20-year run as Fed chairman from 1987 to 2006.

Criticisms of Monetarism

Economists following the Keynesian approach were some of the most critical opponents to monetarism, especially after the anti-inflationary policies of the early 1980s led to a recession.

Opponents pointed out that the Federal Reserve failed to meet the demand for money, which resulted in a decrease in available capital.

Economic policies, and the theories behind why they should or shouldn't work, are constantly in flux. One school of thought may explain a certain time period very well, and then fail on future periods. comparisons. Monetarism has a strong track record, but it is still a relatively new school of thought, and one that will likely be refined further over time.

END OF QUOTES
Monetarism theories change with economic situations (1929, the 70s oil crises, etc...), there are no "universal" theories.

This, to me, is a major point, the monetarist theories needed to adapt to this totally "new" situation which includes meteoric changes in geopolitics and sectoral / per activity changes.

This is where the big problem with the "current" monetarism lies.

Huge inflows of money / liquidity were made, first by the US FED (first to avoid major Too Big to Fail banks' panic), second financing government real estate agencies, third helping corporations like AIG, automobile companies, etc, fourth and not least to boost markets.

Apart from helping major banks to get even Bigger (and more difficult to "save" eventually in case of failure) and helping automobile companies to re conquer market partially, the money inflows did very little to significantly reduce "Total" unemployment, "forgetting" (sic) to tackle underemployment, where the real problems reside, and which is now similar in size and as percent of GDP as "officially" published unemployment which diminished). Total unemployment at 11.5 of GDP in October 2014 and with a close to record low participation rate of 62.8%, is still huge and has a direct effect on growth being too slow in the US.

The Eurozone situation being far worse with "Total" unemployment close to 20% of non farm civilian working population and being in a stagnant situation - *Please refer back to* Chapter 1 *for all this*.

The huge money inflows "helped" weak, but still important in GDP size countries, like France and Italy among others, in the Eurozone to defer the urgent social-economic structural reforms which are at the base of restructuring positively the Eurozone and partially the US also, because the close to zero interest rates of Central Banks allowed for cheap borrowings and increased Indebtedness, obtaining the contrary than what was and is required.

Japan's case is a "model" of failure in Central Banking proceedings.

Personally, I conclude, once more, that the role of Central Banking needs to be changed radically, by instituting as rapidly as possible the Banking Union in Europe, be fully responsible for matters like really controlling private banks' usage of money / credit, continuously control their true financial situations, improve financial regulations, while partially financing a transition period required by the application of structural reforms which have no short -term financial effect, this combined with private ex-Eurozone investments through the IMF.

Pan Eurozone investments, like the 300 Billion proposed by EC president, Mr. Juncker, with no targeting, are theoretical. What is required is to attract private ex – Eurozone investments in targeted projects, country by country, since the Eurozone is probably still the biggest trading area with some 20% of worldwide trade

The ECB should only implement QEs on two conditions: if the measures of asset purchases so far decided mid - 2014 do not bear fruit, If inflation continues to fall and these two conditions are by far not met currently. "The program of asset purchases by the ECB announced so far will not allow to increase its stock of 1 Trillion euros (1 000 billion euros), which is ECB's "goal".

Only purchases of sovereign debt would achieve the goal that ECB has set. And bring down the euro below 1.20 to the US dollar.

Central Banking real challenge - "mission" is to boost markets, this being is the Real Objective.

MY BASIC QUESTION IS "WHY IS MONETARISM FAILING?"
"Blood, sweat and tears" are needed, which means that major – also smaller – weak countries need to help themselves with social-economic in-depth

analysis of the causes / origins of their specific problems (there are no "universal" problems), develop a strategy and an action plan – modus operandi – which must include Social-Economic Structural Reforms.

A big concern the ECB is facing is that low inflation turns into a debilitating bout of deflation that could weigh on growth as consumers delay spending in hopes of cheaper bargains down the line.

This is theoretical and is being repeated all the time, since people will continue buying essentials and even hedonistic products to allow for some "satisfaction", even if it means spending less in essentials – the latter relates to the middle class and not the poor obviously.

Inflation components

Inflation levels are the object of great discussion, in the US and FED, in the Eurozone and BCE.

2% inflation is seemingly (?) the "correct" percentage for inflation…, below it, they say, is a risk of deflation.

Like many macro ratios this is an obsolete concept, because the content of the inflation "basket" reflects only consumption goods purchases.

When a household makes its revenues and expense forecast and compares it with real revenues and expenses, income taxes, health coverage expenses and interest charges are certainly included, because if this would not be the case the exercise would be completely useless. The same occurs with the same items in macro planning and analysis on variations.

This is not the case with macro inflation calculations, as can be seen next.

According to Wikipedia and also BLS in the US as a source, CPI is a measure of all goods and services purchased for Consumption (please refer to below included list).

How is the CPI market basket determined?

The CPI market basket is developed from detailed expenditure information provided by families and individuals on what they actually bought.

For the current CPI, this information was collected from the Consumer Expenditure Surveys for 2009 and 2010. In each of those years, about 7 000 families from around the country provided information each quarter on their spending habits in the interview survey. To collect information on frequently purchased items, such as food and personal care products, another 7 000 families in each of these years kept diaries listing everything they bought during a 2-week period.

Over the 2 year period, then, expenditure information came from approximately 28 000 weekly diaries and 60 000 quarterly interviews used to determine the importance, or weight, of the more than 200 item categories in the CPI index structure.

What goods and services does the CPI cover?

The CPI represents all goods and services purchased for consumption by the reference population (U or W) BLS has classified all expenditure items into more than **200 categories, arranged into eight major groups**. Major groups and examples of categories in each are as follows:

- **FOOD AND BEVERAGES** (breakfast cereal, milk, coffee, chicken, wine, full service meals, snacks) and non alcoholic beverages and beverage material, food away from home
- **HOUSING** (rent of primary residence, owners' equivalent rent, fuel oil, bedroom furniture)
- **APPAREL** (men's shirts and sweaters, women's dresses, jewelry)
- **TRANSPORTATION** (new vehicles, airline fares, gasoline, motor vehicle insurance)
- **MEDICAL CARE** (prescription drugs and medical supplies, physicians' services, eyeglasses and eye care, hospital services)
- **RECREATION** (televisions, toys, pets and pet products, sports equipment, admissions);
- **EDUCATION AND COMMUNICATION** (college tuition, postage, telephone services, computer software and accessories);
- **OTHER GOODS AND SERVICES** (tobacco and smoking products, haircuts and other personal services, funeral expenses).

- It also includes **ENERGY** including Energy Commodities, Fuel oil, Motor fuel, Gasoline (all types) Energy Services, Electricity
- Certain **TAXES** are included in the CPI, namely, taxes that are directly associated with the purchase of specific goods and services (such as sales and excise taxes). Government user fees are also included in the CPI. For example, toll charges and parking fees are included in the transportation category, and an entry fee to a national park would be included as part of the admissions index. In addition, property taxes should be reflected indirectly in the BLS method of measuring the cost of the flow of services provided by shelter, which we called owners' equivalent rent, to the extent that these taxes influence rental values.
- **TAXES not directly associated with specific purchases, such as income and Social Security taxes, are excluded, as are the government services paid for through those taxes.**
- **INTEREST CHARGES** are not included **The effect of interest rates has been included in the New Zealand Consumers Price Index** (please see following résumé)

The current treatment of interest in the index is discussed and the issues are highlighted. The impact of the interest component on the CPI in recent times is presented to illustrate its importance to consumer.

Also included within the major inflation components' are various government-charged user fees, such as water and sewerage charges, auto registration fees, and vehicle tolls. In addition, the CPI includes taxes (such as sales and excise taxes) that are directly associated with the prices of specific goods and services. However, the CPI excludes taxes (such as income and Social Security taxes) not directly associated with the purchase of consumer goods and services.

The CPI does not include investment items, such as stocks, bonds, real estate, and life insurance. (These items relate to savings and not to day-to-day consumption expenses.)

The US consumer price index (CPI) measures the change over time in the cost of a fixed market basket of goods and services. It can be interpreted as a fixed-weight approximation to a conditional cost-of- living index, where the cost of living is defined as the minimum expenditure necessary to achieve a particular level of satisfaction and the cost is defined to be conditional on all the determinants of the level of satisfaction except current quantities of market goods and services.

As a logical consequence of this definition, the CPI is measured gross of indirect taxes, whether imposed at the final or an intermediate stage in the production of consumer goods and services, while income and other direct taxes are excluded from the scope of the index.

Despite its consistency with the theory of the cost-of-living (COL) index, this asymmetric treatment of taxes creates an anomaly for many of the uses to which the CPI is put, including wage escalation and deflation of income.

Most obviously, when the parameters of the income tax system change, escalation of before-tax income by the CPI is un- likely to result in a value aggregate of equivalent real purchasing power. By the same token, if tax structures are shifted away from direct taxes toward indirect taxes (as would occur if a value-added tax were instituted), the CPI will show an increase even if there has been no change in either the overall tax bill or the standard of living. Finally, because of the "bracket creep" resulting from a progressive income tax system, rising consumer prices can lead to more than proportional increases in the income necessary to achieve a base utility level.

Certain taxes are included in the CPI, namely, **taxes that are directly associated with the purchase of specific goods and services (such as sales and excise taxes).** Government user fees are also included in the CPI. For example, toll charges and parking fees are included in the transportation category, and an entry fee to a national park would be included as part of the admissions index. In addition, property taxes should be reflected indirectly in the BLS method of measuring the cost of the flow of services provided by shelter, which we called owners' equivalent rent, to the extent that these taxes influence rental values. Taxes not directly associated with specific purchases, such as income and Social Security taxes, are excluded, as are the government services paid for through those taxes.

For certain purposes, one might want to define price indexes to include, rather than exclude, income taxes. Such indexes would provide an answer to a question different from the one to which the present CPI is relevant, and would be appropriate for different uses.

The US CPI, as it is currently compiled, measures changes in the expenditure necessary to consume a fixed set of goods and services. The CPI is best interpreted within the conditional cost-of-living index framework introduced by Pollak (1975)**. It approximates a cost-of- living index that focuses on the current consumption of market goods, where market goods are defined as those goods to which a user charge is attached, regardless of the supplier.**

Within a multi period framework, it is conditional on the future consumption of market goods, current and future consumption of public goods and leisure, and current and future environmental conditions. That is to say, in comparing alternative price vectors for current market goods, its cost- of-living interpretation is restricted to alternatives in which all other variables affecting satisfaction levels are assumed fixed.

Regardless of the exact coverage, however, there is an obvious alternative to the expenditure focus of the current CPI that lies clearly within its cost- of-living orientation. **For many of the uses to which the CPI is put, it is perhaps more reasonable to measure changes in the income, before taxes, a consumer must receive to achieve a given level of satisfaction.**

Pollak (1972) advocates the construction of such a measure, referring to it as an income cost-of-living index (ICOL) as opposed to the usual expenditure cost-of-living index (ECOL). **In the remainder of this section we derive the form of an exact ICOL and of the fixed-weight approximations, which we compute in Sections IV and V.**

For each of the more than 200 item categories, using scientific statistical procedures, the Bureau has chosen samples of several hundred specific items within selected business establishments frequented by consumers to represent the thousands of varieties available in the marketplace. For example, in a given supermarket, the Bureau may choose a plastic bag of golden delicious apples, US extra fancy grade, weighing 4.4 pounds to represent the Apples category.

Does the Bureau of Labor Statistics calculate the CPI the same way as other nations? Do any differences in method keep the US CPI lower (or higher?) than the CPIs of those other nations?

Yes, the methods described above are used widely by nations in the **OECD and the European Union.** A recent report shows that rental equivalence is the most common method used to measure changes in the cost of shelter by the OECD -- with 13 of 30 nations employing it. The next most common method is for a nation to omit shelter from the CPI. The hedonic method of quality adjustment is used by at least 11 of the 29 other OECD nations, and five of the G-7 nations. Eurostat reports that the geometric mean is used by 20 of 30 countries for its Harmonized Indices of Consumer Prices.

Each nation's inflation experience is the result of its unique economic circumstances, so comparing the change in the U.S. CPI-U with inflation rates in other countries does not gauge the accuracy of US inflation measures.

Nevertheless, over the 1997-2007 period the U.S. CPI-U increased faster than the CPIs of 16 of the other 29 OECD nations, and faster than the CPIs of all of the other G-7 nations, including Canada, the United States' largest trading partner. Similarly, between the first quarters of 2007 and 2008 the U.S. CPI rose by more than the CPIs of 20 of the other 29 OECD nations and by more than any of the other G-7 nations, including Canada.

DEFLATION DEFINITION

In the following discussion, except where prefixed, the term "deflation" means a drop in consumer prices (even though that is a miserable definition).

I use that definition for point-of-discussion purposes only, simply to show the ridiculous nature of widely held beliefs.

Deflation "Theory"

A persistent drop in prices prompts households to delay purchases in anticipation of even lower costs" say the authors of the above article.

I have heard that theory expressed hundreds, if not thousands of times. I suggest a reality check.

Reality Check Questions

- If price of food drops will people stop eating?
- If the price of gasoline drops will people stop driving?
- If price of airline tickets drop will people stop flying?
- If the handle on your frying pan falls off or your blow-dryer breaks, will you delay making the purchase because you can get it cheaper next month?
- If computers, printers, TVs, and other electronic devices will be cheaper next year, then cheaper again the following year, will people delay purchasing electronic devices as long as prices decline?
- If your coat is worn out, are you inclined to wait another year if there are discounts now, but you expect even bigger discounts a year from now?
- Will people delay medical expenses if prices drop?
- If your child has a birthday next week, will you hold off buying him a present because the price of toys will be cheaper next month?
- If your lease is up and you have to move, can you wait six months in anticipation of better prices? Two months? One Month?

If deflation theory is accurate, why are there huge lines at stores when prices drop the most?

Bonus Question
Is any consumer willing to delay purchasing such items simply because prices are falling?

Opposite View
Except in cases of extreme inflation or hyperinflation, I take the opposite view.

I propose people will delay purchases if prices are too high and/or they think they cannot afford something.

Take the worn-out coat as an example. If prices are too high, some will consider making that coat last another year. Perhaps they get the coat, but not the hat they also wanted.

Unless wages keep up, people can only spend what they make or what they can get credit for.

Where's the Evidence?
I cannot come up with a single consumer item that people will routinely delay purchasing simply because prices are falling.

Is there any hard evidence that shows people *significantly* delay purchases (other than asset purchases) when prices fall? (Please do not respond with not really relevant delays ahead of pre-announced sales or year-end car clearances).

Even if people did delay consumer purchases (which they don't), why would it matter?

Can people delay forever?

Contrast between US and Eurozone Monetary policies
The contrast between the monetary policies pursued in the US and the Eurozone since 2012 could not be greater.

Since 2012 the Fed has continued to expand its balance sheet dramatically. From 2012 to 2014 the Fed added 1 Trillion USD to its balance sheet. In doing so, it increased the American money base (liquidity) by approximately the same amount.

The opposite occurred in the Eurozone. After having expanded its balance sheet during the period 2008-11, pretty much as the Fed had done, the ECB started a period of dramatic contraction in its balance sheet (and thus in the euro money base) from 2012 onward. As a result, in 2014 the ECB had reduced the money base by 1 Trillion euros.

This was done after Mr. Dragui's nomination as ECB President in 2011.

Mr. Dragui issued 1 Trillion euros – an increase of 25% - in LTROs late 2011 and in March 2012, which are maturing in 2014 and beginning 2015, and which he wants to "replace" by issuing TLTROs and purchasing covered assets (both actions began with little success apparently), maybe issuing ABS (?), and hoping to make an US type QE (print money), all this for a total of 1 to 1.7 Trillion euros (?), to re increase BCE's balance sheet and bring it back to its 2011 level, all this being questioned by ECB's Board today...

There can be little doubt that the decision of the ECB to reduce the money base by 30% at a time when the euro zone had not recovered from the sovereign-debt crisis contributed to pushing the euro zone into a deflationary dynamic, out of which it still tries to extricate itself.

Why is it then that monetary policies in America and the euro zone diverged so strongly?

My answer is that it had much to do with a different diagnosis of the nature of the economic and financial crisis that hit the industrial world and the role of the central bank in dealing with such a crisis.

The American monetary authorities, correctly, understood that the crisis had led to a balance-sheet recession, i.e. an attempt by private agents to deleverage. Private agents did this by reducing spending. It was the view of the American monetary authorities that this reduction in aggregate demand had to be countered by monetary expansion.

Nevertheless, FED's action which amounted to at least 4 Trillion USD since the Big Crisis began in 2007 were used primarily to save Big Banks Too Big to Fail who got even Bigger, Boost Markets (which was the case!), helped Government real estate agencies (Fanny Mae and Freddy Mac), AIG, the automobile industry, etc…

But FED's actions did not do much for helping Job Creation and correspondingly reducing significantly Unemployment, since some 3-4 years ago it self-appointed itself as "guardian of employment, but only spent "money", without having established a Targeted Plan and worse it "ignored" the huge negative effect of big Under employment.

This is a general "omission", since only "Official" unemployment gets published everywhere, which in September 2014 was 5.9% in the US, with Underemployment, where the real problems reside, being of similar size and also representing 5.9%, which produces Total Real Unemployment of close to 12% (11.8%) of the US nonfarm civilian working population, the participation rate staying at his lowest – 62.8%.

All this not being a significant decrease as compared to before the crisis and even more ("Official" unemployment went down and Unemployment went up, the balance being a favorable 2 -3 points decrease which is not much).

The improvement is wage less (average jobs value went down) and so only favored corporations, it was not Main Street but Wall Street oriented as they say. *Please refer to the first 2 Chapters.*

So, the US monetary actions are not exactly a "universal model" to be followed, this being my personal opinion as a not trained economist, but a very experienced international businessman with actualized notions of macro economics and having acquired practicality and some "horse sense"…

The ECB, on the other hand, was caught in a situation that the problem came from the supply side. There was too much rigidity on the supply side. If these were fixed by structural reforms output would increase by itself. Demand would adjust automatically to the supply.

The inefficient Eurozone "Governance" followed the "de facto" leader, Germany (who had already reformed itself over a decade ago), by establishing the "Golden Rules" some 3 years ago, which created only austerity programs (mainly tax increases and wages / pensions decreases), which were audited by the ineffable "troika" (EU, BCE, IMF) in the bailed-out countries (Greece, Portugal, Ireland, Spain) and modified three to four times per year because the "directives" content, and even worse timing, were totally unreachable!

For too long the ECB believed in this "concept", lecturing governments to do their part by introducing structural reforms. In this view, monetary policies were powerless to move the economy.

BCE only "talked" about structural reforms, but, in reality, helped to defer them with its unreasonable policy of issuing the Trillion euros LTRO which allowed banks to finance sovereign bonds' borrowings by weak Eurozone countries, also allowing banks to make a nice spread between BCE 's refinancing rate (close to zero) and the rate charged of 3-4%! Little credit was given to SMEs and innovation companies...

ALL THIS HELPED TO INCREASE EUROZONE'S INDEBTEDNESS WHICH APPROACHES 100% OF ITS GDP – LIKE THE US!

No social-economic structural reforms were imposed through the "Golden Rules" (3 years ago)or later "directives" by the EC / EU, which by itself shows how bad the content of the EC/ EU Directives were and still are!

Only by the beginning of 2014, did the ECB started to recognize that this situation did not fit the worsening economic macro facts in the Eurozone.

Not one of the Eurozone nations introduced real and complete social-economic structural reforms, (only "reformettes" like in France, totally ineffective). Only Germany had, but this starting in 2000, under Chancellor Schroeder, and followed by Mrs. Merkel until beginning 2014, who is having trouble now -2014 -, due to the Grand Coalition which is imposing social and welfare measures which are making Germany less competitive....

By mid -2014 the ECB announced it would make a QE but found itself in a quandary: Germany's opposition.

Some fear that an increase of central-bank liquidity will only lead to asset inflation. This fear is unfounded. Asset inflation is the mechanism that can pull the euro zone out of its deflationary dynamics. It should be tried.

But BCE and pseudo economists and analysts stressed that failure to do so will keep the Eurozone at a low-growth and high-unemployment "equilibrium", which risks turning away millions of people from a union that instead of bringing them economic welfare leads them into economic misery. By not acting forcefully today the ECB risks unleashing the rejection of the monetary union. This is a much higher risk they maintain than the risk of German ire against the use of a QE instrument, i.e. the purchase of government bonds that in the rest of the world is considered to be standard practice.

This, to me, is the usual monetarists' arguments and it did not work well even in the US, which is One country – a great advantage over a "theoretical union" with Eurozone's 18 totally different countries in terms of tax structure, social protection systems, which used the US dollar with discretionary tactics and with great "flexibility" and used protectionist measures, versus a Euro with a non unified and not economically and financially harmonized area.

The US is a very resilient country, with exceptional innovative corporations which are their real great strength.

Why has Europe not developed a single Apple, Google, Microsoft, etc...?

Monetary solutions will not do it – alone – nowhere (the big error in the US), and even less in the Eurozone, the US has never been "great" in foreign relations – with some exceptions in time (i.e. Nixon – Kissinger), they have always had an isolationist tendency – "why bother with the "others", we are making things work for ourselves" (Germany has a likeness there), and they provide advice which is, generally, not adapted to other countries / economies.

The Eurozone needs to start at the beginning, harmonizing its economies, it has not been done in 2000, when the Eurozone was created and made operational in 2002, it therefore has to start doing it now, with social-economic structural measures, a total revision of myriads of unproductive subventions still alive, far too large governments and bureaucracy, enormous red tape everywhere, etc…

"Money" is necessary, but not "alone", it should be used as an integrated complement of a real social-economic strategy – short, medium and long-term.

What is missing in establishing Eurozone policy is the "Why's" and "How's", as usual.

Low inflation is bearing the torch, but there is no mention as to what the priorities should be, which to me, clearly are the obligation to be imposed on number 2 and 3 Eurozone (weak) countries - France and Italy respectively, and have BCE's money inflows targeted / focused to the firm – in writing "in blood "- commitment to social-economic structural reforms rapid implementation.

It makes no sense to inflict sanctions (which anyhow will not happen, politically not conceivable), what is necessary is to "tell" France (mainly) and Italy that they will not see a "cent" of BCE's projected (and under question) 1 Trillion or 1.7 Trillions (which will end being smaller) of diverse monetary measures if they do not comply with these "obligations" and institute a strict monthly "follow- up" for control purposes.

This situation is basically and structurally the same as when this Great Crisis started in 2008 (nearly seven years ago!), because the economic fundamentals have not changed in Europe / Eurozone (the latter mainly) and to some extent also the US, even being a far more resilient country.

It has not really progressed because of the following factors:

1. Governance in the "Advanced West" (sic), with US - 1 big federal country - doing better than Europe (a "mess" of non harmonized 28 (European Union) and 18 countries (Eurozone) and Europe, and mainly in the Eurozone) has not adapted itself to the requirements of the XXI Century and its meteoric changes in geopolitical and sectoral / per activity structures.
The output of the US economy has surpassed its early 2008 level by about 8 percent, according to data Mr.Draghi presented at a recent –October 2014 - briefing. Meanwhile, the output of the Eurozone's 18 countries using the euro as their common currency - is still 2 percent below its 2008 level.
Private investment has collapsed. It's down about 15 percent from 2008.
It has not progressed because these major countries and the European Unions are still, mainly "politicking" and this has made it possible to limit growth very considerably.
2. Social-economic structural reforms have, in general, not been implemented a realistic and compete sense, this has not allowed for productivity increases, has hindered growth in a big way, and has not allowed for a significant improvement in international competitiveness.
3. Huge indebtedness has been increasing, mainly by the "support" of Central Banking, which due to its cheap money huge inflows of liquidity has allowed major countries to continuously defer the implementation of these essential social-economic structural reforms.

Although Americans are rightly upset about the slow recovery from the 2007-2009 "Great Recession," the US rebound has been speedy compared with the one in Europe:

Since 2008, Europe has experienced two recessions (periods when the economy declined for at least half a year) and may now be on the verge of a third.

For the US Europe is a drag on the global economy since about one-fifth of US exports go to Europe.

Also, about half the overseas profits of US multinational firms originate in Europe, says Dartmouth economist Matthew Slaughter. If these weaken, so could US stock prices and the consumer spending and confidence tied to the market.

But an important portion of this is that large international US (and other nationality corporations) corporations) have installed intermediate "headquarters" in Ireland (tax on income – 12.5% and "legal") and in less legal tax heavens outside of the US.

And there are the political ramifications. Economic stagnation has fed nationalism and populism. Conflict between weak economies (Italy, Spain, Greece, France) and stronger competitors (Germany, the Netherlands) continues. Differences undermine Europe's capacity to act decisively on other issues, from the Middle East to Ukraine.

The US sees the main causes of Europe's economic stagnation as follows:

Here's the conventional list: 1. the euro itself, which prevents weaker countries from devaluing their own currencies to stimulate their economies, 2. high government debt, which leads countries to cut spending or raise taxes — policies that critics denounce as self-defeating austerity; c) over regulation of business, which discourages start-ups, hiring and investment (these policies are obscurely called "structural"), and 3. a "timid" ECB, the rap against the ECB is that it hasn't been as aggressive as the FED. Though –relatively - accurate, the criticism is overdone.

The trouble is that low interest rates won't spur economic growth if lenders don't want to lend and borrowers don't want to borrow.

BCE is putting the cart before horse since it made the 1 Trillion euros offer of LTROs in late 2011 and March 2012.

All these liquidity inflows will not work, to the contrary, they will bring the weak countries like France, Italy and also Spain (doing better) to not implement structural reforms, this is what has been happening since the start of the Great Crisis, and is worsened by a more feeble situation in Germany in 2014 than previously, which will reduce its role a s a "driver".

BCE's "moves" to develop the Eurozone have not been successful, and will not be so, because it was and is (urgently) first necessary to "re arrange" structurally -social-economically, the major Eurozone countries, and then allow for a mix" of private investments through IMF, and public – BCE targeted financing to allow for transitional financing of the not immediate growth process of structural reforms which will be partly costly in the short-term.

It makes no sense to allow huge money inflows before the necessary social-economic matters are underway, because the demand is not there and you cannot put the cart before the horses and give a donkey to drink if it is not thirsty...

What is required is **Indebtedness Reduction**

Western "advanced" countries have generally, with very few exceptions, lived way above their means and this translated into higher Indebtedness which is growing to intolerable levels.

In order to be able to be constructive in making proposals on how to start reducing significantly this huge indebtedness, it is necessary to determine how public debt is composed and the differences between the dozen or so of major countries worldwide.

DEBT ANALYSIS

Debt worldwide, without including household debt, is attaining in 2013 117% of the worldwide GDP (source - OECD), which ratio wise is as high as the level attained in World War II by the 10 most "advanced" economies (*)

(*) After World War II the "advanced" nations were: US, UK, Germany, France, Italy, Spain, Japan, Canada, Australia, South Korea, with debt attaining 116% of their total GDP, to fall to 23.5% in 1965 thanks to high grow and economies' stabilizations.

Nowadays worldwide debt amounts to more than 100 000 Billions (100 Trillions) USD. This is debt contracted by the nations and the corporations, excluding household debt which by itself amounts to 40 000 Billions (40 Trillions) USD!

This of utmost gravity, since a debt needs to be reimbursed and there are two possibilities to do so: A Third World War or Huge Inflation, neither being "acceptable" (sic) "solutions!

What is even worse, this colossal debt has not improved the general state of leading nations' economies, it has served to amortize the huge 2008 crisis shock by "Keynesian" type policies and subsidizing social expense.

Central Banking executed most of this "policy", this being why their "modus operandi" needs to be radically changed, this Chapter will go much further into Central Banking "policies" and the huge problems they have originated.

Speculation has been indirectly financed, with these policies, helping "Banks Too Big to Fail", making them even "bigger", and allowing lending to hedge funds, which is more profitable, but extremely risky business, than lending to, say, "family" SMEs…

The next five points refer to what has been done, or not, to "debt reduction, and relates to 2010 – 2011 data.

How to achieve debt reduction – gradually

I have chosen 5 major macro data "items" per major country, which even if showing 2010 mostly and 2011 data reflect trends which are important to analyze.

Most probably, if not surely, current 2013 - 2014 results are in general worse than the data that follows:

1. 2010 – GDP by major country – US$ Millions – % sector composition
2. 2011 – Q2 Composition of Total Debt as % of GDP -10 major countries and EZ "crisis" countries

3. 2011 - Q2 Debt Deleveraging just begun in same 10 major countries.
4. 2010 - Current Account versus GDP ratio – 2010
5. 2012 - IMF GDP Projections, trying to determine how these major countries differ from each other and also trying to pinpoint where the major opportunities/problems were, by using this macro data, which will be expanded (example : unemployment and job creation latest analysis) to other major macro data in future posts.

All charts and sources are included for consultation after each point of only analytical comments.

The Countries included in these 5 charts (not every country is in all of them) are: **US, China, Japan, Germany, France, UK, Italy, Spain, Brazil, India, Russia, Canada, Australia, and South Korea.**

1. 2010 – GDP BY MAJOR COUNTRY – US$
MILLIONS – % SECTOR COMPOSITION.

SHOWN TO PUT INDEBTEDNESS IN PERSPECTIVE
The European Union (EU - 27 countries) represents 26% of Total World GDP, out of which the 5 major EU countries listed represent 18.5% of total (71% of Total EU), US =23.5%, China= 11.5%, Japan=8.5%, Brazil=3.5%, Canada=2.5%, India=2.5%, Russia= 2.5%.

The total of 12 countries included in the chart represented 73% of worldwide GDP, which provides an order of perspective to the "whole" and constitutes a very representative worldwide "sample"…

The Sectoral analysis shows that Services represent in 2010 63% of Total GDP worldwide, which corresponds to a continuous ascending trend over the last 20-30 years (I have referred in length to this subject previously in this book), at the detriment of Manufacturing (31% of World

GDP), Agriculture's decline (6% of World GDP) which goes further back than the last 20-30 years.

3 out of 4 biggest "emerging" countries (excludes Brazil) in this list still show Agriculture representing 10% and 18.5%, China and India respectively, of Total GDP versus 6% penetration worldwide, and this "phenomena" will not be all that long (?) lasting.

The same differentials exist in Manufacturing for China and Russia who still represent 47% and 37% respectively versus 31% penetration worldwide, this % participation decreasing annually..

These differences are basically related to these countries having huge populations which represent for China and India a total of 2.4 – 2.5 Billion people (equal to 35% of world population of 7 Billion), which still allows for well below average per capita remuneration, with a higher percent of total population still living in a non urban environment.

These 2 differentials are "compensated" by lower Services penetration, which represents "only" 43% (China), and 55% (India) versus 63% penetration worldwide.

But, these big emerging countries are investing heavily in education, formation and training in IT and related technologies, and other "scientific" sectors, and are "picking" up rapidly to become strong competitors with the "Occidental" world.

US, and even more France, with Manufacturing penetrations of only 22% and 18% respectively versus similar European countries average penetration of approximately 25-26%, are in need to re develop their Manufacturing "base", without falling into protectionist traps.

This, and related subjects on work rules, labor flexibility, education, formation/training orientation, re localizations without protectionism, etc..., have been previously commented upon in great length in this book, being related to Job Creation analysis, the most, crucial macro and growth boosting factor.

IMF – Nominal GDP sector composition - 2010 - % incidence on Total and in Millions US Dollars

		Total	Agr.%	Mfg.%	Serv.%	Agr.	Mfg.	Serv.
0	World	62,909,274	6%	30.9%	63.2%	3,585,829	19,313,147	40,010,298
0	European Union	16,282,230	1.8%	25%	73.1%	293,080	4,070,558	11,902,310
1	United States	14,657,800	1.1%	22.1%	76.8%	161,236	3,239,374	11,257,190
2	China(2011)	7,368,187	10.2%	46.9%	43%	751,555	3,455,680	3,168,320
3	Japan	5,458,872	1.4%	24.9%	73.8%	76,424	1,359,259	4,028,648
4	Germany	3,315,643	0.9%	27.8%	71.3%	29,841	921,749	2,364,053
5	France	2,582,527	2%	18.5%	79.5%	51,651	477,767	2,053,109
6	United Kingdom	2,247,455	0.7%	21.8%	77.5%	15,732	489,945	1,741,778
7	Brazil	2,090,314	5.8%	26.8%	67.4%	142,141	560,204	1,408,872
	Italy	2,055,114	1.9%	25.3%	72.8%	39,047	519,944	1,496,123
9	Canada	1,574,051	2.2%	26.3%	71.5%	34,629	413,975	1,125,446
10	India	1,537,966	18.5%	26.3%	55.2%	284,524	404,485	848,957
11	Russia	1,465,079	4%	36.8%	59.1%	58,603	539,149	865,862
12	Spain	1,409,946	3.3%	26%	70.7%	46,528	366,586	996,832

2. Latest – Q2 -2011 – Composition of Total Debt as % of GDP - 10 major countries, including EZ "crisis" countries.

Total Debt is integrated - *see chart please* - by 4 factors, which it is necessary to know, in order to be able to understand the different factors which make up the total debt of major countries worldwide.

These differences in the debt structure prove why it is not possible to impose an universal ratio / "goal" of indebtedness of 60% of GDP, like Eurozone "Governance" does, is totally erroneous, and acts a hindrance to diminish indebtedness to realistic size in each Eurozone country, when other major countries do not impose unrealistic indebtedness ratios, which is finally the objective: make the Eurozone internationally competitive.

The four factors composing Total Debt are:

- Government debt
- Household debt
- Financial Institutions debt
- Non financial Corporations debt.

This "mix"/composition varies considerably between countries, and needs to be evaluated to determine Banking and Corporate financing and indebtedness roles and their relative importance, along with the parallel incidence of Government and Household debts in Total debt.

This chart shows the composition of Total Public Debt for the 10 countries having the greatest total debt as a % of their GDP in Q2 -2011. Countries excluded from previous No_1 chart's 12 countries: China, Russia, Brazil, India because of relative low indebtedness, being replaced by South Korea and Australian who are part of the 10 most indebted countries in 2010.

As a first comment it can be appreciated that the US which is "leading" in the "GDP" ranking, comes "only" as No 7 in "Total Indebtedness as % of GDP" ranking with 279% of indebtedness versus GDP, this being the same *ratio* as Germany.

But Germany's GDP represents only 23% of US's GDP nominal amount, this showing that Germany is a better administered country, since with much lower GDP as a "base", to have the same indebtedness ratio as the US, shows that the US ratio is extremely high having the largest wordlwide GDP.

To stay with the US – Germany comparison, its Total debt structure is very different.

US 's leading debt has no single component having a penetration larger than 31% (Households), but Financial Institutions debt represents only 14% (!) of Total debt, which shows that the banking sector is not that "stretched" in the US, and nevertheless needed huge bailouts during the beginning of the 2007 crisis (?).

If one adds corporate debts (which also needed bailouts), the total % incidence becomes 40% (this is where the crisis "enters" with the real estate agencies (Fanny Mae and Freddy Mac), the automobile industry, AIG, etc, needing support, given by FED).

Household debts plus government debts were, still, the US main problem since they represented together 60% of total US debt, this being highly influenced by, mainly, the still unresolved housing and mortgage crisis at the time, which is improving since Q2 2011.

Germany's debt composition shows Financial institutions representing 31% of total debt (more than double the US's incidence), and if corporate debt is added % incidence becomes 53% of total debt, which illustrates Germany's dependence on administering as best they can its financial and corporate world, which to some extent explains their reluctance to "help" weaker EZ countries, who did "not do the effort", this "non assistance" policy will most possibly boomerang against them in future years (does so already in 2014).

Other European countries listed – UK, France, Italy, Spain's Financial Institutions % incidence is also 31% of total debt (UK weighing more with 43% incidence, the other 3 EZ countries showing 24% incidence). If corporate debt is added to the 4 countries, the % incidence becomes 48% of total debt which is lower than Germany's 53% similar % incidence. This ratio can be safely assumed must have become worse for the "other" 4 countries versus Germany, probably being close to equal in 2011, and worse in 2012-2014?

This is important to keep in mind when referring to Banking role in Europe which is far more determinant than in the US, because European banks finance three quarters of the credit needs of economies in Europe versus US banks financing only one quarter of these needs.

It also shows that Germany's financial institutions plus corporate debt as % of GDP situation, at least in 2010, was higher than that of the other 4 major European countries, at least in this particular analysis, which does not include "deficit analysis", where Germany has a definitive advantage versus the other European/EZ countries.

Japan and UK lead Total indebtedness as % of GDP by far with 512% and 507% (!) respectively (!), third in the list: Spain, showing "only" 363%... Japan's and UK's GDP rating 3rd and 6th respectively in GDP ranking, which makes Japan's indebtedness a major adverse factor (its GDP being more than double than that of the UK), still leaving the UK in a "preoccupying" situation.

Japan's Government debt is by far the highest worldwide with a 44% incidence on its total debt (!), and if Household debt is added it represents a staggering 57% incidence versus US's 43%. This needs to be pointed out, because Japan's indebtedness, having still the 3rd largest GDP worldwide, represents an "immobilization" factor to worldwide growth – please see point 5 on IMF's Growth forecasts for 2012, with Japan coming in with less 0.6%. in 2013 Japan has "adjusted" its exchange rate downwards versus leading worldwide currencies to improve their export situation

UK shows Financial Institutions debt representing by itself 43% of Total debt (!) and if Corporate debt is added, it will become 63% of Total debt, close to Japan's practically inverse debt structure with Government plus Household debt representing 57% of Total debt.

All in all, the above mentioned indebtedness situations do not favor any of these countries in world wide "competition", with the exception of Germany, when it comes to comparing total Indebtedness as a % of GDP.

The big emerging countries like foremost China, and Brazil, India, even Russia (who has in 2014 the Ukrainian problem to deal with), have a distinct advantage with regard to the 2010 situation, and probably even more when extrapolating 2011, 2012, 2013

The US, who was not "performing" economically speaking any better than Europe, but has the great advantage of being a more resilient country and being a "single" big country with a leading GDP, has already in 2012 obtained (slow) growth, but well before Europe, in spite of "poor" budgetary analysis and control which could improve matters in the US considerably, and bring unemployment down faster.

Europe suffers mainly from the absence of an effective European Governance and being a in 2014 28 countries theoretical "union", which is not one because it does not even achieve being a "monetary "union, much less and economic / social-economic one, until it, finally, changes the manner of directing this "union", which is a gradual and long-term process, which needs urgent decision making.

Chart 2 - Composition of Debt

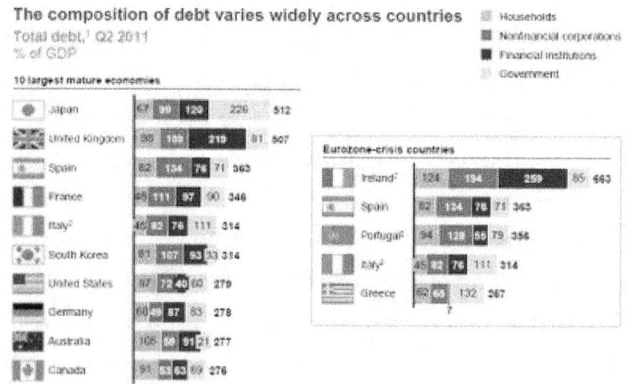

3. DEBT DELEVERAGING JUST BEGUN IN THE SAME 10 MAJOR COUNTRIES – Q2 – 2011 – 10 MAJOR COUNTRIES, INCLUDING EZ "CRISIS" COUNTRIES (THE SAME COUNTRIES LIKE IN POINT 2).

US

Since the end of 2008 all 3 private sector financing debt categories (except government debt) have fallen relative to GDP. Even Household debt has fallen by close to 600 Billion USD, but 2/3 of it is due to defaults on home loans and consumer debt, and this deleveraging process (foreclosing) is far from finished, and constitutes, with unemployment (which is obviously directly related to the housing problem), the biggest problem in the US economy.

When this whole process ends (?), consumption – and growth potential- will continue suffering versus pre-crisis levels during the transition period, where ex-homeowners will be trying to rebuild equity before increasing their consumption.

Meanwhile, US government debt had continued to grow because of the costs of the crisis and the recession. When the crisis started the US already had large deficits, and public debt reached its highest level: 80% of its GDP, in the 2nd Qtr. 2011. The next phase of deleveraging, in 2011 -2012, where government should have started reducing debt, has not occurred, mainly due to political fights, and will prove to be a great problem if "politicking" does not change

US government employment has been decreasing in 2012 and 2013, which favors the decrease of the US deficit, but increases unemployment.

The European situation and its non recovery from the crisis have not been "helping" the US either.

European Union (EU), Eurozone (EZ) and Japan

The subject of the EU / EZ not being able to handle the crisis has been commented already earlier.

I will comment once more that all the EZ countries have different economic, social-economic situations, and are in different phases of recovery or non recovery (recession), and that the solutions involving both "austerity and structural changes" and "growth boosting" programs need to be different in content and timing for each of the 14 EZ countries who do not have a triple A rating, and that "EU/EZ "universal" remedies cannot be applied effectively, other than in eventual infrastructure development.

Everybody knows that all 5 "PIIGs" countries are in different levels of deep trouble, Greece leads on the extreme side, and to me, Italy is the country with the best or least worse macroeconomic fundamentals, but is very much handicapped by its permanent internal political instability and long standing lack of Growth. Until BCE's refinancing facilities in 2012, Italy was "the" target" for speculators, being the 3rd biggest country in the EZ, "too big to fail", etc, whereas Italy's biggest problem has persistently, over the years, been lack of growth. This being why Mr. Monti, technocratic non elected Prime Minister, embarked on a first series of strong austerity changes (but not much on, badly needed "social-economic structural reforms", who are in an incipient stage end of 2012 and in 2013), but has not survived early 2013 elections, which have a split government, including Mr. Berlusconi's "non personal, but "party" comeback.

Mr. Monti had requested from Germany (virtual EZ leader) and Brussels (?) "help" to alleviate too harsh austerity programs which would lead to even larger "non growth", and be given both "money" and time to install growth motivating programs based on higher labor flexibility, new innovation programs with more R & D investment, etc...

He was not listened to, this having been the case by the end of 2012; he has failed in the 2013 elections, because political parties have strongly opposed him. Mr. Lecca, his successor did not fare better, Mr. Renzi who was appointed as PM in 2014 is trying to reform Italy (?)

Spain constitutes a bigger problem because it faces very serious challenges. Corporate debt (42% of Total) plus Financial Institutions add to an incidence on Total indebtedness as % of GDP of 63%, to which one should add Household debt incidence of 17%, for a total incidence of 80% on Total Spain's debt as % of GDP of 363%, which is the 3rd largest ratio of this kind worldwide. Part of the reason for Spain's high corporate debt is its large commercial real estate sector, but corporate debt across other industries is higher in Spain than in other countries. Spain's financial sector has continuing problems as well: seemingly about 50% of loans for real estate development could fail. Spain's young population has over 50% unemployment!

Spain has few arguments for growth, except Exports, since it also has a current account deficit of 4.5%, up to an estimated 6% in 2012. Its total public debt's magnitude does not allow it to increase it further, this leaving restoring business confidence and undertaking social-economic structural reforms to improve competitiveness and productivity as the most important steps this country can take. This shows clearly why comments on "Spain's recovery" due to having placed bonds lately at lower yields are totally "artificial", and only reflects ECB's QEs in disguise to European Banks.

Nevertheless Spain's government has been able to improve productivity of labor to some extent and increased exports, and between the very few has the largest growth in 2014 in the Eurozone.

The chart on "deleveraging", after these comments, shows that deleveraging had only started in the US, see above comments (- 16%), South Korea (-16%) and Australia (-14%). Countries with leveraging below 25 %, meaning that indebtedness as % of GDP ratios have changed less than 25% between 2008 and Q2 2011, are Germany (unchanged), Italy (+12%), Canada (+17%) and UK (+20%). Countries with increases over 25% have substantially increased leveraging: Japan (+39%), France (+37%), Spain (+26%).

This shows that Japan and Europe, in general (and differently per country) have a long way to go and I wager that these situations have worsened in 2012 -2014.

Chart 3 – Deleveraging

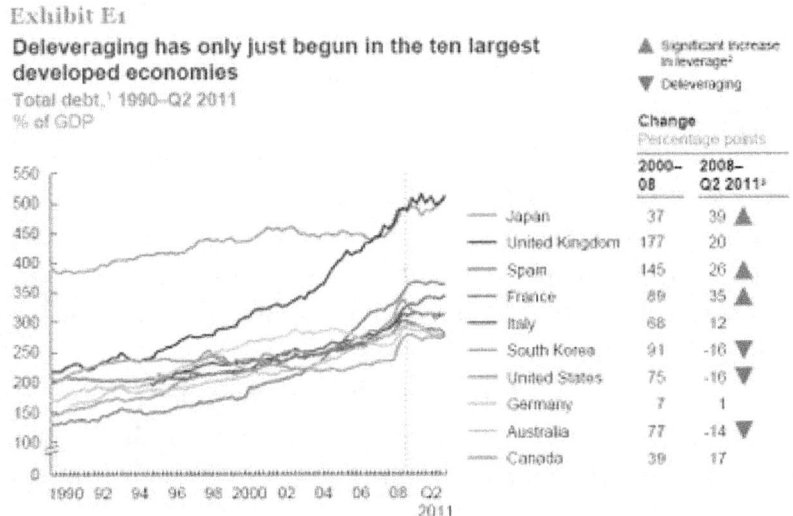

Debt and Deleveraging

Source of these 2 charts : 01/23/2012 article: "Debt and Deleveraging" in Mike Shedlock's blog: citing data of Mc Kinsey Global Institute report: "Debt and deleveraging: Uneven progress on the path to Growth".

4. Latest Current Account versus GDP ratio – 2012

The current account balance is one of two major measures of the nature of a country's foreign trade (the other being the **net capital outflow**).

The chart after these comments includes 9 countries (*) : Germany, China, Japan, France, UK, Australia, Canada, US and India, the same countries listed in the 12 countries included in the GDP ranking in point No 1, except Brazil, Italy, Spain, Russia, and including Australia. (*) The current account chart, allows to find any country worldwide, and I will add 3 countries: Italy with less 3.3%, Spain with less 4.5% and Brazil with less 2.3%

Trade imbalances are one of the major factors of worldwide instability.

Wikipedia writes: David Ricardo, famous economist (1772-1823), *"rgued that there is mutual benefit from trade (or exchange) even if one party (e.g. resource-rich country, highly skilled artisan) is more productive in every possible area than its trading counterpart (e.g. resource-poor country, unskilled laborer), as long as each concentrates on the activities where it has a relative productivity advantage."*

This is very sound, but rather unrealistic now, since no single country will abandon production of products which have traditionally been made and required heavy investment, unless they go "bust" with them. What is desirable, is "healthy" competition and much more focus on "Ricardo's «competitive advantages analysis" in order to obtain growth in "every" country, at different scales.

This seems extremely simplistic, but below coming short comments on the "current account" chart will show that there still are a lot of latent opportunities if these pertinent analyses are "pushed" further.

There is no reason, for example, that in terms of IT innovation, practically all the large companies, like Microsoft, Google, Apple, Amazon, Facebook "grew" in the US and none of that size in Europe.

Also, how come that the US, already twice in the last 30 years, lost huge chunks of market to Asian competition in automobile production, which were not "balanced" out by IT evolution. This is sort of a caricature, but shows how trade imbalances developed.

It is logical, based on comments made in above points 1, 2 and 3, that only 3 countries among 11 major ones: Germany (5.7 surplus), China (5.2% surplus) and (by "exception in this list of macro ratios) Japan (the most positive macro ratio this country is showing, but is greatly falling) with 3.6%, are those showing current account surpluses. It is also logical that the US (3.2%deficit),

4 European major countries, except Germany, but like Spain (4.5% deficit), Italy (3.3% deficit), UK (2.5% deficit), France (2.1% deficit) show current account deficits, whereas both Brazil (-2.3%) and India (-3.2%) show current account deficits (still…).

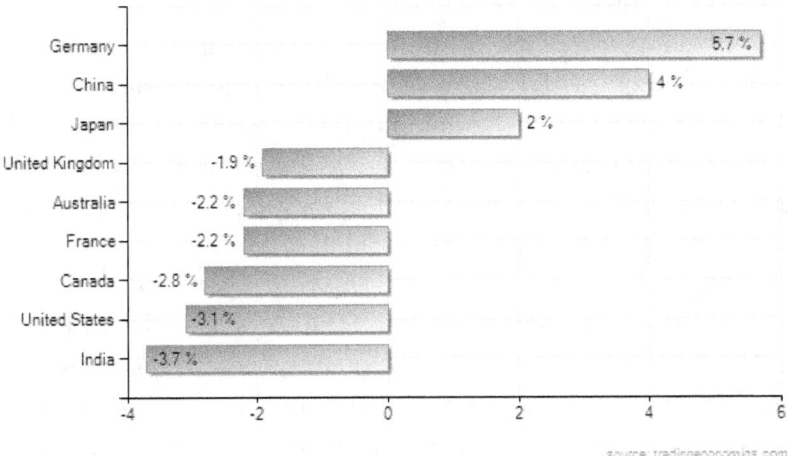

source: tradingeconomics.com

5. 2014 – IMF GDP Projections.

IMF latest – November, 2014 GDP Worldwide growth projections is 2% for G20 countries, it was at 3.3% in 2013 down from previous 4% growth forecast.

 5A. "Advanced" Economies (IMF's "naming"…) Less than 1% growth
  Including : US (+2.5%) / Eurozone (0.4%) , with Germany (+0.3%), France (0.2%), Italy (- 0.5%), Spain (1.7%) / UK (+ 3.0 / 3.5%) / Japan (-%) / Canada (+1.7%)

 5B. "Emerging/Developing" Economies (IMF's "naming") Approximately 3% growth
  Including: China (+7.0 / 7.5%) / India (+6.0%) / Brazil (+ 0.5%) / Russia (less than 1%) and Other Countries.

Conclusions on comments made above on the 5 points shown above:

In a "nutshell", 2012 would have been either a transition year, at best, or a year with very little worldwide growth, since EU/EZ non mobility. If this situation continued (which was the case in 2013 - 2014), it will affect the Eurozone mainly, Japan, Brazil, China somewhat.

 As shown above there are a number of opportunities which can be seized, but that requires far more will full political actions, and better World Governance, and this did not and does not happen "overnight"…

 One of the major conclusions, as far as I am concerned, is that the main reason that debt reduction and deleveraging did not happen in most of these major countries, is that the world of indebted countries at ratios nearing 100%, and some being over it, is more realistic - currently - than the arbitrary 60% indebtedness as % of GDP "golden rule" in Europe.

 This 60% ratio was mainly set by Germany, whose major growth "motor" is exports of quality and durable goods and that it is not a domestic "big spender", so it can live with this rule, whereas other European countries cannot, and the US has "trouble" with it, and prefers to "weaken" its own currency – the US dollar, while criticizing China and in 2013 Japan, for doing the same, the Eurozone being the "loser" with a too high euro…

The second chart - "Latest – Q2 -2011 – Composition of Total Debt as % of GDP -10 major countries, including EZ "crisis" countries, stresses that European banks finance 3 quarters of the credit to European economies, whereas US banks finance only one quarter of these needs, which makes it necessary that European banks be as efficient as possible, which is not the case so far.

So, Europe is being far too dogmatic in trying to respect overdue macro goals, like the 60% indebtedness, the 3% nominal deficit, the 0.5 "primary" deficit (before interest charges), and the vague "structural deficit".

The major conclusion is that you cannot consider "total" debt as a ratio to GDP if you do not know and understand its components, since a given major country with high indebtedness due to- Government debt or Household debt or Financial Institutions debt or Non financial Corporations debt is not the "same", because the "corrective" actions are not the same.

This happens because the G20 does not fulfill its "worldwide" role, does not "discuss" radical changes in Macro Governance, does not "discuss" obsolete macro ratios which serve as unrealistic macro goals, because there is no "auto criticism", only "politicking".

Europe's and mainly Eurozone's Governance are non existing and need to be radically changed and totally revamped in what they should be doing.

The US governments have for various late mandates privileged Financial Ministries (mainly ex-bankers) over and above non existing Economy Ministries and also Labor Ministries, the result being that practically only "monetary" measures were implemented, and the results have shown that they have not been economically and "cost wise" effective, and consequently did not achieve sufficiently high growth increases, which left unemployment / underemployment far too high, but in the general mediocrity the US is performing above average.

2 major countries: Germany and China, among the 12 major ones having the largest GDP, are the economically most performing countries worldwide in 2012 and 2013, but this is changing in 2014 since the worldwide

crisis, which is far from over, has also reached them, as well as Brazil and Russia who are faring far worth, India being in a moderate situation.

Germany and China have two very different government styles: Germany being a democracy strictly governed by a Constitution, and China being an autocracy strictly governed by "the" party, which will, gradually, change policies because of future social-economic changes and related problems, like possible real estate "bubble" and financial – corporations and individuals' credit bad payers' increase.

Europe's debt dynamics keep getting worse in spite of years of cost-cutting and tax hikes designed to return public finances to health.

Eurostat, the EU's statistics office, said government debt as a proportion of the total annual GDP of the Eurozone rose to a record 92.2% in the first quarter of 2013, from 90.6% the previous quarter and 88.2% in the same period a year ago. It will reach 100% in 2014 / 2015.

Battered by a global recession, a banking crisis and in many cases by very lax financial management, a number of Eurozone countries have been forced to take remedial action to deal with their debts, some in return for multibillion bailout loans.

Some type progress has been made – some countries' annual budget deficits are falling.

One side-effect of the austerity measures has been to keep a lid on economic growth - government spending is a key component of the economy while tax rises can choke consumption and investment.

This is totally incoherent in my opinion: How is it possible to start with "economic" growth if the debt continues to increase indefinitely, since it will not diminish to «manageable levels"…?

It is what BCE has been doing, and worse wants to continue doing: feed large inflows of "money" at close to zero interest rate for 3 years, not caring about solvability of users, in the hope these borrowing economies will "recover". If they do not, is the BCE going to inject even more liquidity until the whole Eurozone "explodes", and taxpayers will pay the burden?!

This is a "way" to artificially and very temporarily "arrange a situation with "investors", but it will reach a maximum level.

Many Eurozone countries are actually in stagnancy / recession in 2014, with shrinking economies which make the debt-to-GDP ratio look even worse.

Coupled with the fact that countries continue to add to their debt mountains by ongoing, albeit smaller, budget deficits, the overall debt burden of the Eurozone has continued to rise

The hope of those who have advocated austerity as the main response to Europe's debt crisis is that economic growth will start to emerge as soon as countries get their borrowing levels down to manageable level.

The **US** partial recovery is Lifting Profits, but Not Adding Jobs sufficiently to reduce significantly what I called "Total" unemployment, including Underemployment, this point was already commented in **Chapter 2**, where I referred to the fact that the US - mild - recovery had been a wage less one, and did not create sufficient jobs by a far stretch and accordingly growth was slow.

With the Dow Jones industrial average reaching record highs, the split between American workers and the companies that employ them is widening and could worsen in the next few months as federal budget cuts take hold.

That gulf helps explain why stock markets are thriving even as the economy is barely growing and unemployment remains stubbornly high.

With millions still out of work, companies face little pressure to raise salaries, while productivity gains allow them to increase sales without adding workers.

So far in this recovery, corporations have captured an unusually high share of the income gains, the US corporate sector is in a lot better health than the overall economy. And until we get a full recovery in the labor market, this will persist.

The result has been and is a golden age for corporate profits, especially among multinational giants, listed in selective "top" stock exchanges, that have and now are also partially benefiting from faster growth in emerging economies like China and India

These factors, along with the FED's efforts to keep interest rates ultralow and encourage investors to put more money into riskier assets, prompted traders to send the Dow Jones to record highs.

Other recent positive economic developments, like a healthier housing sector and growth in orders for machinery and some other durable goods, have also encouraged Wall Street but similarly failed to improve significantly the "real" employment picture.

"As a percentage of national income, corporate profits stood at 14.2 percent in the third quarter of 2012, the largest share at any time since 1950, while the portion of income that went to employees was 61.7 percent, near its lowest point since 1966. In recent years, the shift has accelerated during the slow recovery that followed the financial crisis and ensuing recession of 2008 and 2009", said Dean Maki, chief United States economist at Barclays.

Corporate earnings have risen at an annualized rate of 20.1 percent since the end of 2008, he said, but disposable income inched ahead by 1.4 percent annually over the same period, after adjusting for inflation."

There hasn't been a period in the last 50 years where these trends have been so pronounced.

The FED has also played a crucial role in propelling the stock market higher, economists and strategists say, even if that was not the intent of policy makers. The FED has made reducing unemployment a top priority, but in practice its policy of keeping rates very low and buying up the safest assets to stimulate the economy means investors are willing to take on more risk in search of better returns, hence the buoyancy on Wall Street amid the austerity in Washington and gloom on Main Street.

The FED has done a "good job" stimulating financial conditions and boosting markets (!), it's been far less successful in stimulating job growth.

This confirms that in general corporations' policies are short-sighted and 100% profit related, and probably is not conducive to really increasing investment.

The US recovery is "Wall Street inclined and not Mainstream targeted", to say the least!

The FED has contributed to the disconnection between Profitability and Job Creation, while it declares that it is "the guardian of employment". What a (voluntary or not, does not matter) misconception of this role, which should be taken away from this "independent" organization.

"Politicking" has not ceased, but needs to change to adapt to the XXI century requirements and the relatively "new" situation in terms of geopolitics, sectoral / per activity great changes in the last 30 years, where this huge 2007/2008 crisis, which is still present, detonated.

Central Banking Limitations

Central Banking has proved to be a hindrance because of its flooding markets with exaggerated liquidity, not caring about solvability, providing excuses for areas and major nations to defer very necessary and urgent social-economic structural reforms which are those which will bring durable and competitive growth.

The **US FED** in 2 QE's spent **2.3 Trillions USD** (far more if we count the cost of other and remaining credit refinancing facilities). In their self appointed role of **"unemployment guardian"**, they failed and are continuing to do so because according to their own declarations "they" created (?) 2 Million jobs, and even if that was true (and it is questionable). That would mean a cost of **1 Million USD per job created**, which is a very "poor" and greatly expensive result to say the "most"...

As also already mentioned twice, the ECB, before the total passivity of the supposed European Governance (European Commission, European Union, Eurogroup, et al) decided (one does not know if unilaterally or with Germany's - the "real", Eurozone leader - unspoken consent) to create huge refinancing measures – LTROs of 1 Trillion euros at close to zero interest rate over 3 years in late 2011 and March 2012 to allow mainly Spain and Italy to be able to issue sovereign bonds at reasonable and not speculative rates.

This action was wrongly, and on purpose, interpreted by Brussels "authorities", the Eurogroup, some major heads of state, some economists, a lot of analyst, several press editors and journalists, and finally the

markets (who increased like hell!) as being a strong signal of European and Eurozone recovery, which it definitely was and is not, being an artificial and temporary measure.

Central Banks seem decided to "make policy" being "independent" and take onto themselves: FED, ECB, BOJ, BoE and others, to intervene in trying to diminish unemployment with monetary and very costly measures, influence currencies and risk a currency war, because every country (and Central Bank) has as a priority to improve its country or "bloc's" situation, and we are in a globalized world where there is and will be retaliation.

Instead of taking over economic / financial policymaking which are governments' and area governments' responsibilities, Central Banking should assume the role of supervising the whole banking system and its procedures.

Governments let "them do", because it allows them to do more "politicking" and not face the real social-economic issues, which require, in most cases, implementing social-economic structural reforms and therefore changing inapt Governance in the Eurozone mainly.

In the US (also refers to Europe / Eurozone) Banking problems are concentrated on 3 major subjects:
Banks' speculation and lack of management in many instances

I personally think that major banks 'management have been taking advantage and sometimes even abusing of the large QEs and other major credit refinancing facilities given first by the FED during 3 years of crisis and continuing with a steady flux of major monthly financing in the US, and more modestly by the BCE starting late 2011 and on March 2012 in the Eurozone.

Major Banks have been using these funds in non transparent manners and continued paying their executives and traders far too high remunerations, inciting them to take undue speculative risks, which banks management when they failed practically always did not assume their responsibility.

The FED and also the BCE to a lesser degree have taken a rather lax attitude to banks' management.

"Too Big to Fail" – an outdated notion

The European, mainly Eurozone very bad economic and financial situation, shown in 2012, 2013, 2014 published data, was not really and sufficiently "acknowledged" by markets and many top "executives" (sic) in Brussels and Luxembourg "summit "meetings, the EC and EU, Eurogroup, the G7 for Financial Ministers and IMF, and many major countries in Europe in general, all finding "excuses", European shares final swinging downwards, but for an extraneous reason: **the US FED worries**!

Equity traders had thrown a global tantrum, taking chips off the table in a clear indication that they did not want to play without the FED, and BCE, adding liquidity to the pot.

This clearly shows that the "financial world now "lives" with artificial aid support by Central Bankers, and reflects that Central banks were and are increasingly overstepping their roles and that the same needed to be redefined, but by "which worldwide "authority"?!

The notion that large corporations and banks were considered as being **"Too Big to Fail"** should be banned. That some of these huge these corporations, and even more banks, had been abusing the huge relief obtained by continuing to be involved in risky financial situations and paying their executives and traders practically the same huge remunerations in all kinds of modalities. That these large corporations and banks should be treated "normally", and that if they failed, they had to declare bankruptcy, be intervened, and the responsible management needed to be dismissed without any golden parachutes, even if previously convened.

FED's fractional reserve lending, and government (?) or FED's (?) policies benefit mainly those with first access to money: the banks and the wealthy, and have made inflationary policies, which will bust if significant growth and significant reductions in unemployment and underemployment do not happen within the next decade at most.

Mr. Bernanke said he agreed with this, and had commended Dodd-Frank for providing a blueprint to get rid of "Too Big to Fail", this was 6-7 years ago, so when is the US going to get rid of "Too Big to Fail"?

Since the end of 2007, five major central banks have injected some USD 6 Trillion into the global economy, according to figures from the Bank for International Settlements (BIS). This was done to prevent bank runs and revive economies. Panic subsided, but economies are getting worse, mainly in Europe and particularly so in the Eurozone.

As the stimulus forced down interest rates, it eventually whetted investors' appetite for riskier assets like stocks.

Focus on Tax Evasion, Tax Breaks, Mobilizing Cash Savings / Hoarding, Predominance of Dividends' Payout versus creating Investment, all being measures to obtain Growth Resources.

During the whole Great Crisis and currently, with the Crisis not being over, the only "solution" seemed to be to follow Central Banking in its huge money inflows (QEs in the US, LTROs in the ECB) and seemingly more to come from the BCE, all at refinancing rates close to zero.

As already mentioned these "solutions" are not valid if they are the only ones, this has been proved dramatically in the Eurozone which is in a very bad situation, and have not implemented Social-Economic Structural Reforms because they could borrow for sovereign bonds' issues at very low BCE interest rate, which gave them artificial and temporary respite and this has made for at least half a decade of lost time in making Recovery possible.

Since years there is a "lot of talk" on fighting **Tax Evasion and Tax Loopholes** by reviewing the Tax Codes to determine which **Tax Breaks** are "reasonable", and establish coherent Tax policies.

Not much has been done and the amounts to "recover" are enormous in Trillions of USD / euros, and should be an extremely powerful manner to finance transitionally the costs of implementing the structural reforms, plus obtaining large additional Revenue to finance selectively Growth projects.

Another huge source of obtaining Revenue is to make it attractive to **Mobilize Dormant Savings**, which, also, represent Trillions and are not "active" in helping to obtain economic Recovery, the reason being that there is No Confidence in Governments and people and even corporations prefer to keep these "cash savings" under the "mattress"..

The **Japan** situation illustrates this very well, follows a résumé of this situation to illustrate above purposes.

Bank of Japan made massive assets' purchases to "dynamite "Japan's economy, which continued not recovering in spite of Abeconomics now lasting nearly two years.

Japan was concerned that falling energy prices would hurt their inflation target of two percent.

With November 2014 massive inflow of liquidity, the yen fell 2.6%, and import prices will make for more inflation, but hurt the "people"…

The worldwide demand for energy is sinking, a slowdown in China, a slowdown in Europe has hurt energy prices. The one thing that was hurting most Japan's goal of increasing inflation was energy imports sinking, but as mentioned before, this is a worldwide situation.

Why is Japan well noted (AA-) by S &P, in spite of Japan's big economic problems, which are described below?

Because Japan has a very strong exterior position, a prosperous and diversified economy and political stability.

Per capita income in Japan of 73 000 euros is nearly double than that of the Eurozone average!

Why then not having started the "three arrow" plan (see below in Le Figaro's article transcription please) with real and complete social-economic structural reforms, which the business community in Japan is asking for?

Why not have mobilized huge savings, in cash (!), by corporations and households (numbers are staggering, if true?) instead of doing what "everybody else" (US – Europe) does, have Central Banking issue (print) huge liquidity?

Have Abeconomics redressed Japan's economy?

Since last Spring 2014 in Europe a Japan type deflationary scenario has been "scaring" Europe, with inflation close to zero?

This scenario had produced in Japan a spiral of decrease in price which brought about a decrease in wages, entailing a vicious circle with consumption and growth decreasing, this "process" had been lasting for 2 decades, when Abe was elected as Prime Minister in December 2012 to remedy this long lasting very negative situation.

Abe, a charismatic politician, unlike his predecessors, had promised to get Japan out of this "infernal" spiral and created his detailed recovery program, that he himself called Abeconomics.

It basically consisted of lowering the value of the yen versus strong currencies, mainly the US dollar, which provoked euphoria in the Nikkei market, and -less- in other markets.

But in the 2nd Qtr of 2014, Japan's GDP fell 7.1% (!), which was as high as the market fall when the 2007-2008 Great Worldwide Crisis began. And this contraction is not excluded for the 3rd Qtr 2014 (?), and if so making the recession three quarters long, or all of 2014.

As to the so expected re start of inflation, it did not "happen" either in August 2014.

The three "arrows" of Abe's economic policy, as he called them at the beginning of his mandate were the following:

1. Monetary policy, a huge inflow of liquidity to make the yen fall.

2. Economic budgetary re launch program, financing infrastructure programs and social benefit programs with public funds, i.e. the Bank of Japan (BoJ) printed money.

The BoJ is not "independent" in Japan, it generally follows government's programs. Mr. Kuroda, head of BoJ, who shared belief in Abe's program

BoJ printed money in such a manner that BoJ's balance sheet doubled in nearly two years.

The yen devalued 30% versus the US dollar, with the result that currency brought about revenues of export corporations hugely increased their revenue in yens. This increase in revenues spectacularly doped Japan's Nikkei stock exchange.

Japan had suffered, for the first time since World War II, a negative commercial balance in 2011 (before Abe started his mandate in December 2012), due partly to the Fukushima catastrophe which forced Japan to massively import petrol and gas, paid in US dollars, a situation that Abe inherited…

Japan's competitive situation had not increased, therefore Abe increased VAT in April 2014 by 3 points (the last VAT increase was 17 years ago and this increase made it go from 5% to 8% – still relatively low) to finance both the Public Expenses and the Social Security Deficits.

The results were not as expected, Abe thought that consumption would temporarily decrease, but that wages' increases would counterbalance and bring a re launch of demand, but the Japanese had anticipated the VAT increase and anticipated purchases…

The drop in consumption was high and brought about the above mentioned drop of 7.1% of GDP.

The "key" to re launch the economy remained with wages' and salaries' increases.

During 1990 – 2012, over 2 decades of deflation, prices had increased by 5.5% on average, whereas wages / salaries had increased by 3.5 (a 54% difference!), which obviously had considerably reduced purchasing power.

The Corporations' situations improvements made this increase in remunerations possible, but unemployment in Japan being below 4% is not allowing for this, because the corporations found a lack of skilled labor in the jobs' market.

Abe is trying hard to convince big (Toyota, Hitachi, etc…) corporations' management to increase wages and salaries, with some positive results: in August 2014 salaries increased by 2.7% (unheard of since 1997!).

But this progression cannot bring average remuneration to increase, mainly because the ageing "baby boomers" generation which had protected salaries is taking retirement.

Inflation increased to 1.1% (far away from the 2% objective) in August 2014 due to the VAT increase mainly.

3. Structural Reforms, to allow flexibility in the "jobs' market", ration Social Security, modify the pensions' system, favoring work of women

(feeble in Japan), "liberating" agriculture (still an important activity sector in Japan) which was highly subsidized.

The business community feels that Abeconomics did not go far enough with structural reforms, mainly labor flexibility.

But Abe wants to continue his program, this autumn he should announce the reform of public pension plans.

The progressive lowering of corporations' taxes on income from 35% to 29% is planned for 2015.

Abe also wants to make Productivity increase by changing the Governance approach of corporations' management, allowing for more participation of shareholders and of independent Board members, he has created the Nikkei 400 to measure management of corporations.

Abe wants corporations to invest far more, with funds which are in corporations'" safe boxes", it seems there is an accumulation of 1.65 Trillion euros in cash (!) which are not injected into the economy, which would correspond to 44% of Japan's GDP(!).

Households also save enormously, their "stockings /mattresses" seemingly hold 12 Trillion euros (!)

These amounts are enormous (if true?) and if so why has Abe not motivated tax wise or with other financially motivating measures to mobilize these, seemingly (?) huge funds instead of having the BoJ print money, the priority measure ?

The ageing problem is crucial, it increases at high speed, this being a structural problem, that Abe cannot "control" and if you add to this very low unemployment the problem magnifies itself.

It is estimated that extrapolating the current trend the population will have decreased by a third by 2040 (!)

1. Tax Evasion

The "LuxLeaks" affair - November 2014 - is being heavily attacked, but I doubt that there will be any changes in the European Commission "non Governance".

Tax evasion and Tax loopholes considered "legal" once more surfaced dramatically (and politically), now called "LuxLeaks"

Tax evasion "methodology" was known for may decade, only that there was only "talk", with no regulatory actions taken against all these large international corporations, the US doing more than Europe (a "beneficiary") about it.

It will be an uphill and long battle because of not only huge lobbying by these international corporations, but also due to high powered lawyers seeing a gold mine in defending these cases.

But it has to be taken very seriously now, because of the Great Crisis and that Trillions USD / euros in possible Revenue coming out of the elimination of these "arrangements" will avoid continuing with ineffective QEs by Central Bankers, because of the huge losses in revenue to Governments, mainly the US.

American companies have plowed more money into the Netherlands than any other country in the world - for five years running.

It is about the taxes, or lack of them.

The laws in Netherlands shield a variety of profits from taxation, making it attractive for big multinational companies like Starbucks, Google and IBM to set up offices. Even rock stars like the Rolling Stones and U2 have taken advantage of Dutch tax shelters.

The same goes for Luxembourg, Bermuda, Ireland and the British Caribbean countries like the Cayman Islands.

Along with the Netherlands, those places rank among the top destinations for foreign direct investment from the United States, according to a review of data collected by the Bureau of Economic Analysis that shows how entrenched tax avoidance strategies have become.

It is the latest case to focus on favorable and often secretive tax arrangements between big multinationals and tax authorities — deals struck between Apple and Ireland, and Amazon and Fiat with Luxembourg. European authorities have also asked countries about arrangements made with a number of other companies, including Microsoft.

But regulators, if they even make a truly determined effort, face an uphill battle in changing the system.

Companies, for one, are doing their best to minimize the fallout.

Starbucks hired RLM Finsbury, a crisis communications firm, as opposition to the company's tax practices began building in Britain, its largest European market. This year, Starbucks decided to move its regional headquarters to London from Amsterdam as protests grew.

Apple recently tapped Fipra, a prominent lobbying firm with expertise in competition policy and an affiliate of RLM Finsbury, to bolster its defenses in Europe. Apple also hired a top lawyer from the branch of the European Commission investigating it in the tax case.

The financial bite from the European investigations may be limited. American corporations could potentially get credit on their tax bills back home even if they lose their cases, experts said, because the companies are likely to pay back taxes rather than face a fine.

Peter Cussons, a partner at Price Waterhouse Coopers in London, said any funds "in principle should be eligible for U.S. foreign tax credit relief, subject to the usual rules."

In some ways, authorities are performing a futile task: As officials move to close certain loopholes, others are likely to pop up in their place.

Last month, Ireland said it would phase out a loophole that Apple helped pioneer and is currently used by many other companies, known as the Double Irish. The maneuver allows companies to pay royalties from one Irish subsidiary to a second subsidiary incorporated in Ireland and domiciled in another country with low or no corporate tax. The strategy is often paired with a Netherlands subsidiary and known as Double Irish with a Dutch Sandwich.

But Ireland's move seems intended to cushion the blow for multinationals. Not only will there be a long phase-out period, but the country is setting up a so-called patent box.

A similar mechanism in Britain allows a company to pay lower taxes for "its patented inventions and certain other innovations." Here too, European regulators are taking a closer look, viewing it as a potentially unfair trade practice.

Foreign investment figures offer something of a road map to tax sheltering.

Consider that 15.5 percent of American foreign direct investment goes to the Netherlands, and four-fifths of that goes into Dutch holding companies. Companies like Starbucks often have a number of subsidiaries with varying structures in the Netherlands, in Starbucks's case with names like Rain City and Emerald City.

Luxembourg's practices have drawn particular scrutiny, putting its former prime minister, Mr. Juncker, the new head of the European Commission, on the defensive.

The country had inward foreign direct investment of $2.4 trillion in 2012, exceeding the combined intake of Germany and France, the Eurozone's two largest economies, according to International Monetary Fund data.

American companies are fighting efforts in Europe to reverse favorable tax deals.

To put that in perspective, Luxembourg has a population of just over 500 000 people. Germany and France have a combined population of 146 million people.

About 91 percent of the foreign direct investment coming into Luxembourg is through special-purpose entities. Such vehicles are often set up by multinational corporations for accounting purposes, according to the Organization for Economic Cooperation and Development (OECD), a club of developed countries.

Ireland has become particularly popular as a way station for managing taxes. A United States Senate report last year found that from 2009 to 2012, Apple transferred 74 Billion USD in worldwide sales income away from the US to Ireland where Apple has negotiated a tax rate of less than 2 percent. Another Senate report found that Microsoft transferred "rights to the intellectual property developed by American engineers" to a small Dublin office with less than 400 employees, then reported an annual profit of $4.3 billion, which was taxed at 7.2 percent.

Companies defend their tax practices.

Apple has said, "Our success in Europe and around the world is the result of hard work and innovation by our employees, not any special arrangements with the government."

Amazon has said that it received no special treatment. Fiat said it stood by the "legitimacy" of its tax practices. Starbucks said that it had never "sought unfair tax incentives" and complied with all relevant rules.

The most ambitious effort to close loopholes and overhaul the tax system globally is a project being undertaken by the Organization for Economic Cooperation and Development (OECD. The project, which began at the request of the Group of 20 countries, aims to rein in a variety of tax-avoidance practices like transfer pricing.

With that maneuver, companies like Facebook, AstraZeneca and Google have been able to lower their taxes by manipulating the prices one subsidiary charges another for a good or service. The final proposals for the effort are due next year.

Many experts are skeptical about how much this can achieve. The economic development organization's recommendations would need the approval of national governments, all with their own interests and goals.

Will other countries take any steps on their own?

Not the Netherlands. "Unilateral measures may actually increase mismatches and other differences between systems, instead of removing them," the finance ministry said in a statement.

The Luxembourg government recently submitted legislation to make its tax rulings more transparent. Mr. Juncker said last week that addressing corporate tax avoidance "can't be a Luxembourgish answer — it has to be a European answer." Luxembourg tax practices have been widely known for many, many decades, like all above cited tax havens using different "methods" and practices to attract big mainly corporate and individual taxpayers.

The tax loopholes, and tax evasions are huge, you can count them in Trillions, of taxes that Governments in "normal" countries do not receive.

Why?

Because all large international corporations which are extremely successful, have huge lobbying with their local governments

International financial regulations and Central Bankers should "do something" about this.

It would be a larger source of financing to obtain Recovery than all this obsession with cheap huge money inflows, but "Nobody" does anything about it, because its "Too Big" (as the Big Banks Too Big to Fail"…).

As to Mr. Juncker's responsibility as President of the European Commission, it is the same as that of his predecessors.

The author of this book was opposed to his election because I felt he was as "obsolete" as his predecessor, Mr. Barroso, because during 18 years he has been part of inefficient European / Eurozone "non Governance" and during 8 years headed the Eurogroup from which he resigned before the end of his second mandate.

I wrote a book in 2014:"Why Macro Governance is Obsolete and Killing the World Economy", published mid 2014 by Amazon-Kindle (e-book) and by Amazon-Create Space in September 2014 (paper version), in which I make concrete alternative proposals on "modern governance".

Between 2002 and 2010, according to a survey published Thursday – 11/06/2014 – by 40 international media, the Grand Duchy of Luxembourg passed tax agreements with 340 multinationals, including Apple, Amazon, Ikea, Pepsi, Heinz, Verizon, AIG, Axa to minimize their taxes.

These are definitely not "new" practices, they are, to some extent, even legal, and do not only apply to the Luxembourg.

The survey "highlights the "unfair" practices of tax havens in the heart of Europe and a large series of other places worldwide, and whose "new" European Commission President, Mr. Juncker, was obviously aware of this situation during the eighteen years he passed as being an executive member of the EC.

For Mr. Juncker, the new president of the European Commission, the honeymoon is over and some in Europe already want a divorce.

The prime minister of Luxembourg for the better part of 18 years, Mr. Juncker took over the European Union's top job on Nov. 1, 2014, only to be hit by calls to resign a few days later.

The sniping came after a group of investigative journalists issued a report detailing secret deals struck by major corporations with Luxembourg that allegedly allowed them to shave billions of dollars off their global tax bills.

On Wednesday - *11/12/2014* – Mr. Juncker personally responded to the allegations for the first time, taking political responsibility "for what happened in each and every corner and quarter" of Luxembourg during his tenure.

But he said the deals in question had been struck with independent tax authorities, while also insisting that they complied "with national legislation and international rules."

But he conceded that some of his country's tax rules might not have been in line with "ethical and moral standards that are generally applicable."

Nevertheless, he said he would push for streamlined tax codes across Europe and vowed that he could be relied on to fight tax evasion.

He said he would not step down.

The EU's Competition Office is investigating Luxembourg - as well as Ireland and the Netherlands - for super tax deals.

But thus far, there have been no official charges of wrongdoing.

Mr. Juncker pledged not to discuss the case with E.U. Competition Commissioner Margrethe Vestager to avoid the impression of impropriety.

A host of critics, however, are calling the fresh revelations evidence that Mr. Juncker is the wrong man for the job. Some are going even further, saying the scandal is exposing a woeful lack of democracy at the top of EU power structures.

Indeed, EU's president is a mighty post, with the person in that job wielding sweeping authority over the creation of laws and the legislative agenda for the 28-nation bloc. But it is a job that is still not filled by voters and that, especially this year, was decided on via a backroom political deal.

Before assuming his new role, Mr. Juncker had been forced to step down as prime minister in December 2013 amid charges of corruption and over reaching within Luxembourg's spy agency.

He denied any wrongdoing and sought to continue "his career" by slipping into the job of European Commission president (sic).

Previously, Europe's elected heads of state had largely nominated candidates. But despite strong reservations from a number of E.U. leaders — chiefly British Prime Minister David Cameron — Mr. Juncker managed to secure the job through a lead-candidate system that came into effect in 2014.

Political groups in the European Parliament, including members of German Chancellor Mrs. Merkel's Christian Democratic Union, agreed to support certain candidates depending on the results of the May 2014 elections for the European Parliament.

As it turned out, the bloc backing Mr. Juncker emerged the strongest. But a study by one group, *Open Europe*, showed that the center-right parties backing Mr. Juncker were supported by only 9.7 percent of the European electorate.

The scandal now is another example of the view that there is a huge democratic deficit at the center of the European Commission (EU).

No one really was making the connection between tax issues and Mr. Juncker's candidacy beforehand, and this also highlights the lack of scrutiny going on at the very highest levels of the EU.

For the EU, the scandal could not have come at a worst time.

Mr. Juncker is being charged with restoring confidence in Brussels, the EU administrative capital. But particularly after the European debt crisis, that is no easy job. Today, its image as a hub for knotted bureaucracy, inefficiency and "Machiavellian" (sic) deals is as strong as ever.

A pull-no-punches Bloomberg View editorial this week declared:"Jean-Claude Juncker needs to go."

It accused him of presiding over Luxembourg as it used "Swiss-style bank secrecy" and "government-blessed tax avoidance schemes" to become a haven for 340 major corporations and investment funds eager to avoid taxes.

How did the little Grand Duchy do it? By granting some firms a corporate tax rate below 1 percent for profits funneled through Luxembourg, providing an avenue for to exploit loopholes in the countries where the majority of their profits were being made.

In the UK, in particular, Mr. Juncker was facing calls to resign.

The US has calculated for 2011 that it had lost 1.38 Trillions USD in lost income taxes - close to 10% of the US GDP of USD 16 Trillion (?!), in Europe the same type of loss is estimated for 2011 at 1 Trillion euros, equal to 10% of European Union 27 countries' GDP (?!).

OECD feels that it would take them 2 years to "clean up" (?), but the opposition/lobbying of large international corporations will make this "task" extremely difficult if there is no major - G20 - countries' political will.

In a concerted move to quiet fears of a so-called currency war, finance officials from the world's largest industrial and emerging economies expressed their commitment beginning of 2013 (sic) to "market-determined exchange rate systems and exchange rate flexibility." In a statement issued at the conclusion of a conference here of the Group of 20, the finance ministers from the Group of 20 promised: "We will refrain from competitive devaluation. We will not target our exchange rates for competitive purposes."

In its statement, the G20, in 2013, also vowed to "take necessary collective actions" to discourage corporate tax evasion, particularly by preventing companies from shifting profits to avoid tax obligations. For instance, a number of big American companies, including Apple and Starbucks, have come under scrutiny recently for seeking out the friendliest tax jurisdictions.

Over all, the statement largely echoed one by seven top industrial nations' pledging to let market exchange rates determine the value of their currencies. Currency devaluation can be used to gain competitive advantage because it makes a country's exports cheaper.

In the statement, the Group of 20 pointedly avoided any criticism of Japan, where stimulus programs backed by Prime Minister Shinzo Abe – Abeconomics - have kept interest rates near zero and flooded the economy with money — leading to a roughly 30 percent drop in the value of the yen against the dollar to date – November 2014. The Japanese policies, which have reduced the cost of Japanese products around the world, were the primary cause of fears of a currency war."

In essence, the G20 expressed a view that loose monetary policy, including steps that weaken currency values, are acceptable when used to stimulate domestic growth but should not be used to benefit in global trade.

This is a "fine", vague and incoherent statement, since how does one make the distinction between "domestic growth simulation" and "benefit in global trade"…?

Critics of that view say that it amounts to a distinction without a difference because loose monetary policies stimulate growth and bolster exports at the same time.

The US - always in 2013 - had also used a loose monetary approach to aid in the economic recovery, in the form of "quantitative easing" by which the FED buys tens of billions of dollars in bonds (85 Billions USD at the time) each month." The chairman of the Federal Reserve, Mr. Bernanke, who attended the 2013 G20 conference, gave brief remarks "indicating support for Japan's efforts"…

In the meantime, November 2014, the FED has stopped with Quantitative Easing (QE) but left a close to zero interest rate, not indicating yet at which date it would increase it.

Faster-growing, developing countries like Brazil and China –now having far more moderate growth (China with below 2 digits 7.5% growth, Brazil with close to nil growth…) had expressed concerns about the loose monetary policies of more established economies like Japan and the United States. The money created by policies like the FED's quantitative easing can prove destabilizing as it enters faster-growing economies.

The Group of 20 (beginning 2013) acknowledged this concern in its statement, saying: "Monetary policy should be directed toward domestic price stability and continuing to support economic recovery according to the respective mandates. We commit to monitor and minimize the negative spillovers on other countries of policies implemented for domestic purposes."

A "very" general, vague and unfulfilled statement by the end of 2014…

2. Tax Breaks

They began more than 90 years ago as a small tax break intended to help family farmers who wanted to swap horses and land. Farmers who sold property, livestock or equipment were allowed to avoid paying capital gains taxes, as long as they used the proceeds to replace or upgrade their assets.

Over the years, however, as the rules were loosened, the practice of exchanging one asset for another without incurring taxes spread to everyone from commercial real estate developers and art collectors to major corporations. It provides subsidies for rental truck fleets and investment property, vacation homes, oil wells and thoroughbred racehorses, and diverts billions of dollars in potential tax revenue from the Treasury each year.

Yet even with those generous terms, some major American companies, and also majorEuropean ones, have routinely pushed the boundaries while claiming lucrative tax savings, according to evidence recently presented at a federal trial in New York.

President Obama and Congressional leaders had agreed 2 years ago to a limited agreement to raise taxes on the wealthy, and **the** president said over the weekend that he would press this year for broader reform in the tax code.

The expansion of the tax breaks once intended to help farmers illustrates the challenges ahead and how special interests have learned to use the tax code to maximum effect."

The federal government allowed in 2012 more than1.1 Trillion USD a year in this and other tax expenditures.

Each of those incentives — which include hundreds of exemptions, exclusions, deferrals and preferential rates — either adds to the budget deficit or shifts the cost of government to other taxpayers.

Tax expenditures are very similar to an entitlement program, so they're easy to start, but once a tax break gets started, people think they're entitled to it, so they are very difficult to end.

Many tax breaks began with narrow targets and expanded into vast, expensive subsidies far beyond their original intent or the Internal Revenue Service's ability to monitor them.

Most have developed constituencies of taxpayers, lobbyists and elected officials who fiercely defend them, making it politically treacherous to limit or eliminate them.

With hundreds of thousands of transactions a year, it is hard to gauge the true cost of the tax break for so-called like-kind exchanges, like those used by Cendant, General Electric and Wells Fargo.

The government estimates that it diverts less than 3 Billion USD a year from the Treasury, but industry statistics suggest the number could be far higher.

The tax breaks also expose one of the greatest vulnerabilities of the US tax system: it depends on voluntary compliance.

The I.R.S. staff is so outnumbered by tax lawyers and accounting departments at major corporations that there is often little to prevent taxpayers from taking a freewheeling approach to interpreting and administering the rules.

What's more, the tax breaks are so numerous that they tend to escape attention. The independent Simpson-Bowles deficit commission appointed by Mr. Obama in 2010 raised the possibility of eliminating it and other tax expenditures, however, and some budget experts argue that the program should be severely limited or repealed.

Some financial planners and economists say that the tax breaks even favored real estate investors unfairly by allowing them to defer capital gains taxes that those who invest in securities and other ventures have to pay.

A crucial element of the tax breaks is that companies cannot use the proceeds of an asset sale for any purpose other than buying a replacement.

Because the tax breaks are intended to encourage reinvestment in a business, companies that sell an asset are required to deposit the proceeds from the sale into an escrow account, which must be controlled by a third party.

At least half-dozen companies were allowed unrestricted access, according to evidence at the trial. For at least 30 months, Wells Fargo had unfettered access to billions of dollars intended to be held in escrow, the records show. And American subsidiaries of Volkswagen and BMW had so much control over the money that they used it as collateral to obtain lines of credit.

There is a deep conviction in the real estate business that it is justified. Advocates for the real estate industry say that a large majority of transactions are conducted in strict compliance with I.R.S. regulations. Because the asset exchanges spur investment and help create jobs, industry officials say they would strenuously oppose any effort to end them.

Real estate business leaders continue arguing that this seemingly "greatly fouled" tax breaks "system" is good for the economy!

Somebody" in the Governments (the "missing" Minister of Economy in the US) should take the whole Tax Codes "in hand" and review them extensively and then revise them, taking into account all that happened during the existing crisis (since 2007) and before, and making a total "cleanup" which will take years, but needs to be started like "now"...

3. Motivating Mobilization of Cash Savings / Hoardings

Corporate Cash Hoarding

According to Wikipedia - In March 2013 Moody's Investors Service published their report entitled *Cash Pile Grows 10% to $1.45 Trillion; Overseas Holdings Continue to Expand* in their Global Credit Research series, in which they examined companies they rate in the US non-financial corporate sector (NFCS). According to their report, by the end of 2012 the US NFCS held "$1.45 trillion in cash," 10% more than in 2011. At the end of 2011, US NFCS held $1.32 trillion in cash which was already a record level.[28] "Of the $1.32 trillion for all the rated companies, Moody's estimates that $840 billion, or 58% of the total cash, is held overseas."[28]

In his article in April 2013 FED's Economist, Mr. Kliesen investigated some of the causes of the "recent upsurge in hoarding of cash by firms" or "increased accumulation of cash on corporate balance sheets" in the US. He suggested a number of valid reasons including "increased levels of economic uncertainty," "increased competition, especially in the information technology sector" and "financing of research and development." Mr. Kliesen also argued that another reason for cash hoarding in the US is the "relatively high U.S. corporate tax rate on income generated from foreign operations and subsidiaries."

According to Economix many corporations are holding vast amounts of cash and other liquid assets, using them neither for investment nor to benefit shareholders. These assets are largely earned and held overseas and not subject to American taxes until the money is brought home.

Such tax-avoidance techniques, while legal, have come under increasing political attack. On Thursday, Senator Bernie Sanders of Vermont introduced legislation to end deferral and force multinational companies to pay taxes on their foreign-source income.

According to the Federal Reserve, as of the third quarter of 2012 nonfinancial corporations in the United States held $1.7 trillion of liquid assets – cash and securities that could easily be converted to cash.

By any measure, corporate cash holdings appear to be high and rising.

According to the Federal Reserve, nonfinancial corporations historically held liquid assets of 25 to 30 percent of their short-term liabilities. But this percentage began rising in 2001 and now tends to be in the 45 to 50 percent range. In the third quarter of 2012, it was 44.9 percent.

A recent study by Juan Sánchez and Emircan Yurdagul of the Federal Reserve Bank of St. Louis looked at the ratio of cash to assets at all publicly held nonfinancial, non-utility corporations. They found that, historically, such corporations held cash equal to about 6 percent of their assets, but that began rising in 1995 and is now more than 12 percent, as seen below.

Ratio of Cash to Net Assets

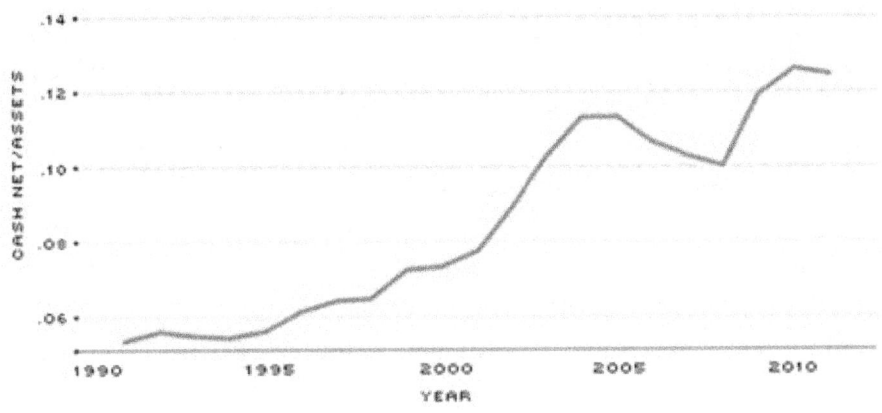

Credit Federal Reserve Bank of St. Louis analysis of Compustat data

One obvious explanation for higher cash holdings by corporations is the uncertainty of the economic environment in the aftermath of the financial crisis. They may also face greater difficulty in getting credit on short notice and need to hold more cash as a precaution.

Another explanation, put forward by the economists Thomas W. Bates, Kathleen M. Kahle and René M. Stulz, is that the growing research-and-development intensity of corporations forces them to hold more cash than they used to. They also note that companies hold fewer inventories and accounts receivable than they used to. And, they say, these factors make corporate cash flow less dependable than previously, thus necessitating the need for higher cash holdings.

However, the dominant explanation for the increased liquidity of nonfinancial corporations appears to be the growing role of multinational corporations and the profits of their foreign operations.

In a 2006 speech, the Federal Reserve Board governor Kevin Warsh noted that higher corporate cash holdings were dominated by those with foreign operations. Between 2001 and 2004, the ratio of cash to assets at domestic-only corporations increased 20 percent, while it increased 50 percent among multinational corporations.

Individuals' Cash Hoarding

Japan - "Abe wants corporations to invest far more, with funds which are in corporations'" safe boxes", it seems there is an accumulation of 1.65 Trillion euros in cash (!) which are not injected into the economy, which would correspond to 44% of Japan's GDP (!)."

Households in Japan also save enormously, their "stockings" - seemingly - hold 12 Trillion euros (!?)"

This seems surprisingly high in view of following data:

8% of "individuals' " worldwide wealth is in tax havens, equal to 7.6 Trillion (7 600 Billion) USD

Source – Le Figaro – 11/24/2014

Some 7.6 trillion USD, or 8% of global wealth is held by individuals in tax havens, says a recent study in the Journal of Economic Perspectives.

European households arrive first with some 2 600 billion USD (2.6 trillion) located in countries that combine low taxes and financial secrecy, says French Grabiel Zucman, assistant professor at the London School of Economics.

Behind them, the Asian taxpayers (1 300 billion USD) distancing few Americans (1 200 billion USD), which are followed by individuals in the Gulf countries (700 billion USD), says the author of "The Hidden Wealth of Nations. Survey the tax havens "(2013).

The study takes into account the financial assets and not the real or personal property that can also be kept out of the national treasuries.

It can superficially conclude that Cash Hoarding / Savings is mainly with Corporations with Overseas Operations, the main motivation being to not pay taxes, which if this is the case rejoins the "Tax Breaks" point above, there is still the point of great incertitude about the future.

Individual's holdings seem to largely exceed corporate holdings, and this is mainly based on uncertainty on the future.

Conclusions on Diminishing strongly Tax Evasion and Tax Breaks versus huge money inflows by domineering Central Banks, be it QEs or any other financial instruments.

Undoubtedly, Cash Hoarding represents a great many Trillions of inoperative funds for economies, and it would be necessary to "join" Tax Evasion / Loopholes, Tax Breaks and Cash Hoarding to obtain an approximate amount of these not or badly utilized funds in economies.

In order to do something other than "Talk" about this huge opportunity to recover Trillions of USD / euros Revenue for major countries in order to re invest them in structural reforming and selective Growth Projects, it is required that the G20 decades on which supranational organization/ s will tackle this huge "Project", where data exits all over the place – worldwide.

I believe that OECD, IMF and the five most important worldwide Central Banks (FED, People's Bank of China (PBC or PBOC), BCE, BoJ, BoE) should be made responsible to:

- First, determine amounts involved and categorize them into Tax Evasion / Loopholes, Tax Breaks and Cash Hoarding.
- Second, identify what "carrots"/ incentives can be used to allow for as large as possible recovery of funds.

This will only be effective if an agenda is prepared and responsibilities are defined.

4. Corporate Dividends' payout increases versus Corporate Investments decreases.

Worldwide corporate dividend payout has been increasing considerably while corporate Investments have been decreasing since the Great Crisis began, and this is continuing.

Many investors think of dividend-paying companies as boring, low-return investment opportunities. Compared to high-flying small cap companies, whose volatility can be pretty exciting, dividend-paying stocks are usually more mature and predictable. Though this may be dull for some, the combination of a consistent dividend with an increasing stock price can offer an earnings' potential powerful enough to get excited about.

The important indication of "dividend power" is not so much a high dividend yield but high company quality, which you can discover through its history of dividends, which should increase over time. If you are a long-term investor, looking for such companies can be very rewarding.

The dividend payout ratio, the proportion of company earnings allocated to paying dividends, further demonstrates that the source of dividend profitability works in combination with company growth.

For decades, many investors have been using this dividend-focused strategy by buying shares in household names.

These are basically the arguments in favor of paying out dividends.

The counter side is that there has been a decrease in worldwide Investments as a parallel to this Dividend increase, which has been a great factor in hindering Growth.

A steep fall in FDI (Foreign Direct Investments) in 2012 reverses the recent recovery in developed economies, this trend continued in 2013 - 2014

The sharp decline in inflows reversed the FDI recovery during 2010–2011. Inflows fell in 23 of 38 developed economies in 2012.

The 32 per cent nosedive was due to a 41 per cent decline in the European Union and a 26 per cent decline in the United States.

The overall decline was due to weaker growth prospects and policy uncertainty, especially in Europe, and the cooling off of investment in extractive industries.

The falling prices of oil in 2014 must have accentuated the trend.

Conclusion

A superficial, but credible conclusion is that investments fell due to economic uncertainty, which has been increasing worldwide in 2014 due also to problems encountered in some of the large "emerging" countries' development.

In order to reverse this trend, it would be a great mistake to penalize dividend payout by applying extra / higher taxes to dividends.

A far more positive and motivating measure would be to motivate corporations who have large dividend payouts to invest a large part of them by allowing attractive tax motivation measures.

Conclusions on the great interest of giving priority to achieve success in achieving to the highest degree success in applying these four making revenue measures

I firmly believe that to spend a great amount of time in trying to make these four big measures work to the highest possible degree and re create three huge potential sources of Trillions in revenue s is going to be far more productive and far less costly than continuing devising artificial and temporary huge money inflows by Central Banks.

To allow the preceding measures to be able to work, the Banking sectors need to be far more transparent.

This is where the long awaited Eurozone Banking Union is going to be a greatly needed institution, which will be under BCE's control and needs to go through the following process, which is "in progress".

The Eurozone Banking Union

The Eurozone Banking Union Project, is one of the projects that is most badly needed to be able to coordinate efficiently Banking behavior in the Eurozone, but will take some years to be operational and function.

This time period is necessary to obtain the agreement of the now - 2014 - 18 nations of the Eurozone which will be extremely difficult, also as usual, because the preparatory work by the Eurogroup in conjunction with the European Commission and the European Union was not done in-depth.

Agreement on "principle" happened in 2014 and implementation will not happen before 2 to 3 years, led by the ECB, whose main function should be to regulate, analyze quarterly and control permanently the Banking sector.

This crucial and necessary project had been evoked since years, but since the European / Eurozone "non authorities" have not succeeded in achieving any project because of not sufficient preparation and definition of "workable" functionality, all these projects have never reached a final stage of implementation in the last half decade.

It is also related to already mentioned exaggerated role/s of Central Banking, especially the FED and the BCE later, "independent" organizations who assume functions they did not have years ago (like the FED being "guardian of employment").

The purpose of the Banking union is to de-link banks from their sovereigns.

- Putting the ECB in charge of supervision and creating a common resolution mechanism should help, but this is not enough.
- European banks hold too much government debt of their own governments to really sever the sovereign-bank link.

The BCE had a far more difficult "job" of fulfilling its "right" role in the Eurozone, because of the European / Eurozone (non) Governance, its inertia and incapacity and total indecision, because Germany really directs the Eurozone and also is not capacitated to do it, and should not to it.

The Eurozone Banking Union Project is very important to the Eurozone because European banks finance 3 quarters of the credit to

European economies, whereas US banks finance only one quarter of these needs, which makes it necessary that European banks be as efficient as possible, which is not the case so far.

The European Union has failed to agree rules on who should pay in the event of a global banking collapse after Eurozone countries clashed with those outside the single currency over how flexible the system should be. Germany wants to ensure the tax on savings that formed part of the Cyprus rescue in March 2013 is repeated in al future bail-outs.

The Eurozone Banking issue will not be really remediated if banks continue to hold far too much of their own countries' sovereign debt and the enormous risk that this represents for the banks, the countries, and the Eurozone as a whole.

This basically happens because sovereign bonds are construed to be riskless, and since the "Greece" hair-cut, his is known not to be true, but, still, is not taken into consideration, at least "officially", and should be so imperatively.

The link between banks and national governments played a dominant role in the Eurozone crisis. ECB being in charge of Eurozone's Banking supervision and creating a common resolution mechanism is not enough, because European banks hold too much government debt of their own governments to really cut the sovereign-bank link.

A simple solution would be to apply the general rule that banks are prohibited from holding more than a quarter of their capital in government bonds of any single sovereign.

Data on share of own-government debt in bank holdings

The concentration of public debt on bank balance sheets is not just a result of the euro crisis (Figure 1). The numbers show that French and Italian banks always held a considerable fraction of total public debt. The data for Germany are surprising. They show that in the not-so-distant past more than one half of the country's total national debt was held by German banks. The German banking system has diversified its holdings of government debt only since the creation of the euro.

Figure 1 (National) government debt held by domestic banks in France, Germany, Italy and the US (% of total)

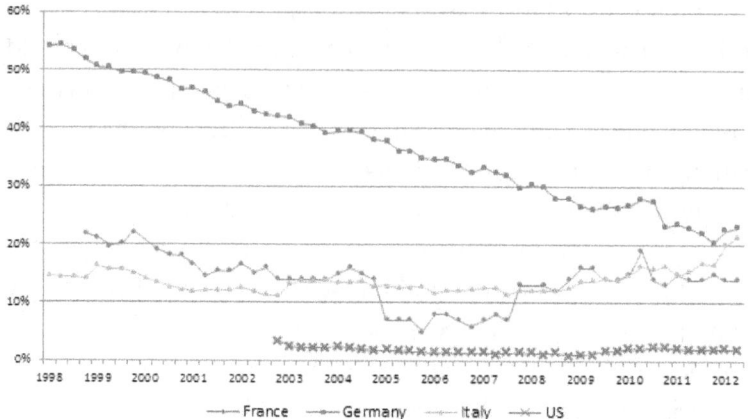

Source: Agence France Trésor, Bundesbank, Bank of Italy and FED.

- Why do banks hold so much government debt?

The answer is simple – regulators have made it attractive for them to hold such debt, because:

Banks do not have to hold any capital against their holdings of government debt.

Banks hold capital against their investments only if regulators assign a risk weight to this investment. But the risk weight is zero on sovereign debt. This assumption that government debt is riskless permeates all banking regulation and thus contributes indirectly in many ways to induce banks to hold government debt.

It is difficult to understand why this assumption has not been changed after the 'PSI' (private-sector involvement) operation in Greece showed that banks can lose money on their holdings of Eurozone sovereign bonds. Moreover, PSI is now also official policy since the ESM Treaty foresees explicitly the possibility of a haircut on public debt if a debt sustainability analysis shows that the country cannot service its debt in full.

There is thus no reason to continue with the regulatory fiction that sovereign debt is always riskless.

Introducing risk weights for government debt will not be enough to prevent a crisis because of the 'lumpiness' of sovereign risk. Experience has shown that sovereign defaults are rare events, but the losses are typically very large (above 50%) when default does materialize. In many peripheral countries, banks hold sovereign debt equal to (or greater than) their total capital. Even with a risk weight of 100%, these banks would only have sufficient capital reserves to cover losses of 8% (!).

- Large banks are allowed to "selective" regulatory approaches.

There is an obscure but very important clause: "Permanent Partial Exemption". This term refers to one of the many wrinkles in the way the EU has implemented the Basel agreements on banking regulation in its own capital requirements Directive (CRD).

In essence large banks are allowed to use their own models to assess the riskiness of their own assets. But when these models would signal that government debt has become risky (for example because the debt has become unsustainable or CDS spreads signal risk), the normal risk models are put aside in favor of the general presumption that government debt can never be risky.

Accordingly, large banks can be "selective". Most large banks use their internal risk models to calculate the riskiness of their lending to households, the corporate sector and their other assets. By doing so they can generally arrive at a lower level of capital requirement than under the so-called standardized approach in which all lending falls in certain risk classes determined by ratings levels. However, these internal risk models are put aside in the case of government debt. Given this, there is little wonder that European banks lack the capital to weather a sovereign debt crisis (which by regulatory definition should not be possible).

Liquidity requirements favor government bonds.

Another reason why banks hold large amounts of government debt on their balance sheets is that they have to hold a certain amount of 'liquid' and safe assets. Until recently, only government bonds were recognized as liquid. However, experience over the last few years has shown that at times even government bonds can become illiquid.

Forcing banks to hold large amounts of government bonds might make sense if it were true that that this is the only class of liquid and safe assets, but this is manifestly no longer true.

Fortunately the latest version of the so-called liquidity cover ratio (LCR) allows banks to also hold other assets to satisfy the requirement of the LCR, whose purpose is to ensure that a bank can always offset potential outflows of funds by selling liquid assets. This incentive to hold government debt might thus be somewhat diminished.

There is no limit on the concentration of sovereign risk.

The most basic principle of finance is reducing risk through diversification. The need to diversify risk is the reason why all regulated investors (banks, insurance companies, investment funds, pension funds) have to limit their exposure to any single counterparty to a fraction of their total investment or capital (for banks). For banks, the limit on the exposure to any one borrower is 25% of their capital, but this limit does not apply to sovereign debt.

The logic of this exemption was simple: since there was thought to be no risk in sovereign debt, there was no reason to put any limits on its concentration.

The result of this lack of exposure limits has been that banks in the Eurozone periphery have too much debt of their own government on their balance sheets which has greatly contributed to the deadly link between sovereigns and banks.

It is apparent that in most countries the domestic banking system would not survive a Greek-style 'haircut' on public debt. (In the context of the PSI operation of March 2012, holders of Greek bonds had to accept a nominal haircut of over 50%, and on a mark-to-market basis the haircut was over 80%. It is apparent that no bank that has a sovereign exposure worth over 100% of its capital would survive such a loss.

Conclusions

The belief that government debt is riskless is a fundamental assumption in banking regulation. In Europe this has induced banks to hold large amounts of government debt and, even worse, to concentrate their holdings on their own sovereign – thus ensuring that a sovereign-debt crisis also becomes a banking crisis.

The key aspect for the stability of the euro and its banking system is the concentration of bank holdings of their own sovereign.

If this was changed, and it needs to do so, the banking system would become much more resistant to sovereign-debt problems.

A simple solution would be to apply the general rule that banks are prohibited from holding more than 25% of their capital in government bonds of any single sovereign.

This rule could be applied only to new investment during a transition period so that it would not force any abrupt selling of the existing holdings.

The treatment of government debt in banking regulation is kept silent.... The EU has recently completed a wide-ranging overhaul of its banking regulation framework in the context of the renewal of the capital requirements Directive (CRDIV).

The regulatory treatment of sovereign debt was not even discussed in this context. Why? Simply because governments want to maintain a source of demand for their own bonds!

But this self-serving treatment of government debt in banking regulation is short-sighted because it leads to a situation in which Eurozone banks hold a large proportion of government debt – much more than in the US.

These are the dangers of considering sovereign bonds riskless and having Eurozone countries hold too much debt in their own sovereign bonds.

This is dangerous given that banks are highly leveraged and that sovereign debt is inherently subject to default risk within the Eurozone. For financial-stability reasons, it would thus be preferable if a higher proportion of government debt were held by unleveraged investors, e.g. directly by households or via investment funds. But this would of course reduce the income of the banks.

The unholy alliance of short-sighted finance ministers and bankers interested in keeping their business will be very costly because it perpetuates the negative links between banks and sovereigns.

The 1 Trillion euros LTROs issued by ECB end of 2011 and in March 2012, directly to banks' main usage was for banks to lend to governments at "normal" open market interest rates and keep the spread between these rates and the below 1% ECB refinancing rate - a "nice business" financed by ECB!

International supranational organizations like IMF, European Commission, Eurogroup, OECD, et al, often, on a quarterly, change their declarations, going from "bad" when evidence shows that banks are not lending "adequately" (i.e. to finance working capital needs to help expand locally and export wise SMEs and innovation corporations, as an example) to "good", when stress tests and other analysis show that their financial structure is adequate.

This seems to be the case with the stress tests conducted by ECB in 2014 on the 130 major banks and where only 25 Banks did not "pass", Italian banks for the largest portion, but not all conclusions have been made yet.

One reason the Eurozone is in such a mess is that it has not had the courage to clean up its banks.

The US gave its lenders a proper scrubbing, followed by recapitalization, in 2009.

ECB now has a great opportunity to press the reset button in advance of taking on the job of banking supervisor in 2014 - 2015.

It must not miss the cleanup. Mr. Draghi, ECB president, must be ready to the opportunity and the threat.

His fear is that, even if the supervisor does its job properly, there will not be a safety net for troubled banks that cannot recapitalize themselves.

This is why he called on governments to make an explicit commitment to provide such a "backstop".

This is the real problem since most Eurozone member countries abhor "intervention", rightfully so with the "troika" in the last years, but ECB has to be able to do it, and should use the 18 "local" Central Banks to obtain results.

Mr. Draghi highlighted the contrast between the US stress test, in which Washington committed to plug any balance sheet holes, and the last stress test conducted by the European Banking Authority (EBA) in 2011 and 2012, which lacked such a commitment by governments.

The US tests started the American economy on the road to recovery - the European ones set off a new phase in the crisis.

The moral is obvious: Without a type of safety net, exposing problems and being "transparent" and not "political" can provoke panic. The supervisor may as a result be tempted to continue sweeping problems under the carpet. The Eurozone's recovery would then be further delayed, and ECB's credibility destroyed.

Who exactly has been reviewing the 130 major banks' assets which were included in the 2014 stress tests?

Has ECB acquired the necessary manpower to do it? If not, it has to rely on national supervisors. The snag is that these supervisors could have an incentive to hide problems in their banks, so the cost of bailing them out is borne by the Eurozone as a whole.

Mr. Draghi's answer is to get supervisors to cross-check the balance sheets of banks in other countries — and to reinforce the audit's independence by involving private-sector assessors. The latter suggestion originally provoked unhappiness in France. But at a recent dinner with central bank governors, Mr. Draghi pushed his solution through. This is why I feel that the "supervisors" should be the local member countries' Central Banks who have relative "political independence"...

ECB should have determined whether lenders have used appropriate "risk weights" for their assets. A risk weight determines the size of the capital buffer a bank is required to hold. There was a widespread suspicion that many lenders are using artificially low weights to give the misleading impression that they are well-capitalized. This is a capital point, as above mentioned, the bases for calculating risk need to ne as realistic as possible in order not to camouflage reality, as has been the case since 5 years!

Yet another issue is whether capital shortfalls will be expressed as an absolute number — like 1 Billion euros, or 1.3 / 1.5 Billion euros— or as a percentage of risk-weighted assets. The last banking authority tests opted for the percentage method, with the disastrous consequence that many banks solved their capital problem by selling assets and stopping lending — and thus further crushing the economy.

Once all this is dealt with, the question then becomes who will provide a backstop in the event that a bank has a capital shortfall that it cannot fill itself, and its government has too much debt to help out.

The **European Stability Mechanism (ESM)** the Eurozone's bailout fund, should be the one to inject capital directly into banks.

Single Supervision Mechanism (SSM)

A division of labor has been established between the ECB and national supervisors. Banks deemed "significant" will be supervised directly by the ECB. Smaller banks will continue to be directly monitored by their national authorities, though the ECB has the authority to take over direct supervision of any bank. A bank is deemed significant when it meets one of the following 5 conditions:

1. The value of its assets exceeds 30 Billion euros.
2. The value of its assets exceeds both 5 Billion euros and 20% of the Gross Domestic Product of the member state in which it is located.
3. The bank is among the three most significant banks of the country in which it is located.
4. The bank has large cross-border activities.
5. The bank receives, or has applied for, assistance from Eurozone bailout funds (the European Stability Mechanism - ESM) or European Financial Stability Facility - EFSF).

Around 130 major banks will be supervised directly by the ECB, representing approximately 80% of bank assets. All other banks in the SSM (more than 6 000 in the Eurozone alone) will be supervised by the national supervisor, although the ECB will keep final supervisory authority over these banks.

Banks have abused of rescue funding and the European Committee, the European Union, the Eurogroup, the EBA, the IMF, et al had not been able to construe this SSM, which will represent a type of "insurance fund" for banks which will have to fund themselves to cover against their own eventual defaults, this being a justified prerequisite that Germany demands – see next more extensive comments please.

Banking Capitalization

Banking Capitalization needs to be reviewed and changed, adopting the same rules in all "Western" countries - Europe and US – because the various "stress test" held in 2010 and 2011 proved totally unrealistic and the agencies like EBA in Europe were not "in tune" with realities anymore. To require excessive capitalization from banks impedes them to be competitive with other financing sources like hedge funds and other financing instruments.

As is well known there is a severe opposition between the BCE and the Bundesbank, the German Central Bank.

The results of stress tests partially revealed in November 2014 by Mr. Dragui, need more in-depth review as to necessary capitalization and transparent explanations on how they were determined / calculated.

"Currency War"

The Eurozone is and will be increasingly be plagued by the not so called "currency war", imposed by China, the US and Japan (the latest considerably – 30% in two years - devalued the yen), who have left their currencies undervalued to benefit from international trade advantages, while the euro has increased its value against most currencies, because being now a 18 nations bloc it is far more difficult to "monitor" its single currency - the euro.

The FED has stopped in October 2014 the QEs but left its close to zero interest rate unchanged, being vague as to when it would increase it, this hopefully giving emerging markets a respite.

This rethink is also affecting the Eurozone, whose bond and equity markets have soared since 2012 / 2013, when in 2012 ECB President Mr. Draghi promised to do whatever it took, within certain constraints, to defend the euro's existence.

This first widely applauded, and later partially criticized by analysts and economists, statement of Mr. Draghi: "ECB will do everything to save the euro", and consequent measures by implementing very generous QE type re financing offers at 0.75% rates, has to a great extent failed, because it has, to a great extent, been misused by banks and not served to finance performing SMEs and Innovation companies, in general.

ECB wants to renew the 1 Trillion in LTROs issued late 2011 and March 2012 for three years which is maturing end 2014 and In 2015 by new monetary inflows, like purchasing of securitized assets, TLTROs, ABS (?) and also wants to issue (print money for the first time) an US style QE to allow purchasing of sovereign bonds.

Priority should be given to economic growth rather than a share buyback program of sovereign bonds whatsoever, said on 11/24/2014, Mr. Weidmann, BUBA's president and member of the Board of Governors of the ECB – Reuters.

"Instead of focusing our attention on the buyback plan we should focus on ways to find growth," said the president of the Bundesbank in Madrid, in response to a question about the possibility that the ECB buys bonds sovereign in the context of a policy of quantitative easing.

He warned it would be difficult to go further in the measures to fight against low inflation.

"Of course there are other measures that are more difficult because they have not been tested because they are less clear (..) and of course, they reach the legal limits of what is possible to do, "said Mr.Weidmann. "That is why discussions are so difficult" he added.

Mr. Weidmann also suggests that "legal impediments" exist for ECB's proposed "actions".

The ECB is likely to face "legal obstacles" if it decides to embark on redemptions of government bonds, warned Mr. Weidmann.

These statements of the president of the German Bundesbank and member of the Governing Council of the ECB illustrate once again its opposition to a sovereign debt buyback program.

Mr. Draghi expressed its determination to quickly lift the inflation rate in the euro area, which has been interpreted by many investors as the promise of a sovereign debt buyback program, or quantitative easing in 2015.

When asked about this during a speech in Madrid on Monday Jens Weidmann said: "Instead of focusing our attention on the redemption plan we should focus on ways to find growth."

He warned it would be difficult to strengthen existing measures against the low inflation.

The Bundesbank, in Germany, the largest economy in the Eurozone, is not the only one to manifest hostility to redemptions of sovereign debt by the ECB. Much of the German political class is afraid that such a policy will accrue to fund countries unable to undertake reforms intended to strengthen the competitiveness of their economies.

BCE's TLTRO wil have low demand in December 2014. Banks should borrow only 150 Billion euros according to ECB in December 2014 at the second refinancing longer-term target (TLTRO), according to a Reuters survey.

Mr. Draghi, ECB president, wants to bring the institution's balance sheet to its level in March 2012, about 3 000 billion euros against 2 000 billion today. The objective is to raise the rate of inflation in the Eurozone to 2%.

Mr. Dragui's obsession with monetary expansionist measures is hindering progress in the Eurozone to finally start real and complete social-economic structural measures, which are the real solution to Eurozone stagnancy.

Governments do not "make financial / economic laws" anymore, Central Banks do, and this is very dangerous, because economic analysis and development evaluation have been and still are in the hands of so called "monetary experts", who have not been successful in spite of at least 4 Trillions USD of printed money and spend in the US over 3 to 4 years and over 1 Trillions euros by the BCE since end of 2011, to decrease significantly unemployment / underemployment and have not obtained more than 2% growth in the US in 2013, and may reach close to 3% growth in 2014, but with continued very high "total" unemployment (including under employment) - with a stagnant Eurozone in 2014!

This state of affairs has to change since if it does not GDP stagnancy will start installing itself, gradually, also outside of the Eurozone (which represents 20% of world trade!).

INVESTMENT IN THE EUROZONE

Mr. Juncker, "new" European Commission (EC) president has started his five year mandate with his November 2014 "idea" to issue a 3 years' Eurozone Plan to be financed by only private investors with a Eurozone guarantee requiring extremely high leverage.

My anticipated comments

If below comments are based on a true basis, I believe that the leverage multiplier required by Mr. Juncker's total unrealistic plan of 59 times (!!!) guarantees offered is a sure "No - No".

There is no other answer than "blood, sweat and tears" by going through the implementation in the whole Eurozone of the implementation of real and complete social-economic structural reforms, because it f this "happens, private investors to finance selective with great potential growth projects, which exist, can be attracted, through the IMF, not through the EC or EU.

Last week France asked for a Plan with "real Money", wanting to receive 20% - 60 Billion euros - of the Plan funding.

French Minister of Economy, Mr. Macron, who is basically right in the proposals he makes, should start by convincing his own government party of applying "real" social-economic structural reforms, which have already been denied in France by his party last and this week, before making Eurozone proposals which will not float

France makes this request because it does believe (rightfully so in my personal opinion) that the leverage will be way too high and that France will not receive anything.

Question remaining is should France receive anything if they do not - finally - commit "in blood" with implementing structural reforms as requested by the EC in its "shopping list".

Seemingly Mr. Juncker's Big "Plan" is as follows (this is not from official sources, it is what the press, FT in this case, in general, leaks).

EC's Mr. Juncker's Plan should seemingly (?) correspond to 315 Billion USD over 3 years, composed of:

* EU Budget - 16 Billion USD - 5% of Total.
* European Investment Bank (EIB) guarantee - 5 Billion USD - 1.6% of Total (!!!)
* Private Investments - 294 Billion USD - 93.4% of Total.

Which means that there needs to be 59 times leverage (294 Billion / 5 Billion), which seems "quite " impossible.

This reminds me of previous ideas, far less ambitious, of leverage by the EC in its previous five year mandate, which all failed.

How can a totally mismanaged area like the Eurozone, even if it still probably represents close to 20% of worldwide trade - the "big" arguments in its favor - obtain 59 times leverage?

This "plan" needing "administration" (sic) this should fall on a new "Investment Advisory Hub" (?) run by "Financial Experts" (?) under the direction direction of the European Commission and EIB.

The European Union (EU) will seemingly offer a *"first-loss"* guarantee, where EU "money" would absorb any initial investment losses in an effort to attract private investors looking for more secure guarantees.

France requests the EU to inject up to 80 Billion USD of "real money" into the stagnant at best Eurozone economy, warning that a big investment plan being drawn up in Brussels risks flopping if not sufficient hard cash is not used to stimulate demand.

Mr. Macron, France's Minister of Economy said "I'm convinced we need real money and we need to use it in an effective way."

Mr. Macron proposed a new independent entity to oversee what some are calling a "New Deal". The overseer would increase the fund's firepower by raising debt on the markets to fund investments in projects such as fibre optic networks and renewable energy. It would also set up panels of European experts to select projects after a competitive process.

Problem is who puts up 80 Billion in funding, the EU cannot, France cannot, Germany probably will commit either 10 or 20 Billion euros to their own economy, so it would have to be the BCE?

EU officials briefed on Mr Juncker's 'plan" said there was unlikely to be any new money. Instead, only existing public resources will be used, with the hope that this will attract private capital to bolster the fund.

Mr. Macron insists on his "proposals", saying: "We have 10 per cent unemployment, 25 per cent youth unemployment. What is the alternative solution? Spend more money that we don't have? It's not conceivable. It's a real leftwing package, it's a package for the outsiders, it is aimed at restoring equal opportunities."

Mr. Macron spoke frankly of past "fake" reforms in France. He says "real" reforms are now the pre-requisite for a matching stimulus from European partners. "It is our job to create a momentum for the stimulus package. And our reform package is key because this is how we can be demanding in return."

The Eurozone countries require investments, because very little has been done in the last decade, including in Germany.

These Keynesian types of investments can only be implemented if the funding is realistic, which in this case I do not believe it is.

To start with what is important is the content of such an Eurozone investment plan, and this content can only be potential growth projects in mainly the four largest economies in the Eurozone plus some other smaller countries.

If lobbying / politicking for inclusion of "favorite" projects by country starts, the Investment Plan will be an ineffective "mix" and a pre announced failure.

It will be seen what emerges out of all this?

Conclusions

I will start by further illustrating the lack of Governance by quoting my 11/16/2014 post in my blog: "Macrovolatility.com" of the **G20** Brisbane's 11/15-16/2014 meeting:

This G20 meeting spent a great amount of its time agenda in attacks on Mr. Putin and Russia's attacks on Ukraine, to the point that Russia's president, Mr. Putin, left before meeting "concluded", pretending "tiredness" from a long flight back home.

President Obama is repeating 7 months errors in foreign policy by trying to sanction Russia, the European community is "tired" about this attitude, since the Eurozone, already in a very bad economic and financial situation, is ten times more hurt trade wise by this conflict than the US.

It is obvious that Russia cannot exceed international rules I unilaterally. This crucial problem needs to be debated at "high level" (Presidents / PMs and FO Ministers) f of the countries involved (Russia, Ukraine, a representation of the Ukrainian Separatists, Europe, and the Us, but not in a single huge meeting like the G20, but in as many meetings as it takes to obtain consensus

The G20 's Communiqué is a 21 point "Shopping List" of mostly all that needs to be done worldwide, problem is that most points were already in the last G20 minute meeting/s…

It was most probably (?) written before the meeting, since most of the 21 points individually would probably require a full fledged meeting, this showing the relative ineffectiveness of these global meetings which never stick to an agenda.

How can G20 enforce its "recommendations", because realistically speaking that is all they are, letters of intent?

G20 Leaders' Communiqué – My Résumé – My Comments in italics

The key objective is to raise growth to deliver better living standards and quality jobs worldwide.

I would have changed the order, create durable jobs which require social-economic structural reforms in order to obtain durable growth.

G20 wants to strengthen global institutions.

This is great priority since supranational organizations like the European Commission, the IMF, OECD, Central Banking, et al can be far more productive if they were not so bureau technocratic in general and knew far more of what is happening "in the field" – the countries, and not through "directive" letters and x number of meetings.

G20 says they are (?) implementing structural reforms.

Very few countries so far have done so, so far, it is a crucial problem, and even more a great opportunity, but there is no political will in general, the big majority, so far.

G20 says that monetary authorities have and are committed to support the recovery and address deflationary pressures when needed, consistent with their mandates.

I have been commenting with great repetition in my blog – macrovolatility. com - since its creation in April 2011 and in my former book – "Why Macro Governance is Obsolete and Killing the World Economy" that to allow monetary authorities to do the job alone is the biggest problem along with obsolete governance. There is no master guide, no strategy and "modus operandi" which builds on in depth economic and social analysis and planning, and decision making should be based on this type of analysis and precede monetary ones, which are a complement, this seems not to be understood by the G20 either?

This year the G20 has set an ambitious goal to lift the G20's GDP by at least an additional two per cent by year until 2018. Analysis by the

IMF-OECD indicates that G20 commitments, if fully implemented, will deliver 2.1 per cent.

This will add more than US$ 2 trillion to the global economy and create millions of jobs. G20 measures to lift investment, increase trade and competition, and boost employment, along with our macroeconomic policies, will support development and inclusive growth, and help to reduce inequality and poverty.

G20 does not refer to "how", this is and has been the big problem – general statements, with no concrete follow-up, and no agenda referring to "who" is responsible for "what", at least not a published one. They now refer to a "Brisbane Action Plan", which for transparency purposes should be published.

G20 states that to tackle global investment and infrastructure shortfalls is crucial to lifting growth, job creation and productivity. We endorse the "Global Infrastructure Initiative", a multi-year work program to lift quality public and private infrastructure investment.

Again, this multi-year program: "The Global Infrastructure Initiative" is probably one of the techno bureaucratic programs, and if so they should be revealed, because these great infrastructure plans, which are of Keynesian origin mostly, have not been initiated so far during decades, because they are complex and difficult to finance.

To support implementation of this Initiative, G20 has agreed to establish a Global Infrastructure Hub with a four-year mandate. The Hub will contribute to developing a knowledge-sharing platform and network between governments, the private sector, development banks and other international organizations. The Hub will foster collaboration among these groups to improve the functioning and financing of infrastructure markets.

Again, this "Global Infrastructure Hub" should be explained, since it sounds like past projects which never saw the light.

To strengthen infrastructure and attract more private sector investment in developing countries, G20 welcomes the launch of the World Bank Group's Global Infrastructure Facility, which will complement the above stated projects' work. They will support similar initiatives by other development banks and continued cooperation amongst them.

This "World Bank Group's Global Infrastructure Facility", is the fourth "big title" so far, I wonder what will become reality out of all this "techno bureaucratic" language.

Trade and competition are powerful drivers of growth, increased living standards and job creation. In today's world we don't just trade final products. We work together to make things by importing and exporting components and services. We need policies that take full advantage of global value chains and encourage greater participation and value addition by developing countries.

G20's growth strategies – *Which (?), name one please* - include reforms – *Which?* - to facilitate trade by lowering costs, streamlining customs procedures, reducing regulatory burdens and strengthening trade-enabling services.

G20 say they are promoting competition, entrepreneurship and innovation, including by lowering barriers to new business entrants and investment. G20 reaffirms its longstanding standstill and rollback commitments to resist protectionism.

This is all "old hat" and said innumerable times in such G20 meetings and other "summit" meetings – where are the results of past meetings and general "considerations"?

G20 says that their actions *(Which?)* to increase investment, trade and competition will deliver quality jobs. They add that more needs to be done to address unemployment, raise participation and create quality jobs.

G20 agrees to the goal of reducing the gap in participation rates between men and women in our countries by 25 per cent by 2025, taking into account national circumstances, to bring more than 100 million women into the labor force, significantly increase global growth and reduce poverty and inequality.

These are great objectives for...2025, "how" does the "world" get there (?), and what about now and in-between?

G20 is strongly committed to reducing youth unemployment, which is unacceptably high, by acting to ensure young people are in education, training or employment. Our "Employment Plans" *(Which?)* include investments in apprenticeships, education and training, and incentives for hiring young people and encouraging entrepreneurship.

G20 remains focused on addressing informality *(?)*, as well as structural and long-term unemployment, by strengthening labor markets and having appropriate social protection systems. Improving workplace safety and health is a priority.

We ask our labor and employment ministers, supported by an Employment Working Group, to report to us in 2015.

"Employment Plans" and "Employment Working Group", two more "titles"....

Where are they, who makes them up, what are their results so far, what are their plans, have they already dealt and they deal with Under Employment which is as big as Officially published Unemployment?

G20 request strengthening the resilience of the global economy and stability of the financial system are crucial to sustaining growth and development.

G20 reforms to improve banks' capital and liquidity positions and to make derivatives markets safer will reduce risks in the financial system.

G20 welcomes the Financial Stability Board (FSB) proposal as set out in the Annex requiring global systemically important banks to hold additional loss absorbing capacity that would further protect taxpayers if these banks fail.

Progress has been made in delivering the shadow banking framework and we endorse an updated roadmap for further work.

G20 has agreed to measures to dampen risk channels between banks and non-banks. But critical work remains to build a stronger, more resilient financial system. The task now is to finalize remaining elements of our policy framework and fully implement agreed financial regulatory reforms, while remaining alert to new risks.

G20 calls on regulatory authorities to make further concrete progress in swiftly implementing the agreed G20 derivatives reforms.

G20 encourages jurisdictions to defer to each other when it is justified, in line with the St Petersburg Declaration. G20 welcomes the FSB's plans to report on the implementation and effects of these reforms, and the FSB's future priorities. G20 welcomes the progress made to strengthen the orderliness and predictability of the sovereign debt restructuring process.

It is true that progress has been made, but there are huge "tasks" ahead, like cutting the link between private banking in the Eurozone and financing sovereign loans (which are considered as risk less!) as one large example, the preceding feeding even higher indebtedness in the Eurozone.

G20 is taking actions to ensure the fairness of the international tax system and to secure countries' revenue bases. Profits should be taxed where economic activities deriving the profits are performed and where value is created.

G20 welcomes the significant progress on the G20/OECD Base Erosion and Profit Shifting (BEPS) Action Plan to modernize international tax rules.

G20 is committed to finalizing this work in 2015, including transparency of taxpayer-specific rulings found to constitute harmful tax practices.

Never in their life will OECD (alone) "clean" up this "mess" which is at least half a Century long, of Tax Evasion and Loopholes and Tax Breaks by 2015, with all the adverse lobbying and now trails of and by large international corporations. It will take at least half a decade and this is a great priority since the Revenues which can be retrieved are many Trillions USD or euros!

The G20 must be at the forefront in helping to address key global economic challenges. G20 welcomes the increased representation of emerging economies on the FSB and other actions to maintain its effectiveness. G20 is committed to maintaining a strong, quota-based and adequately resourced International Monetary Fund (IMF).

G20 reaffirms their commitment in St Petersburg and in this light they are deeply disappointed with the continued delay in progressing the

IMF quota and governance reforms agreed in 2010 and the 15th General Review of Quotas, including a new quota formula.

"Who will follow up until the next G20 meeting in ... 2015 and 2016?

The implementation of the 2010 reforms remains G20's highest priority for the IMF and G20 urge the United States to ratify them.

If this does not happen by year-end, G20 asks the IMF to build on its existing work and stand ready with options for next steps.

G20 needs a strong trading system in an open global economy to drive growth and generate jobs.

To help business make best use of trade agreements, G20 will work to ensure bilateral, regional and multi lateral agreements complement one another, are transparent and contribute to a stronger multilateral trading system under World Trade Organization (WTO) rules.

These rules remain the backbone of the global trading system that has delivered economic prosperity.

"Who will follow up until the next G20 meeting in ... 2015 or 2016?

Increased collaboration on energy is a priority. Global energy markets are undergoing significant transformation. Strong and resilient energy markets are critical to economic growth.

Today G20 endorses the "G20 Principles on Energy Collaboration". They ask energy ministers to meet and report to us in 2015 on options to take this work forward. Gas is an increasingly important energy source and we will work to improve the functioning of gas markets.

Improving energy efficiency is a cost-effective way to help address the rising demands of sustainable growth and development, as well as energy access and security. It reduces costs for businesses and households.

G20 have agreed an Action Plan for Voluntary Collaboration on Energy Efficiency, including new work on the efficiency and emissions performance of vehicles, particularly heavy duty vehicles; networked devices; buildings; industrial processes; and electricity generation; as well as work on financing for energy efficiency.

G20 reaffirm its commitment to rationalize and phase out inefficient fossil fuel subsidies that encourage wasteful consumption, recognizing the need to support the poor.

G20 supports strong and effective action to address climate change. Consistent with the United Nations Framework Convention on Climate Change (UNFCCC) and its agreed outcomes, G20 actions will support sustainable development, economic growth, and certainty for business and investment.

G20 will work together to adopt successfully a protocol, another legal instrument or an agreed outcome with legal force under the UNFCCC that is applicable to all parties at the 21st Conference of the Parties (COP21) in Paris in 2015.

G20 is deeply concerned with the humanitarian and economic impact of the Ebola outbreak in Guinea, Liberia and Sierra Leone. It supports the urgent coordinated international response and are committed to do all we can to contain and respond to this crisis.

End of G20 Communiqué and of my comments on it.

This book's objective is to present the social-economic problems of the so called "Advanced Western" world - US and Europe" - in the most simple and understandable manner, limiting economists' "jargon" usually used, to a minimum.

The 3 themes I have developed in this book are:

Under Employment data needs to take a major part in all unemployment data in major countries.

Social-economic structural reforms need implementation in practically all major countries.

Reforms need to be targeted: general, supply side, demand economics - a well thought out "mix".

Monetary policy cannot act alone since it failed doing so.

- Monetary policy must follow and not precede Economic Strategy and Action Plan to complement it.

- Central Banking role to be first totally reviewed and then revised worldwide.
- Focus on Tax Evasion, Tax Breaks, Mobilizing Cash Savings / Hoarding and Developing corporate

Investments by reducing corporate Dividends, all "topics" having the same objective - to obtain Large Growth Resources

The preceding requires the urgent need to change the approach to Governance in most Eurozone countries and the European / Eurozone "area" Governances, and to some extent also in the US, in order to adapt it to the requirements of the XXI Century with its meteoric developments and change.

This requires a change in how the heads of countries' Governments, their Ministers and their top executives" make politics", the old style of avoiding "hot" subjects like necessary social-economic structural reforms, being afraid of losing votes does not work anymore, because they are losing increasingly credibility with their «people", who want to understand where their countries «are going" and what they are "doing" to get there.

Some major countries have been for decades and continue being "prisoners" of labor unions / syndicates, while the degree of representation/ adherents to extreme unions has been strongly decreasing, but these minorities "act" with strikes and public manifestations and cause total disruption, confusion and increasing anger with the population, but the "silent" majorities have never been "active", unless there is war, and not even then did it create reactions like those obtained by these obsolete but "acting" minorities …

What is needed are "clones" of Margaret Thatcher who changed the UK"s social- economic situation by "fighting" excessively negative, always opposing any improvement measures and therefore obsolete labor unions at the prize of "sweat, blood and tears", to quote another transcendent figure: Winston Churchill, and finally ending by reforming them to the benefit of the UK population in general.

This change in Governance approach and methodology is even more needed for "areas'" Governance, like the European Union and the Eurozone, since it is far more difficult to integrate a large number of "independent" countries economically, financially and politically, the latter being utopia.

The Brussels' European Commission, the European Union, the Eurogroup, the BCE, the IMF, OECD et al have not only not "understood" but do not have the capacity to act differently, not being able to assume that changes in concept and approach were necessary and continued with their techno bureaucratic, procedural and politicking attitudes.

It also requires, as above commented, redefining the role of Central Banking, which during the last decade, mainly in the US, and since 3 years in the Eurozone, have overstepped their responsibilities as "independent" organizations and assumed and taken over roles (like being the employment" guardian" in the US), which does behoove countries' or areas' governments as policymakers.

Stock Exchanges have become accustomed to Central banks providing "tons /Billions" of liquidity, without caring about solvability, and therefore real economic and financial non performance got and still remains "disguised", but hopefully this will change when it comes to acknowledging that no Recovery is underway, in some major cases the contrary is happening. To be stagnant is to recede.

This implies an urgent need to make social-economic structural reforms, instead of covering bad administration of spending with increasing taxation and social charges, plus creating government "supported" jobs. Government should not be "employers", either directly or indirectly.

This constant macro "mismanagement" is causing havoc and is behind this huge and biggest ever crisis, which started in 2007/08 and is continuing, pushing some major countries into recession.

Governments think that very necessary structural reforms take away acquired benefits from the "people" and will make them lose voters, and "prefer" to tax more which is totally illogical, but has immediate, but temporary results, and kills growth.

Governments have "gotten away" with this type of mismanagement because when they increase taxes and social charges they promise the "people" that the result of this increase in Government revenues will be used in measures which will increase employment and favor those taxed more than the increased taxation they were subjected to, but the contrary has been happening for decades – and record unemployment and underemployment is the final result - "people", in general, do not believe their governments anymore.

Too much taxation kills the revenue planned on taxation, meaning that a certain –very high – level of taxation, the result will be that the revenue on taxation will progressively decrease, and that the income planned for financing growth measures will not exist, and push countries further into recession.

Presidents and Prime Ministers are "generalists", they need to understand the various "functions" of well organized Governance, but the various Ministers who direct functions (Economy, Finance, Labor, Education, Health, Foreign Affairs Defense, Interior, et al) need to be "professionals". The habit of playing "musical chairs" and change Ministers from one function to the other is not anymore adapted to the ferocious international competitiveness which globalization, highly increased technology and permanent innovation requires.

Presidents in Western countries have, in general, good educational background, and a vocation for politics which, in most cases, becomes deeply ingrained. They, generally, have no previous business experience, some have been lawyers.

Their "performance ' is judged by elections, not "business success", and they cannot be involved –directly – in a "myriad" functional topics, even the most vital ones, because they cannot be more than generalists with good "understanding" (not know-how) of the main government functions. It's like with "medical general practitioners" today, with increasing and very "technical" scientific progress, they need to recur to specialists.

There is one virtue they need to have: to have outstanding leadership and to be able to make decisions (like "the buck stops here" – President Truman's famous expression).

The more Government there is, with too many Ministers, too many cabinets, too many "advisors", too many expensive "ad hoc" studies or analyses which, in general are never used and applied, too many levels of intermediate government to reach a, say, municipality through the various de centralization processes, in résumé: too much "Government, the more difficult decision making becomes, the worse a country gets "governed".

This applies even more to supranational "organizations".

The biggest single conclusion is that after the beginning in the US of the so called "'sub – primes" of real estate, this opened - as a detonator - all the factors which led, gradually, to all past mismanagements of mainly "Western" (US - and more so in Europe / Eurozone) countries / areas became manifest, without that fundamental social-economic factors which were at the "origin of evil" (way before the crisis "detonated") have been taken seriously into consideration, most measures taken so far have been mainly "reactive" and not really in-depth analyzed, letting monetary measures take the overhand over social-economic ones.

Politics, and even more "politicking", has and is interfering with adopting policies which I have tried to describe, and which I feel will represent major improvements in Governance efficiency and related results, if implemented.

Most governing politicians have not really realized that these XXI Century requirements for efficient Governance need to be adapted to rapidly, time does not stand still.

Governments do not govern in order to make the people they govern happy through proselytism,   people do not "govern", they need to express themselves through their regional / municipal representatives…) or based on too frequent surveys, but on the basis of "vision" and short / medium, long-term strategy for their country, and clear and transparent communication of these objectives in a pedagogic manner.

No country nor area governance can continue working in a procedural manner and with little "professionalization".

Governments need to have as their primary function to be their own policymakers and decision makers, taking into account the globalized competition they are increasingly facing.

Governments need to be able to define their own "vision" of what their countries' future should and can realistically be / become, and reliance on "ad hoc" external analysis should be far more limited, the various functional Ministers need to have sufficient know-how to analyze themselves their situations and what can be done in each function.

Macro goals - on primary and total deficit and on indebtedness - as ratios of GDP, are to a great extent obsolete because the composition of the GDPs of the various countries and supranational "areas" need re evaluation on an "individual" bases, and not on "universal" criteria anymore.

Goal setting - to be redefined - is necessary, without it there can be no planning nor budgeting, nor control and follow-up, but it needs to be done differently.

The inflation "measuring basket" should be reviewed / actualized in terms of its "product mix", like because the official inflation numbers for the Eurozone being in 2013 for the first 2 months below 2% seem, and are low because they are "incomplete" because in some countries they exclude income taxes, social security charges and interest expense and real estate value fluctuations, these items weighing very heavily on household's expenses and on macro expenses.

The attached **Addendum** shows a concrete proposal of evaluating stock exchange listed corporations following both profitable results and social-economic performance.

Governments need to finally understand that they cannot continue "ignoring"(sic) Underemployment which in the case of the US is a big as "officially published unemployment and is where the origins of real unemployment are. Targeted measures are needed and subsidized employment has never worked and very costly failures happened.

To be successful in reducing significantly "total" unemployment, and not only "official" unemployment, targeted measures are necessary and to start with what is required is to implement social-economic structural reforms starting with labor and eliminating unproductive subsidies / subventions.

Targeted measures relate to reviewing in-depth education orientations and create intermediate levels which correspond to making integration possible into different sectoral activities which are in need of filling jobs with adequately trained people.

Governments need to reduce to a minimum to be employers, this requiring that State Business units be increasingly "transferred" to private business.

As can be appreciated in Chapter 1 comments and propositions, the matter of improving conditions to increase Job Creation is crucial to obtain a far better economic situation and the needed growth.

In order to be able to start again having "real" durable growth it has to be based on basic economic fundamentals, not any more - nearly solely - on temporary monetary measures which do not respond to the origin of this very problematic social-economic situation in Europe, the US being in a less difficult (sic) situation, because it has a more resilient economy and is a "single" country, and not a (theoretical) "union", but still is far from being "out of the hole".

This is a long-term evolution, but needs to be started far more seriously now, because if this does not happen the gap between the "scholars" entering the market and their acceptance by those sectors which are the most dynamic ones, will widen. This is the main reason for extremely high "youth" unemployment and under employment.

Long-term unemployment concerns 5 Million workers in the US or 3% percent of total civilian working population, and represents one of the hardest challenges to start resolving, length of unemployment representing the biggest handicap workers face, because employers will not be prone to hire people who have mismatched skills to requirements, and the long unemployed lose confidence and trust in themselves, and reach the point where they abandon looking for jobs.

Young population is the great priority, because in an "older" and ageing population they have to be able to "enter" the jobs' market for a self-motivation, but also to increase the "active "population to fund an increasingly ageing populations' retirement needs.

These include a major review and then revision of education orientation adapted to the needs of each country's government defined future "vision" (strategy), which needs to be accompanied by a new approach to formation and training, and much more interaction between "schooling", at various levels, and corporations to define the most productive support. This is getting away from government programs creating mainly jobs for the young and spending "good and scarce money" for non discriminated and non targeted programs.

It requires reviewing all possibilities, on a sectoral / per activity basis on possible re locations of jobs which left the US because labor cost far more cheaper years ago in, say, Asia / China, see previous example on APPLE and how to calculate real cost of delocalization, this should be applied in general.

It requires having powerful Ministries of Economy and Labor, and not only rely on Ministries of Finance's and Central Banks' measures which should not be and are not responsible for Job Creation.

Contrary to what most" Western" politicians claim, jobs start not with government but with investors.

Investors are people in a position to invest money in a business endeavor. They could be owners or managers who want to grow their companies, and must invest in order to do so.

Whatever the case, the investor intends to create output, to increase productive capacity, and to make money. The jobs come as a result of the investment, which is expensive activity.

Everything takes time, and many projects face government obstacles. On top of that, the risk is very real. In fact, most investments fail and many fall short on the profit side.

Governments should therefore consider how every regulatory decision impacts investment. Regulations may be completely necessary but they needn't be punitive. Regulatory agencies need not be staffed with zealots eager to control industries they despise. When onerous regulation discourages investment, jobs will not be created.

This is even truer in most "troubled" European / Eurozone countries.

I have also included comments on the urgent needs to implement financial regulations to diminish drastically tax evasion, tax breaks through maybe legal but damaging loopholes which diminish the taxes that they should be paying in their "home countries", which hurts the financial situation of these countries, and by the same token affects negatively job creation. Savings / hoarding of cash needs to be motivated to get out of the individual private mattresses and corporations' reserves and be invested through motivating financial measures.

These three "points" are worth many Trillions in "hidden" Revenues

Governments should aim to create certainty because important business investment decisions should be mostly long-term. The payoff, if it comes at all, will come over time, not next year. The more uncertain the future, the more difficult it is to make investment decisions, and in an uncertain environment the easiest decision is to say "No" – and that dynamic employs nobody.

Even so, human creativity and the entrepreneurial spirit can produce useful products that people are willing to buy. That generates profits and jobs, but it all begins with investors, not government.

Government can create only government jobs that must be paid for out of taxes.

Government works projects may employ independent contractors, but such jobs are temporary, and this has nothing to do with creating jobs in the long run. There is, however, plenty the government can do to help the job creation process, which in a nutshell is "making it easier to work for workers"…

Government works projects may employ independent contractors, but such jobs are temporary, and this has nothing to do with creating jobs in the long run.

The US has grown used to FED's massive interventions since the crisis began, and it has become a "way of living". This is also becoming true in the Eurozone, since 2011 / 2012 with BCE's massive interventions.

This needs to change because real "economic performance" is being disguised and accordingly the necessary social-economic structural reforms are not being realized as rapidly as needed and with insufficient depth.

The US partial recovery from the 2007-2009 recession, during the period: 2nd Qtr. 2009 - 2014 is both a jobless and wage less one - proving that massive injections of "stimulus" / money do not "do the job", but social-economic structural reforms will do it, in due course of time, since the effect of such reforms is not "immediate" but medium to long-term, and therefore needs to be started in earnest – now...

Since mid 2012 there has been a disconnection between European markets' (stocks) and countries' performances, markets are becoming more bullish on the basis of injection of rather non discriminated and non targeted monetary "support" by ECB, but these need to be temporary measures because if countries do not really "perform", the economic reality will "catch up" with unrealistic monetary support, with grave consequences.

This disconnection is partially justified, because the large international corporations are all listed in the selective Big Stock Exchanges and make more than 50% of their Revenues and even more of their Net Earnings (through utilization of tax loopholes and tax breaks) and therefore their consolidated "home country" assessment includes "intercompany" tax advantages which make their "home countries" markets swing due to "events" that do not occur in the "home countries" of these corporations, and this contributes to what is called " disconnection".

Finally, there must be far more **Investments.**

I have shown in Chapter 3 the Eurozone "Investment Plan" by the European Commission"s president, Mr. Juncker, which I believe is doomed from the beginning because it is erroneously conceived.

Such an Investment Plan can be successful if it is based on realistic foundations and fundamentals and not "wishful thinking".

I finally included as an **Addendum** a concrete proposal to go to the "origin of good or evil", which is not attained by "ism"s (capitalism, communism, socialism, liberalism, et al) anymore, but is designed to provide improved and more general possibilities for analysis and appraisal / evaluation on corporations' global performances, and not only "profit", which has made a great number of corporations to be extremely short-sighted and allowed for loss of development on a medium-long term basis because of shareholders greed.

This proposal diverts from the classic "Price/Earning" (P/E or "PER") ratio, which at the time of the emergency of the first large IT corporations did not reflect what these corporation market capitalization was based on, which was how much "audience" they had, i.e. how many people adhered to their systems of communication, and not profitability – they actually practically all made losses, a concept which, blew up in pieces with the 2000 "IT Bubble". It is not certain that "social media" corporations will not also blow up, but they have the advantage of the year 2000 "bubble" experience, and nowadays the cost of technology investment has gone down drastically.

These social-media corporations have recognized that they need to create / bill revenue and cannot continue with free services and "applications, and this might be a "turning point", since the revenue mainly comes from subscription fees and publicity - which is not "all extensive" to all medias, having its cost limitations and needing media targeting.

Since the "Digital" world is the highest job creation contributor, if the concept fails, even partially, it will have very negative consequences on job creation - directly and indirectly (suppliers) - and therefore needs to be "integrated" into a new and different valuation system.

This proposal on a new valuation system for corporations' performance is not another "discourse" with a lot of economic / technical" jargon on economic Nobel Prize winning economic models (there are a lot of them to "choose "from), nor the failed "treaties system" which were, seemingly, built on economic" guidelines but did not include "economic integration" policies which could realistically work knowing that "area union" countries were very different in many aspects. See Maastricht treaty and other European Union "development treaties" as being maybe the worse examples, because they were not thought out in-depth and were not practical in terms of "where" they wanted "to go"," what" they wanted to "achieve", and "how" and "when".

The major "forum" and source of "expression" of confidence has been and still is, in a more mitigated manner, the Stock Exchanges, where corporations' results are regularly (daily) published and where the "market" (analysts) expresses its "feelings" and therefore "judges" results in a periodical manner.

The worse tendency that has predominated in the last decade is the short-sightedness of corporations' management and their Boards, and the very much insufficient evaluation process of financial analysts.

This reflects itself in various manners : pushing for immediate profit which is to the detriment of medium (I don't even mention long-term because of no macro "visibility") development, repurchasing their own stocks which causes share value dilution, paying themselves huge dividends, paying huge remunerations to their executives and traders (and by the latter stimulating speculation).

All of the preceding points are in summary and in general not acting in a social-economic manner, which increases unemployment and underemployment, and this requires drastic changes, because if it not, this will be one of the principal causes of continuing with slow growth, if not contraction, and finally, recession.

I feel that to evaluate corporations listed in Stock Exchanges by a new "Performance" evaluation method which would replace the longstanding PER (Prize/Earnings/ Ratio), would allow for far more objective, complete and not short-term evaluation, and better respond to the huge changes already made and to come in our societies. The attached **Annex** explains this proposal extensively.

Machiavelli said "that counselors are not payers", very true, I have nevertheless tried to do so hoping to contribute to a more practical way of taking macro decisions and adapt macro evaluation to the increasing requirements of a meteoric changing world.

Addendum

Establishing a new method to evaluate Performance of Market listed Corporations.

The "PPR" (Prize/Performance/Ratio) to replace the PER (Prize/Earnings/Ratio).

For Stock Exchanges' utilization and corporations' performance improvement

This is a proposal for a new and different appraisal method of Stock Exchange listed corporation's performances.

It justifies itself because the appraisal methods of analyst are outdated and short-sighted and harm innovation and economic development.

The world has not found a new and adequate "ism" to relate to since the "opposition" between capitalism and communism practically disappeared through Mr. Gorbatchov's policies to change the former USSR, and Mr. Geltsin who broke them down prematurely, into so called "independent" (???) Republics efforts, and the fall of the Berlin wall which in some way consecrated the fall of Communism, which if still prevailing in many countries as a party, does not obtain large shares of voting population at election time.

The remaining "capitalism" is not a concept which proved it could "live by itself", it became increasingly a system which is generally speaking short-sighted, with only immediate results to validate shares valuation.

The "IT" first developments diverted from the classic "Price / Earning" (P/E) ratio when the first large IT corporations started to be very successful, but not profitable, since what counted was how much "audience" they had, i.e. how many people adhered to their systems of communication, and this "non-profit" concept, actually loss-making valuation concept, blew up in pieces with the 2000 "IT Bubble".

it is not certain that "social media" corporations will not also blow up, but they have the advantage of the year 2000 "bubble" experience, and nowadays the cost of technology investment has gone down drastically. These social-media corporations have recognized that they need to create / bill revenue and cannot continue with free services and "applications, and this might be a "turning point", since the revenue mainly comes from subscription fees and publicity - which is not "all extensive" to all medias, having its cost limitations and needing very sophisticated media targeting.

Since the "Digital" world is the highest job creation contributor (see Chapters 2 and 3 please), if the concept fails, even partially, it will have very negative consequences on job creation - directly and indirectly (suppliers) - and therefore needs to be "integrated" into a new and different valuation system.

This proposal on a new valuation system for corporations' performance is not another "discourse" with a lot of economic / technical "jargon on economic Nobel Prize winning economic models (there are a lot of them to "choose" from), nor the failed "treaties system" which were, seemingly, built on economic" guidelines but did not include "economic integration" policies which could realistically work knowing that "area union" countries were very different in many aspects.

See Maastricht treaty and other European Union "development treaties" as being maybe the worse examples, because they were not thought out in-depth and were not practical in terms of "where" they wanted "to go", " what" they wanted to "achieve", "how" to go about them, and "when" they could realistically be implemented.

Politicians have not adapted, in general, to this meteorically, in all aspects, changing world and the XXI century, and continue "politicking" in the "old way", and that this makes obsolete both the countries and supranational "organizations" Governance systems, which need radical changes.

A lot has been written on opposing large international / multinational corporations to medium - large SMEs. The general opinion is that large stock exchange listed corporations, which are all international, and where most of them do a very sizable part of their business (at least 50%) and even more of their net earnings (tax loopholes and tax breaks utilization) outside of their "home countries", will "dominate".

This is not so to a large extent, a large part of these large international corporations create suppliers' jobs in their home countries or "elsewhere" if the "real" costs (which need to be permanently verified and compared with foreign outsourced costs) are much lower, that is what globalization is all about: to choose freely where the "work" will be done.

Medium-large (and surely small) SMEs, who are the biggest employers, by far, in practically all countries, tend to do most of their business in their "home "countries, because, in general, the most successful ones are not provided with necessary funding to enable them to grow by scales (mainly in Eurozone "Latin" countries) because banks do not sufficiently finance working capital needs for growth purposes, and because most of these SMEs do not export, because of lack of experience and know-how, and insufficient financing.

Consumer fidelity to the so called "established" brands, is increasingly not the case anymore, because competition through all medias and "in-store" is ferocious and eats up considerable margin.

Confidence has always been a major source of success for private "ventures", and the increasing macro volatility and insufficient visibility in the macro-economic areas they "perform in" is vital. As shown in this book in its 3 preceding Chapters, confidence resides in the "people" and in how they adhere (or not) to the policy making and decision making processes in their countries.

If policymaking is not "transparent" and is mainly a "number crunching" exercise which practically nobody really understands (including partially those who talk about these "numbers"), and if the decision making process is slow or nil, people will not have confidence, and will reflect in poorer demand and lower business results.

Many millions of workers are sitting on the sidelines and so are not counted in the total tally of unemployed. Some are merely waiting for the job market to improve, and others are trying to invest in skills to appeal to employers who are already hiring.

The major "forum" and source of "expression" of confidence has been and still is, in a more mitigated manner, the Stock Exchanges, where corporations' results are regularly (daily) published and where the "market" (analysts) express their "feelings" and therefore "judge" results in a periodical manner.

Stock Exchanges / "Markets" have to some extent disconnected - in the second half of 2012 - with the "real" (poor) performance of "Western" (US / Europe) economies, more so in Europe than in the US. Remember the composition of the large Stock Exchanges (already mentioned) and that they all list big international corporations who do more than 50% of their Revenues outside of their "home countries" and even more of their Net Earnings (tax loopholes and tax breaks utilization), and this needs to be taken into consideration when appraising the "PER" of these corporations, where most of them benefit from having very low consolidated income tax rates through this "maneuvering, which is practically "legal" (to some extent…), and needs to be fully revised.

Why? Because the "analysts" are always looking for some kind of relevant statistic: in the US, in China, in Germany, or wherever, to influence investors and those many individuals who have not got a clue of what is happening. Actually practically "nobody« really does, because this huge crisis is "new" and there are no valid reference points to similar crises in the past. Analysts work, quite a bit, on "promises" and "declarations", which in the last years turned sour in general.

This way, they, and some economists / financial "experts", et al, who write all over the place and where each one has an "undisputed" (sic) opinion, create confusion, stress and increasing macro volatility.

The worse tendency that has predominated in the last decade is the short- sightedness of Corporations' Management and their Boards, and the very much insufficient evaluation process of financial analysts.

This reflects itself in various manners : pushing for immediate profit which is to the detriment of medium (I don't even mention long-term because of no macro "visibility") development, repurchasing their own stocks which causes share value dilution, paying themselves huge dividends while making large personnel decreases in order to increase the quotation in stock exchanges, paying huge remunerations to their executives and traders (and by the latter stimulating speculation). One of the biggest issues is the power of markets '"analysis" to influence corporations' behavior, the main effect for the last decades has been that it championed "shortsightedness", pushing for immediate profits and hindering development plans that did not "capitalize" rapidly.

In February 2013 a rare event happened, it concerns the DELL corporation, where Michael Dell decided to "go Private".

This decision to take Dell private puts the company more firmly under the control of Michael S. Dell.

Dell announced on 02/05/2012 that it had agreed to go private in a USD 24.4 billion deal led by its founder and the investment firm Silver Lake, in the biggest leveraged buyout since the financial crisis began.

Under the terms of the deal, the buyers' consortium, which also includes Microsoft, will pay USD 13.65 a share in cash. That is roughly 25% above where Dell's stock traded before word emerged of the negotiations of its sale. Michael S. Dell will contribute his stake of roughly 14% toward the transaction, and will contribute additional cash through his private investment firm, MSD Capital. Silver Lake is expected to contribute about 1 Billion USD in cash, while Microsoft would loan an additional 2 Billion USD. As a newly private company – now more firmly under the control of Mr. Dell – the computer maker will seek to revive itself after years of decline. This "deal" has not yet been consummated as of June 2013 – to my knowledge?.

The takeover would represent Mr. Dell's most drastic effort yet to turn around the company he founded in a college dormitory room in 1984 and expanded into one of the world's biggest sellers of personal computers.

But the advent of new competition, first from other PC manufacturers and then smart phones and iPads, tablets and all IT successors, severely eroded Dell's business. Such is the concern about the company's future that Microsoft agreed to lend some of its considerable financial muscle to shore up one of its most important business partners.

"I believe this transaction will open an exciting new chapter for Dell, our customers and team members," Mr. Dell said in a statement. "Dell has made solid progress executing this strategy over the past four years, but we recognize that it will still take more time, investment and patience, and I believe our efforts will be better supported by partnering with Silver Lake in our shared vision."

"Michael Dell is a true visionary and one of the pre-eminent leaders of the global technology industry," Egon Durban, a managing partner at Silver Lake, said in a statement. "Silver Lake is looking forward to partnering with him, the talented management team at Dell and the investor group to innovate, invest in long-term growth initiatives and accelerate the company's transformation strategy to become an integrated and diversified global I.T. solutions provider."

This is a very good example that DELL's decision - if finalized? – would be one that "frees" his corporation from short-sighted analysis by markets, this being what this Chapter 4 is all about.

The 3 first Chapters in this book show that, in general, Western "Governance", be it that of nations and / or Supranational area organizations (European / Eurozone), are, in general, not acting in a social-economic manner, which increases unemployment and underemployment, and this needs to change radically, because if it does not, this will be one of the principal causes of continuing with slow growth, if not contraction, and finally, recession.

In these first 3 Chapters of this book I have tried to eliminate as much as possible "economic jargon", and tried to propose and present priority subjects for in-depth analysis, valid and practical discussion, which should end with policymaking and decision making, and get away as much as possible from general "politicking" and half-way and not realistic "ideas", which have regularly failed.

The place where results are sanctioned for large and medium sized listed corporations are the Stock Exchanges – the "Markets", as already previously mentioned.

I feel that in order to get away from the "isms" (capitalism, socialism, liberalism, extreme parties in both "right" and "left" vertices, et al), a way of trying to analyze and evaluate as impartially as possible, is a social-economic composite "P & L, which is makes up (see further on please) the PPR (Prize/Performance/Ratio", which would replace the "PER" (Price / Earnings Ratio analysis.

"IT" has greatly improved analysis mechanisms, to some extent stressing people with just too much information they cannot apprehend, this facility to use all kinds of information and process them enables to use a more elaborate and objective "social-economic composite "Index", which can be handled easily by all listed corporations.

The Government or the State must restrict its role as an employer and let corporations primordially exercise this role which corresponds to their vocation as "businesses", this a pre requisite for good functioning of this "social-economic composite Index".

What am I referring to?

Social-economic coefficients will be applied to specific items in different "real /official" P & Ls to show how these "coefficient compose P & Ls", called "PPR" P & L, which vary from their "official" P & Ls.

The "PPR" P & L includes 9 Coefficients, applied to 9 "official" P & L items. Those P & L "items" which lead to a realistic evolution of a corporation, and correspond to equivalent "macro items" in the economy which are favored by minus coefficients to show that these positive expenses are granted "realistic" treatment

The opposite happens to P & L items which are influencing negatively the corporations' evolutions, and they get applied plus coefficients to "penalize" their effect on the "official" P & Ls.

This total corporation's "PPR" P &L "Performance ", which finally is "represented" by the Corporations' "PPR" Net Income amount has to be divided by the total number of Shares listed in the Stock Exchange by the corporation and will accordingly represent the "PPR Performance per share".

This "PPR Performance per share" will be called "PPR", instead of the current "PER" (Prize/Earnings/Ratio), and will provide a far more complete and fair evaluation of a corporation's performance

The most important positive points included in the first 3 Chapters of this book to improve "Western" countries' economies are, to some extent, and in a practical way, reflected in the following 9 "PPR Coefficients".

Please see chart that follows which will make this matter practically understandable and it is totally feasible nowadays with the Computing programs available.

This proposal is based on making 3 examples of corporations working in the same activity sector, let's say in a non massive / selective distribution / sales corporation like selling music, or clothing, domestic appliances, etc…, but not in hyper / super markets.

The sales levels are different, because the 3 corporations are differently managed. The P & L components are organized in such a manner that they show the differences in cost of sales ratios to revenue, some operating expenses ratios on revenue, investment depreciation, financial expense, and tax on income ratios on revenue.

Different items of the P &L will be applied a coefficient to prepare 3 P &Ls which will better reflect the 3 manners of management – long, medium and short-term.

US Dollars – Millions	Coefficients	PPR Numbered Demo			Long Term Managed Corporat. w/Coeff.	Med. Term Managed Corporat. w/Coeff.	Short Term Managed Corporat. w/Coeff.
		Long Term Managed Corporat.	Medium Term Managed Corporat.	Short Term Managed Corporat.			
		P & L	P & L	P & L	P & L	P & L	P & L
Revenue		10000	8000	6000	10000	8000	6000
Cost of Sales	-5%	5500	4800	3800	5225	4560	3610
% on Revenue		55%	60%	63%	52%	57%	60%
Gross Margin		4500	3200	2200	4775	3440	2390
% on Revenue		45%	40%	37%	48%	43%	40%
Operating Expenses - Excl. :							
Formation, Training, Apprenticeship Expense/							
Top Mgt Total Expenses/							
Private Health programs /							
Environnemental Expense		1550	1250	1150	1550	1250	1150
% on Revenue		16%	16%	19%	16%	16%	19%
Formation, Training, Apprenticeship Expense/	-10%	400	240	100	360	216	90
% on Revenue		4%	3%	2%	4%	3%	2%
Top Mgt Total Expenses/	+10%	300	300	300	330	330	330
% on Revenue		3%	4%	5%	3%	4%	6%
Private Health Programs	-10%	200	100	50	180	90	45
% on Revenue		2%	1%	1%	2%	1%	1%
Environnemental Expense/	-10%	200	150	50	180	180	45
% on Revenue		2%	2%	1%	2%	2%	1%
R & D Expenses	-10%	400	200	100	360	180	90
% on Revenue		4%	3%	2%	4%	2%	2%
Operating Expense Total		3050	2240	1750	2960	2246	1750
% on Revenue		31%	28%	29%	30%	28%	29%
Operating Profit		1450	960	450	1815		640
% on Revenue		14%	12%	7%	18%	15%	11%

Investment Depreciation	-10%	200	100	50	180	90	45
% on Revenue		2%	1%	1%	2%	1%	1%
Financial Expenses	+10%	300	300	300	330	330	330
% on Revenue		3%	4%	5%	3%	4%	6%
Income Before Taxes		950	560	100	1305	774	265
% on Revenue		9%	7%	2%	13%	10%	4%
Taxes on Income	-10%	250	130	30	225	117	27
% / Income Before Taxes		26%	23%	30%	11%	15%	10%
% on Revenue		3%	2%	1%	2%	1%	0%
Net Profit		700	430	70	1080	657	238
% on Revenue		7%	5%	1%	11%	8%	4%

This whole proposal is based on applying the same coefficients to all 3 corporations

These corporations are part of the same sector of activity and compete with each other. They are differently managed.

COST OF SALES

The "long term «managed corporation reaches higher sales because it is competitive, meaning:

Its cost of sales is at 45% of Revenue, which is a "good" ratio, and is obtained because this corporation analyzes carefully its "mix "of products sold, and eliminates products which are not at the core of the business and not performing sales wise, and replaces them, eventually with other "new" products which will gain more sales and be more profitable, it also obtains better prices from its suppliers because it is well cash managed and pays in accordance with terms set. The "medium" and short" term corporations are less well managed, do not analyze in-depth their sales "mix «and carry higher cost of sales.

Cost of Sales gets a minus 110 coefficient to recognize better management of cost of sales, a crucial P &L item

OPERATING EXPENSES

Those expenses which will create additional sales and a good working situation for employees: Formation, Training, Apprenticeship expenses, Private Health Plans, Environmental expenses

All these expenses receive a minus 110% coefficient to demonstrate that these expenses are favorable to the corporation and its human environment.

R & D expenses will provide medium, long-term growth to the corporation.

A minus 110 coefficient will be applied to these expenses.

Top Management expenses, including remuneration, fixed and variable, all kinds of bonuses, perks, share options, and social benefits of all kinds paid to the top management including their "executive staff, are applied a plus 110 coefficient to "penalize" those corporations where this type of expense represents too high ratios on revenue.

OTHER NON OPERATING EXPENSES

Depreciation on Investments receives a minus 110 coefficient to favor investments in the corporation, which if adequately targeted will influence future sales.

Financial expenses reflects the annual cost of borrowings and if it too high, the corporation will have trouble in its P & L and also trouble in getting additional financing. Therefore it will be applied a "penalizing" plus 110 coefficient.

Taxes on Income, will be favored with a 110 minus coefficient, because a number of corporations evade taxes on income through semi legal loopholes which favor the corporation, but deprive the home –country of considerable tax revenue

The end result can be seen if one compares the P &Ls with PPR coefficients' applied to the 3 corporations with their "real" P & Ls.

It shows clearly that the long-term approach is the right one.

It shows that the well managed corporations, which are those who work based on a long –term strategy, which is re analyzed every month, and may be corrected at different stages, do far better than those who "react" and have no real strategy and no medium – long-term planning.

Short-term led corporations, are influenced every day with how the market "judges" them, and makes them look only at the short-term, will, in general, not have the same evolution in revenue and net income as the long-term led corporations, the table above shows this clearly.

The data to obtain these "PPR coefficient made P & Ls" is easily obtainable (daily, weekly, monthly, quarterly, bi annually and yearly, and on moving averages, with today's computer "ability «and versatility.

The "PPR" P & Ls shown above reflect also the macro problems that are, to some extent, comparable to those of corporations, the 'solutions" are different…

The 9 PPR coefficients relate to macro problems:

1. Cost of Sales management very much relates to the need for governments to have a strategy and a realistic plan for their countries and not be only "reactive".
2. Formation, training, apprenticeship expenses very much relate to the needs of practically all Western countries to reduce unemployment / underemployment.
3. Private health programs relate to the needs of Western countries to finance increasing health programs with the ageing of populations.
4. Environmental expenses relate to the increased ecological problems in the Western world (and worldwide)

5. R & D expenses relate to the need for development and innovation projects to be developed in Western countries.
6. Top Management expenses relate to the need to control exaggerated remunerations by top public and private executives in countries and supranational "Governances"
7. Investment Depreciation expenses relate to the need of investing in Western countries on Innovation and developing sectors of activity.
8. Financial expenses relate to the need of good administration of financial instruments and controlling exaggerated liquidity offers on a macro basis and keeping control on solvability.
9. Taxes on Income relate to the fact that many corporations take advantage of semi legal tax loopholes and tax evasion, and therefore diminish tax revenue in their "home countries".

The P & L "items" that this approach of re qualifying "official" P & Ls into "PPR" P & Ls is trying to demonstrate, corresponds to the "macro" problems that many countries are suffering and not resolving. These can be summarized as follows, and have already been commented in this book's preceding 3 Chapters.

1. A country and area's social- economic and financial performance should be analyzed far more in depth than in last decades. "Remedies" should not anymore be exaggerated inflows of liquidity by Central Banking, without regarding solvability. Social-economic structural reforms should be the number one priority.

2. Re orientation of the Education / Schooling system at different stages to adapt to the needs of the XXI Century activity sectors needs in workers skills. This requires a permanent dialogue between corporations, education establishments at different stages of education, representative labor unions and corporations / employers' associations, in order to also improve and far better target pertinent and adapted Formation and Training efforts.

It must also take much more into consideration the "Reconversion" efforts made for a large portion of dismissed personnel.

It requires what Germany has done successfully over decades, create real and efficiently managed apprenticeship jobs, not with non discriminated / "support" jobs, which have failed and will continue to do so.

Many Governments created "support" jobs and continue doing so, mainly for political reasons to – artificially - decrease unemployment, and whose costs are very heavy and do the contrary of what is needed: decrease the cost of labor, contribute to increasing their "deficits" to no avail and use unproductive badly needed funds which are "subsidies". These "subsidies" (which I have referred to – in length - in past Chapters) are, in general, so confusing that potential beneficiaries do not even know how many exist and their purpose, because mostly they remain "superimposed" one on the other because they have been "budgeted" and represent an "acquired benefit" which a great number of people "in need" ignore !

A corporation should be evaluated in terms of the efforts conceded in formation and training and creation of apprenticeship jobs and their evaluation of results in terms of lack of stress of their employees. This can be measured mainly by how many apprenticeship jobs were created as a % of total payroll, formation and training costs as % of Revenues, if workers are part of management councils and have participation in the corporations' results, increased monthly productivity, days of manifestation/strike every month.

3. Social-economic structural reforms, including far less work rules, work flexibility in hiring and dismissing employees/workers who performed badly or have become unaffordable because of a deterioration of the corporation's situation (without having to go through endless paper work and heavy delaying bureaucratic procedures), job security obtained by allowing employees/workers to stay for an x period with lower remuneration until the affected corporations return to an acceptable profit level, increasing retirement age due to the ageing of population, in general lower amounts in unemployment benefits versus past salaries, and also in general lower length of these unemployment benefits, discrimination and targeting of all other labor subsidies – all factors which will make a

corporation more efficient and create a good human relations corporate environment.

A corporation should also be evaluated in terms of how worker's right to work is made easier, which will bring higher productivity and output. It can be measured in quantifying monthly absenteeism, output and productivity increases.

4. Management of health coverage of workers by corporations. This is a complex issue since it depends from macro health coverage systems in every country whose levels of "generosity" can be very variable, but health coverage is increasingly affected by the ageing populations and in most cases will become unaffordable for total coverage, and corporations will need to "privately" partially cover parts of health programs for their employees.

5. Research and Development (R & D) spend plus other Investments as a percent of corporations revenues. Corporations need to Innovate and Invest in it, practically whatever the field of activity (not only "IT"), which requires investment in R & D. Innovation is the most important "competitive pole", and other types of investments should be considered as positive (depending on their targeting).

6. Environmental behavior and contribution to communities. Corporations need to contribute to national energy and environmental policies and programs in the communities where they operate.

7. Top and high staff Management's total cost (including all sorts of benefits and participations) versus employees and workers' remuneration and benefits and participations of all kinds.

A corporations' management should be evaluated in terms of the various spreads between top management, intermediate management, skilled workers and unskilled workers global remuneration including salary, benefits and participation.

8. Cash Flow Management. This reflects management's performance in controlling, and eventually improving, the level of spend in working capital and investments, representing the "investing effort" in a corporation's assets. It also shows the level of capitalization and indebtedness of a corporation.

A balanced cash flow with limited and affordable indebtedness is a very good criteria of evaluation of a corporation's management.

9. Taxes and Social charges supported by corporations. There is a macro percentage level of imposition on taxation and social charges which is the end result of all impositions levied by Governments. If corporations pay far less than the national level of total imposition, they need to justify how they manage to do so.

Many multinational corporations take advantage of "legal loopholes and tax breaks" in consolidation, establishing "intermediate" fiscal head quarters in countries like Ireland with a 12.5% tax rate and benefit from "unfair" tax advantages. "Real" corporations' income tax consolidation (excluding utilization of tax loopholes and tax breaks (even if "legal" – see Ireland case) for multinational corporations who represent a large share of Stock Exchanges.

10. Profitability before Taxes on Income Management. This reflects management's performance in controlling, and eventually improving, the level of revenues and expenses which make a corporation profitable.

This "PPR" P & L approach should be applied in all Stock Exchanges/Markets in the world, which sounds like "utopia", but is totally feasible.

This is not "utopia", since this approach to examining P & Ls is far more realistic and "doable" than all the pseudo economic "theories" that are being published and are reflected online; they represent a realistic and pragmatic approach to evaluating in Stock Exchanges the "value" of corporations, than most complicated texts which compare the still current 2007 / 2008 ….crisis with past huge crisis like 1929/30 and the oil crises in the 70s, which are totally "obsolete" as references, because the world has totally changed in practically all geo-economic aspects. It will be also more "efficient" as a regulator than all these "incomplete Treaties".

I am calling this a "practical proposal", which is in no way animated by political considerations, nor any "isms".

Politics need to adapt to this globalized world and the "ferocious" competition which exists and will be increasingly so between rich in "per capita GDP" Western countries (US and Europe), with acquired benefits, and "emerging" BRICS and other fast developing countries, which are either partially "dictatorially" directed in both politics and social - economics, like China, or have developed by exploiting their natural wealth in commodities and making social-economic structural reforms (still very incomplete) like Brazil.

The objective of this "PPR" P & L is to make it necessary to analyze the factors (based on 9 coefficients) which will make corporations' performance more efficient and attract investments, and eliminate factors which false comparisons.

It will reduce spectacularly the level of speculation, because corporations will be required to have short, medium and long-term planning and follow a "line", which, in general, has not been the case in at least the last decade, and analysts will have to evaluate corporations not on the short term only, which is what has been happening, and is very shortsighted and opposed to dynamic evolution and innovation.

Macro volatility will greatly diminish, and accordingly the "utilization" of hedging methods and creating non understandable derivative "products" will have far lesser importance, and speculation will subside considerably.

www.ingramcontent.com/pod-product-compliance
Lightning Source LLC
Chambersburg PA
CBHW051636170526
45167CB00001B/212